Apple Pro Training Series
Final Cut Express 4

Diana Weynand

Apple Certified

Apple Pro Training Series: Final Cut Express 4
Diana Weynand
Copyright © 2008 by Diana Weynand and Shirley Craig

Published by Peachpit Press. For information on Peachpit Press books, contact:

Peachpit Press
1249 Eighth Street
Berkeley, CA 94710
(510) 524-2178
Fax: (510) 524-2221
http://www.peachpit.com
To report errors, please send a note to errata@peachpit.com.
Peachpit Press is a division of Pearson Education.

Editor: Nancy Peterson
Production Editor: Danielle Foster
Project Director: Shirley Craig
Technical Reviewers: Brendan Boykin, K.D. Gulko
Media Reviewer: Eric Geoffroy
Copyeditor: Darren Meiss
Indexer: Jack Lewis
Cover Illustration: Kent Oberheu
Cover Production: Happenstance Type-O-Rama

ISBN 13: 978-0-321-53467-5
ISBN 10: 0-321-53467-0
9 8 7 6 5 4 3 2 1

Printed and bound in the United States of America

For digital video enthusiasts everywhere.
May your stories spring to life with Final Cut Express.

Acknowledgments

I'd like to thank my business partner, Shirley Craig, for guiding our Weynand Training team, as I wrote. Together we'd like to thank:

Susan Merzbach and Brendan Boykin for their editorial feedback and contributions; K.D. Gulko for technical editing; and Carol Soh and Erik Buckham for their illustrations; and Manny Gaudier, Alejandro Navarro, and Steve Ruiz with Sony Electronics, Inc. for the use of the HVR M15U HDV deck.

Special thanks to Nancy Peterson at Peachpit Press for guiding this book along its path, and to the rest of the Peachpit editorial and production team: Darren Meiss, Eric Geoffroy, Danielle Foster, and Jack Lewis. Thanks to Dion Scoppettuolo at Apple for his feedback, patience, and support, and to Patty Montesion for continuing to raise the bar of excellence with every new Apple Pro Training Series book.

Stories need pictures and sound. Our grateful thanks to Tina Valinsky, Dave Schwartz, and Daniel Grant for shooting the surfing footage, and Jim and Cindy Borland and their son, Jimbo, for sharing their surfing experiences with us. Thank you Ron Chapple and Graham Smith at Thinkstock Footage—they were always there when we needed them. And finally, thanks to Andrew Robbins of Megatrax, for the always inventive music tracks.

Table of Contents

Getting Started

Welcome to the official Apple Pro training course for Final Cut Express 4, Apple Computer's powerful, fun, and exciting nonlinear digital video editing software. Whether you're a first-time editor, an experienced iMovie user, or have worked in Final Cut Pro or other editing software applications, this book will take you from basic editing through outputting your Final Cut Express project complete with music, titles, and effects.

The Methodology

Editing can be the most exciting aspect of video production. It's where the little pieces come together, and you begin to see all your hard work pay off. Editing can be a simple process of stringing shots together, or a highly complex process that includes building layered effects and creating titles.

Using step-by-step exercises and practice projects, this book will teach you all you need to know about editing and delivering professional-looking projects using Final Cut Express. Each lesson builds on the previous lesson and continues to step you up through the program's functions and capabilities.

Course Structure

The lessons begin by introducing some necessary computer and application basics and follow with the editing and trimming techniques of Final Cut Express. Next you will learn how to customize and capture your own project. Finally, you will learn how to incorporate the higher-end features of Final Cut Express, such as effects and titling.

The lessons fall into the following categories:

Lessons 1–2	Mac OS X features and nonlinear editing basics
Lessons 3–4	Project organization and interface basics
Lessons 5–8	Editing techniques
Lessons 9–10	Trimming and adjusting edit points
Lessons 11–12	Customizing and capturing a project
Lesson 13	Audio features
Lessons 14–15	Transitions and titles
Lesson 16	Finishing a project

Special Training Aides

There are three training aides that support the learning process throughout this book. After Lesson 3, each lesson begins with a "Preparing the Project" section. This section guides you through opening the correct project file, organizing that project's elements, and viewing the completed project. You will then follow step-by-step exercises to produce that project.

At the end of each lesson is a section called "Lesson Review." This section contains questions and answers that summarize the functions covered throughout the lesson. Following this is a section called "Keyboard Shortcuts," a quick reference to all the shortcuts mentioned in the lesson.

In addition, "Project Tasks" sections, which appear throughout the book, let you practice what you've learned before moving on to new material.

> **NOTE ▶** This book works with more than one version of the Mac OS. Throughout this book, you will see a mixture of images from both Mac OS 10.5 (Leopard) and OS 10.4.9 (Tiger).

Final Cut Express Book Files

The Apple Pro Training Series Final Cut Express DVD-ROM includes a folder titled FCE 4 Book Files. This contains two folders: Lessons and Media. (In Lesson 1, you will be instructed how to load these files onto your computer.) These folders hold the lessons (called *project files*) and editing material (called *media files*) you will need for this course. Each lesson, except Lessons 1 and 2, has its own project file. In Lesson 12, you will create your own project file from within Final Cut Express.

In the Media folder, you will find primary audio/video media file folders organized according to topic. For example, there are folders of media files called Vacation Fun, Working Out, and Surfing. Each of these folders contains media files that pertain to that topic. In the Music and Sound Effects folders, you will find the music tracks and sound effects used throughout the book. The Import-Export folder is used in the last lesson on finishing. Each lesson will guide you in the use of all the project and media files.

In addition to the lessons in the book, there are additional lessons on the DVD. These PDFs cover some of the more advanced features of Final Cut Express, such as motion effects, color correction, and advanced trimming, as well as the additional application, LiveType, that comes bundled with Final Cut Express. Each of these PDFs also have a lesson project. Those projects can be found in FCE 4 Book Files > Lessons > Lessons on DVD.

Final Cut Express can work in both NTSC and PAL standards and in DV, HDV, and AVCHD formats. Although the project files on the DVD were created in NTSC, you can work with them successfully even if you are in a PAL system. Standards and standard settings are discussed in more detail in Lessons 2 and 3.

Also on the DVD is a folder called FXScript DVE's by CGM. This folder contains an effect you will use in Appendix D. You will be instructed in that lesson how to add that effect, and any other third-party effects, to the Final Cut Express effect collection and access it during the editing process.

Reconnecting Media

It is important to keep the Lessons and Media folders together in the FCE 4 Book Files folder. If you keep them together on your hard drive, you should be able to maintain the original link between the files.

It is possible, however, to break the original link between the project files and media files in the process of copying them from the DVD. You will know this has happened if a dialog appears when you open a lesson project file, asking you to reconnect the project files. Also, you will see a red diagonal line over some of your material. Reconnecting the project files is a simple process and is covered in more depth in Lesson 16 in the "Reconnecting Media" section. But if this happens when you're opening a lesson project file, just follow these steps:

1 If an Offline Files dialog appears, click the Reconnect button.

2 When the Reconnect Files dialog appears, click Search.

  Final Cut Express will automatically find the missing file for you.

3 Click Choose.

4 In the Reconnect Files window, click Connect.

  Final Cut Express will reconnect a link to the file at this location.

Loading Software

Before you get started, you will need to load the Final Cut Express application onto your hard drive. To do this, follow the directions that came with the application.

> **TIP** It's important to download and install all the latest updates to Final Cut Express. In addition to including additional features, these revisions often include minor fixes to the software. Download updates from www.apple.com/support/finalcutexpress.

About the Apple Pro Training Series

Apple Pro Training Series: Final Cut Express 4 is part of the official training series for Apple Pro applications developed by experts in the field. The lessons are designed to let you learn at your own pace. If you're new to Final Cut Express, you'll learn the fundamental concepts and features you'll need to master the program. Although each lesson provides step-by-step instructions for creating specific projects, there's room for exploration and experimentation. Each lesson concludes with a review section summarizing what you've covered.

System Requirements

Before beginning this book, you should have a working knowledge of your computer and its operating system. Make sure that you know how to use the mouse and standard menus and commands and also how to open, save, and close files. If you need to review these techniques, see the printed or online documentation included with your system.

Basic system requirements for Final Cut Express 4 include the following:

▶ Macintosh computer with 1.25 GHz or faster PowerPC G4, PowerPC G5, Intel Core Duo or Intel Xeon processor

▶ An AGP or PCI Express graphics card compatible with Quartz Extreme or an Intel GMA integrated graphics processor in MacBook or Mac mini

▶ Mac OS X v10.4.10 or later

▶ QuickTime 7.2 or later (included)

▶ 1 GB of RAM

▶ 500 MB disk space required for applications; additional 500 MB of additional storage space for LiveType content (can be installed on separate disks)

Resources

Apple Pro Training Series: Final Cut Express 4 is not intended as a comprehensive reference manual, nor does it replace the documentation that comes with the application. For comprehensive information about program features, refer to these resources:

▶ Final Cut Express user's manual.

▶ The Reference Guide. Accessed through the Final Cut Express Help menu, the Reference Guide contains a complete description of all features.

▶ Apple's Web site: www.apple.com.

▶ Final Cut Express Web site: www.apple.com/finalcutexpress.

1

Lesson Files	None
Media	Lesson 1 Media folder
Time	This lesson takes approximately 30 minutes to complete.
Goals	Work with Finder windows and column views
	Locate and screen media files
	Customize the Dock
	Load DVD lessons and media onto the hard drive
	Add Final Cut Express application icon to the Dock

Lesson **1**

Covering the Basics

This lesson demonstrates a few fundamentals of Mac OS X to prepare you to work with Final Cut Express 4. It shows you how to view the contents of your hard drive and screen media files in a column display. In addition, you will load the Final Cut Express lessons onto your hard drive and add Apple Final Cut Express 4 to the Dock, making the program easy to open and access.

Working with Finder Windows

Like previous Apple operating systems, Mac OS X uses icons to represent applications, documents, and other files. The hard-drive icon looks like an image of a hard drive; it is located in the upper-right corner of the Desktop. The applications and documents you will be organizing and working with are stored on the hard drive and can be accessed through that icon.

Viewing Columns in a Finder Window

In Mac OS X, there are three ways to view the contents of your hard drive: by icon, as a list, or in column view. The latter is especially helpful when working with media files.

> **NOTE ▶** An icon is a visual representation of something.

1   Turn on your computer and double-click the hard-drive icon to open the contents of the hard drive in a Finder window.

> **TIP ▶** The keyboard shortcut to opening a Finder window on the Desktop is Cmd-N. The Command key is on either side of the spacebar.

2   Click and drag any portion of the outer silver area in the Finder window. This is how you reposition a window on the Desktop. In Final Cut Express 4, you drag from the window's title bar.

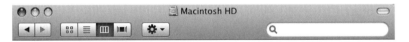

3   In the upper-left area of this window are backward and forward arrows and four view options (three options for Mac OS 10.4.9 or earlier). If it's not already selected, click the third view option to sort by column layout.

4   The first column is a sidebar divided into devices and places. In the upper area of the sidebar for devices, click the Macintosh HD icon once to select it. The Macintosh HD is the *root level* of the computer.

The content in the hard drive is displayed in the next column.

5   In the Places section of the sidebar, click the Applications icon to display applications.

A list of all the applications on your computer appears alphabetically in the next column, including Final Cut Express 4, if installed.

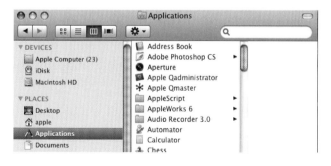

Resizing Windows

Resizing, minimizing, and hiding windows in Mac OS X is necessary at times to see additional columns of computer content in the Finder window. Final Cut Express windows are also manipulated this way.

1   Drag the lower-right corner down and out to enlarge the window.

This allows you to view more columns and more content within each column.

2 Look for the tiny double vertical lines at the bottom of a column. Drag one of these column markers right or left to expand or contract that column width.

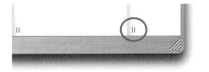

TIP ▶ If you want to resize all columns to the same width, press the Option key as you drag a column's vertical marker. If you want to resize the sidebar, move the pointer over the silver column divider. When the pointer changes to a resize arrow, drag left or right. Dragging left all the way hides the sidebar entirely.

3 Click the green Zoom button in the upper-left corner to enlarge the window to show additional information, if available, or to shrink it to hide empty areas.

NOTE ▶ When the pointer is positioned over the window buttons, they each display a symbol. The Zoom button displays a plus sign.

4 Click the green Zoom button again to return the window to its previous size.

NOTE ▶ Later, you will click the yellow button to minimize the window and store it in the Dock, and you'll click the red button to close the window.

Loading Lessons and Media onto the Hard Drive

Before you begin working with the material from the Final Cut Express 4 DVD, you will need to load the files onto your hard drive.

1   Insert the DVD included with this book into your computer.

The APTS (Apple Pro Training Series) Final Cut Express 4 DVD icon appears in the first column of the Finder window. It also appears on the Desktop.

2   Click the APTS Final Cut Express 4 DVD icon in the sidebar of the Finder window to view the contents of the DVD in the next column.

3   Click the FCE 4 Book Files folder in the second column and then the Lessons folder in the third column.

There is a Final Cut Express project file for each lesson, beginning with Lesson 3.

4   Click the Media folder in the third column.

All of the media files you will use in the lessons are organized by topic into individual folders.

TIP To ensure that each project knows where to locate its associated media files, do not separate the Lessons and Media folders. Keep them together in the FCE 4 Book Files folder and move only that folder.

5   To copy the media files to your hard drive, drag the FCE 4 Book Files folder from the second column of the Finder window onto the Macintosh HD icon in the sidebar.

NOTE ▶ Make sure you see an outline around Macintosh HD before releasing the mouse button. The outline indicates that the target has been selected.

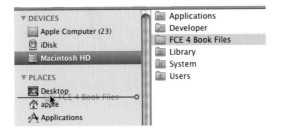

A Copy window appears, listing what is being copied and how long the process will take to complete.

6   After the copying is complete, eject the DVD from your computer.

The additional folder on the DVD, FXScript DVE's by CGM, holds an effect you will use in Appendix D (on the DVD). You will install it in that lesson.

7   To make the FCE 4 Book Files folder easily accessible from the sidebar, click the Macintosh HD icon, then drag the FCE 4 Book Files folder from the second column into the Places section of the sidebar, somewhere beneath the Desktop icon. Look for an insert line before you release the folder.

This action does not remove the folder from its original location but simply places a copy of the folder icon, called an *alias*, in the sidebar for easy access.

Viewing Media in the Finder

At this point, you should have the FCE 4 Book Files folder (containing the Lessons and Media folders) from the DVD loaded onto your hard drive as outlined in the previous steps. The Lessons folder contains individual Final Cut Express project files for each lesson. The Media folder contains media files (video clips) used in the lessons.

Using the column view, you can access your lesson files quickly and easily and preview or screen your media files as well. You can also access other information about a media file, such as when it was created, the date it was last modified, and its duration, file size, and frame size. For the moment, you will work with media files from the Media folder. Later, you can work with your own media.

1   Click the FCE 4 Book Files folder in the sidebar of the Finder window, then the Media folder in the next column.

     A third column appears, displaying individual folders that organize the media by topic. If necessary, expand the width of the column to read the filenames.

2   Click the Lesson 1 Media folder.

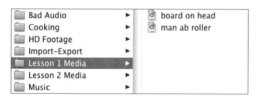

3   Click **man ab roller** once. A single frame appears in the next column. Expand this column to see a larger preview of the media file image.

TIP When you select a media file, such as a QuickTime movie, in column view, you can play the file in the far-right column to screen it or use the displayed file information for reference. (QuickTime files are discussed in more detail in Lesson 2.)

4   To play and navigate a media file in Mac OS 10.5 (Leopard), follow these steps:

▶ Move the pointer over the image area. When you see the Play icon appear, click it. Press the Stop icon to stop playing the clip.

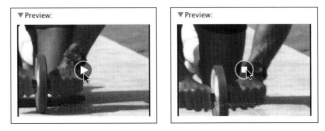

▶ To quickly preview a selected clip, press the Space bar. This opens and plays the clip in the Quick Look window. Press the Space bar again to close the window.

▶ Click the Space bar to open the clip, then click the Pause button to stop the clip.

▶ Click the Full Screen arrows to make the preview window full screen.

▶ From the Full Screen mode, click the Close button (X) to close the window.

TIP ▶ When the Quick Look window is open, you can select or navigate to another clip and that clip will begin playing in the window.

5 To play and navigate a media file in Mac OS 10.4.9 or earlier, follow these steps:

▶ Click the Play button beneath the image area to play the media file.

▶ Click the Pause button to stop the media file.

▶ Drag the frame slider to move quickly through frames.

▶ Click the left and right frame buttons to move backward and forward through the clip, frame by frame.

▶ Click the audio speaker to the left of the image and drag up or down to adjust the volume.

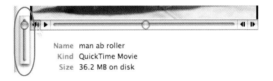

6   Play the other media file in this lesson, **board on head**.

Working with the Dock

On the Mac OS X Desktop is a strip called the Dock, where application icons can be conveniently stored for easy access.

If multiple users log on to your computer, OS X allows each user to have his or her own personal Dock and Desktop configuration. The Dock can be placed on the bottom, left, or right of the screen. It can be sized to your preference and can be hidden when you're not working with it.

1   In the menu bar, click the blue Apple icon.

2 Slide down and choose Dock.

```
About This Mac
Software Update...
Mac OS X Software...

System Preferences...
Dock                  ▶    Turn Hiding Off      ⌥⌘D
Location              ▶    Turn Magnification Off

Recent Items          ▶    Position on Left
                        ✓ Position on Bottom
Force Quit...    ⌥⌘⏻       Position on Right

Sleep                      Dock Preferences...
Restart
Shut Down
```

Some Dock options, such as position, magnification, and hiding, appear in the Dock submenu.

3 Choose Dock Preferences from the Dock submenu.

The Dock preferences window appears, offering ways to personalize your Dock.

```
●  ●  ○                        Dock
 ◀  ▶    Show All                              Q

            Dock Size:  ├──────────●──────────┤
                          Small             Large

      ☑ Magnification:  ├────────●────────────┤
                          Min                Max

   Position on screen:  ○       ⊙       ○
                        Left   Bottom   Right

       Minimize using:  [ Genie Effect    ▼ ]

                        ☑ Animate opening applications
                        ☑ Automatically hide and show the Dock      (?)
```

4 In the bottom of the window, make sure the "Automatically hide and show the Dock" option is deselected.

```
☐ Automatically hide and show the Dock
```

NOTE ▶ Deselecting this option keeps the Dock visible on the Desktop while you adjust your preferences. At other times, you can show or hide the Dock by using the keyboard shortcut Cmd-Option-D or by selecting the hiding option from the Dock submenu.

5   Move the Dock Size slider to change the size of the Dock.

6   In the Dock, move your mouse pointer over the dividing bar until the pointer changes to a double arrow resize icon. Drag up and down to make the Dock larger or smaller.

7   Select the Magnification box in the Dock preferences window, and drag the slider to the middle of the bar.

8   Move the mouse pointer over the application icons within the Dock.

The application icons enlarge as the mouse pointer moves over them. If you like this option, leave it selected. If not, deselect the Magnification box.

9   Click the yellow Minimize button in the Dock window's title bar.

When the pointer moves over the button, a minus sign appears.

Dock

Show All

The Dock window hides from the Desktop by squeezing itself into the smaller portion of the Dock next to the Trash icon.

10 Click the Dock window icon to bring the window back to full size. Reselect the "Automatically hide and show the Dock" option.

11 Click the red Close button in the Dock window to close it.

When the pointer moves over the buttons, an X appears.

NOTE ▶ Clicking these buttons has the same effect on any OS X window in any application, including Final Cut Express.

TIP ▶ You can use the keyboard shortcut Cmd-W to close any open window on the Desktop and within Final Cut Express.

Adding Final Cut Express to the Dock

A Macintosh computer straight out of the box will have a Dock that contains some of the icons for applications that come with the computer. But once you install additional software applications, it's a good idea to add icons to the Dock for applications you use frequently so you can have easy access to them.

When you add the Final Cut Express icon to the Dock, you will be using a copy of the application icon, or an alias. Clicking an alias icon of a program in the Dock will open the original application wherever it is located on your hard drive. Let's add the Final Cut Express icon to the Dock.

1   In the Finder window, click the Macintosh HD icon in the sidebar column, and then click the Applications folder in the next column.

   NOTE ▶ If the Applications icon appears in the sidebar, you can just click that icon instead.

2   Click the Final Cut Express application icon once. If it is not in view, scroll down until you see it.

   A large Final Cut Express icon appears in the next column, along with some information about the program size, version, and so on.

Name Final Cut Express
Kind Application

3 Drag this icon into the Dock where you want it to be placed, and release the mouse button.

NOTE ▶ For this icon, use the area to the left of the dividing bar. The area to the right is usually saved for the Trash, temporary documents, and certain other icons.

4 To remove the Final Cut Express icon from the Dock, simply drag it out of the Dock and release.

A little puff of smoke appears, indicating that you have successfully removed the icon from the Dock. However, you have not removed the application from the hard drive.

5 Repeat step 3 to add the Final Cut Express icon back into the Dock.

NOTE ▶ In another lesson, you will open Final Cut Express by clicking its alias icon in the Dock.

6 Close the Finder window.

Lesson Review

1. Which view option is recommended when viewing media files?

2. How do you resize the Finder window?

3. How do you make a window hide into the Dock? How do you close a window?

4. How do you view a QuickTime media file from a Finder window?

5. How do you change the Dock preferences?

6. How do you add an application icon to the Dock?

7. How do you remove an item from the Dock?

8. Where can you place your FCE 4 Book Files folder for easy access?

Answers

1. The column view.

2. Drag the lower-right corner or click the green Zoom button.

3. To hide a window, click the yellow Minimize button. To close a window, click the red Close button.

4. In Mac OS 10.5, you click the Play icon in the image area, or press the space bar to open the file in the Quick Look window. In OS 10.4.9 or earlier, locate and select the file, then click the Play button under the preview image.

5. Click the blue Apple menu and choose Dock and then Dock Preferences from the submenu.

6. In the sidebar, click the Applications icon, then select the specific application and drag its icon into the Dock.

7. Drag the item from the Dock and release it. You will see a puff of smoke.

8. Drag the folder to the sidebar of a Finder window. When you see a horizontal insert bar, release the folder.

Keyboard Shortcuts

Cmd-N	Opens a new Finder window
Cmd-Option-D	Hides the Dock or shows a hidden Dock
Cmd-W	Closes any open window on the Desktop
Space bar	Opens and closes a selected media file in the Quick Look window. In full screen mode, it starts and stops the clip.

2

Lesson Files	None
Media	Lesson 1 Media folder, Lesson 2 Media folder, Cooking folder, Music folder, HD Footage folder
Time	This lesson takes approximately 30 minutes to complete.
Goals	Understand video standards
	Understand and work with digital video
	Learn about and view QuickTime movies
	Learn shooting and composition terminology
	Understand the nonlinear editing process

Editing Video

You may be a first-time editor or have a few editing projects already under your belt. Whatever your background in video editing, it will be helpful to review some basic concepts and terms about video standards and formats and take a look at the nonlinear editing process you will use in the following chapters.

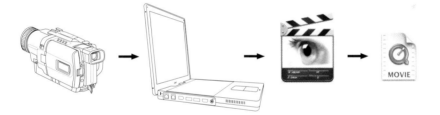

Preparing the Lesson

Make sure you have loaded the FCE 4 Book Files folder from this book's DVD to your hard drive, as detailed in Lesson 1.

1   Open a Finder window by pressing Cmd-N or double-clicking the Macintosh HD icon on the Desktop.

2   In the View button area, click the third option to display the column view. Do not open Final Cut Express just yet.

   TIP ▶ In Mac OS X, you can change the default window layout to column view by choosing Finder > Preferences. Click the General icon and select the "Open new windows in column view" option.

Working with Video Formats

Before you begin to edit in Final Cut Express 4, it's important to understand some of the DV and HD properties that will affect your editing options. Final Cut Express 4 can edit three types of video sources or formats: DV, HDV, and AVCHD. Each of these formats produces digital video but goes about it in a different way, which creates different results in image quality and file size. While DV is a standard digital video format, AVCHD and HDV are both HD, or high definition, formats.

Depending on what country you live in, some formats allow you to choose between two standards: NTSC and PAL. NTSC is used in most of the Americas, Taiwan, Japan, and Korea. PAL is used in most of Europe, Brazil, Algeria, and China. Each video format has its own set of rules or protocols that defines how video will be recorded, transmitted, and played within a certain country or region. These protocols define several aspects of the video signal, such as the image quality or resolution, the frame rate, and the size of the image. It also defines how the image is compressed during the recording process.

Understanding the DV Format

Within each standard, there can be many different video formats. For example, the tape you use to shoot at-home videos is a different videotape format from the one that was used to broadcast an on-air program. DV is a high-quality, low-cost format you can use to make professional-looking projects. DV formats exist in both NTSC and PAL standards.

When a video camera is recording an image, it converts the light it sees through the camera lens into an electronic signal on tape. The electronic image is recorded as individual frames. NTSC DV records and plays back 29.97 frames per second (fps). This is the *frame rate*. The PAL frame rate is 25 frames per second. Each frame is broken down into picture elements, or *pixels*. One NTSC DV frame is made up of 480 horizontal lines of 720 pixels each. You will often see a reference to these two numbers as 720x480. PAL is 720x576.

1   Click the FCE 4 Book Files folder in the sidebar of the Finder window.

2   Click the Media folder in the next column, and then the Cooking folder in the third column.

3   Click the **mushroom sliced** QuickTime file.

4   In the QuickTime Preview area, look at the Dimensions information for the image.

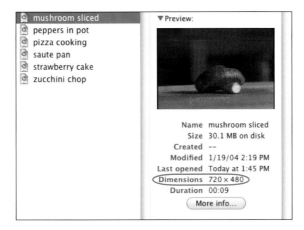

The dimensions of this image are 720x480.

Understanding Aspect Ratio

All videotape formats record a video image in a rectangular shape. The shape is defined by comparing two aspects of the video image: the horizontal width to the vertical height. A square would be a 1-to-1, 2-to-2, or 3-to-3 comparison. These comparisons are written 3:3 or sometimes 3x3. Most standard definition television sets are 4:3, which means they are a little wider than they are tall. High definition television sets are 16:9, and are referred to as "widescreen" because they are wider proportionally than the older sets. In video formats, this screen ratio is referred to as the *aspect ratio* of the image.

In DV, there are two possible aspect ratios. One is the 4:3 you are accustomed to seeing on standard television sets; the other is a 16:9 ratio. This widescreen 16:9 aspect ratio is often used to shoot low-budget DV films.

4:3   16:9

Understanding the HD Format

Final Cut Express 4 can also edit material shot in the high definition video format. High definition video has a better-quality image than DV because there is simply more information that makes up the image. Rather than the 480 lines that make up a DV-NTSC image (576 lines in DV-PAL), one HD video format has 1080 lines of video information, and another format has 720 lines. The more lines of picture information (called pixels) a video image has, the better the overall image resolution you will see.

Final Cut Express 4 can edit HD footage in either the HDV or AVCHD format. Both of these formats can have the same frame size, line count, and aspect ratio, but each has a different way of compressing the image. Compressing HD video makes the video file size smaller than uncompressed HD and allows you to capture and utilize more video for editing. While HDV uses an MPEG-2 type of compression, AVCHD uses MPEG-4, specifically H.264. The HDV video formats record on tape and can use the same type of tapes as DV video. The AVCHD formats, however, record directly onto disks or hard drives, creating digital files of what you've shot.

1   Click the Media folder, and then click the HD Footage folder in the next column.

2   Click the **on the beach** QuickTime file. This footage was shot using an HDV camera.

3   In the QuickTime Preview area, look at the Dimensions information for this HDV image.

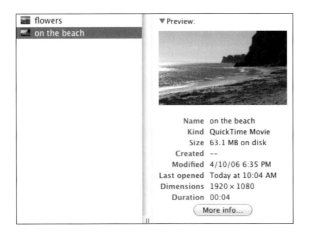

This HD image has the wider 16:9 aspect ratio. Its dimensions are 1920x1080, which means it has 1920 pixels across one line and 1080 lines of video information. Because HD clips have a wider image area, you can see more action in the clip.

4 Click the **flowers** clip and play it.

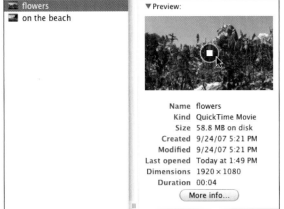

This is an AVCHD clip. Since it's an HD format, it too has the wider 16:9 aspect ratio. Notice the size of the image. The AVCHD format uses a different type of compression than HDV, so the media file, although similar in length of time, is a slightly smaller size than the HDV clip.

Connecting via FireWire

Final Cut Express can edit DV or HD video. That means the material you choose to edit has to be shot with an HDV or DV camera or transferred to one of these formats from its originating source. If you shot with an HDV or DV camera, you can simply hook up your camera directly to your computer and you're ready to input, or *capture*, material into the editing program. Or if you have a DV or HDV VCR, you can take the tape from your camera and play it back from the VCR to the computer.

FireWire is an Apple technology used to connect peripheral devices to your computer. With a FireWire connection, you can input, or capture, video images directly into your computer. You can also output your final edited project through FireWire back to a DV or HDV recording device.

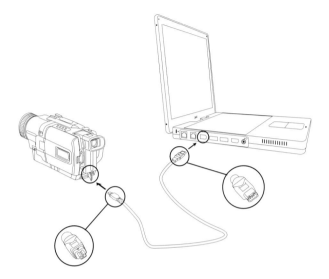

NOTE ▶ In Lesson 12, which discusses inputting your video into the computer, you will plug your camera source into your computer using a FireWire cable and then capture video. Often the FireWire connection that goes to the camera or VCR is smaller than the one that goes to the computer.

However, if you want to edit something that was shot on a nondigital format, such as Hi-8 or VHS, you will first have to dub that material to a digital format before bringing it into Final Cut Express. You can purchase a converter box that will convert a nondigital or analog video format into a digital video signal that you can input into your computer. Capturing is discussed in detail in Lesson 12.

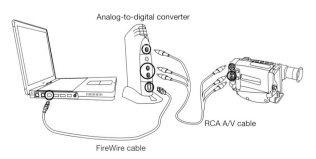

Analog-to-digital converter

RCA A/V cable

FireWire cable

Working with QuickTime

QuickTime is software that allows you to play dozens of different types of files, including audio, video, and graphics. QuickTime files can originate from any number of video formats or sources.

Playing QuickTime Files

When you begin to input and capture your DV material into your computer, Final Cut Express automatically creates QuickTime files from the video. Any length of tape you import is turned into a file. Each file is referred to as a *clip* and is usually only a portion of the whole tape. QuickTime clips can include video, audio, or video and audio. You will often see or hear a QuickTime file referred to as a *QuickTime movie,* and sometimes you will see the extension .mov at the end of the QuickTime filename.

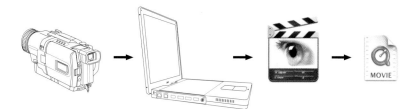

During the course of editing in Final Cut Express, QuickTime will be used in many ways. As mentioned, when you input source material into your computer, Final Cut Express automatically creates QuickTime files or clips from this material. If you want to export a single frame from your video to use in a graphics program such as Adobe Photoshop, you use QuickTime to convert the video image to a graphic file such as TIFF or PICT. When you output something you have edited, you also use QuickTime to create the file. You will work more with QuickTime options in later lessons.

1   Click the Lesson 2 Media folder in the third column of your Finder window, single-click the **jimbo name** QuickTime file (or clip) in the fourth column, and click the Play button in the Preview area. The clips are listed alphabetically.

TIP ▶ Remember you can enlarge the Preview column to see a larger image by dragging the double vertical lines in that column.

This QuickTime clip contains both audio and video.

2   In the Cooking folder, select the **peppers in pot** clip and play it the same way.

This clip has no audio, so there is no speaker icon in the controls beneath the image area.

3   In the Music folder, select the **surfing voices** clip and play it.

This clip has no video, so the video image area does not appear. But a play bar appears with the same controls to listen to the audio.

4   Change the volume on the music clip.

TIP ▶ You can also double-click the QuickTime clip icon to open and view the clip in a QuickTime Player window.

Viewing File Size

Extra seconds can add up very quickly in terms of computer space. So be sure to choose shots you think you will actually use to edit your project. Although everyone's hard drive capacity is different, it is helpful to keep a simple piece of information in mind as you weed through your source material looking for good shots to transfer to your computer: 5 minutes of DV footage takes up approximately 1 GB (1024 MB) of hard drive space.

1   In the Lesson 2 Media folder, select the **with dad long** clip and play it.

2   Look at the file size and duration in the Preview area.

3   Select the **with dad short** clip and play it.

This clip has been pared down to exclude the unusable material.

4   Compare the file size and duration of the two clips.

> **NOTE ▶** It's a good idea to have a few seconds of media on either side of the action of a clip. These media *handles* give you options during the editing process. The right balance is getting all the important action or dialogue, plus a little more for handles.

Shooting Terminology

Although this is a book about editing with Final Cut Express 4, it's always helpful to understand certain terminology regarding how the subject was framed in the shot and how the camera moved. This allows you to discuss the footage more precisely during the editing process. The following sections discuss a few frequently used terms.

Identifying Camera Moves

A camera can be used in many ways. It can be locked down, pointing at a subject or object so that there is no movement; it can follow a subject as he or she moves left or right or stands up and lies down; or it can move back and away from a subject to include other action. Follow these steps to see examples of camera movement:

1   In the Lesson 2 Media folder in the Finder window, select and play the **high 5** clip.

In this *zoom in,* the camera view magnifies, and Jimbo and his dad seem to get bigger and bigger.

2   Select the **jimbo and board** clip and play it.

In this *zoom out,* Jimbo seems to get smaller as the camera pulls back, and the image area expands to include more of the scene around it.

3   In the Cooking folder, select the **pizza cooking** clip and play it.

In a *pan shot* like this, the camera lens moves left or right horizontally.

4   Select the **strawberry cake** clip and play it.

In a *tilt shot* like this, the camera lens moves up or down vertically.

Identifying Shot Composition

However the camera may be moving, the size of the main subject in the shot is another consideration in video storytelling. The positioning of the subject in relation to the rest of the image is called *framing* or *shot composition*. Here are some examples of framing terminology.

In telling a story with video or film, you often begin by using a shot that is wide enough to indicate where the subject is. This is referred to as a *wide shot* or an *establishing shot*.

1   In the Lesson 2 Media folder, select **surfer-ws** and play it.

This is a wide shot of a surfer on a beach. In the wide shot, you can see where he is located and some of the ocean behind him. This gives the viewer a sense of place.

2   Select **surfer-ms** and play it.

In this *medium shot,* the surfer's size makes it appear as if the camera has moved forward a few feet. In fact, it has only zoomed in to make the surfer appear larger in the frame.

3   Select **surfer-mcu** and play it.

In this *medium close-up shot,* we seem to have come even closer as the surfer is framed around his chest. Again, the camera zoomed in to get a tighter shot.

4   Select **surfer-cu** and play it.

In this *close-up shot,* or CU, the surfer's face is framed tightly. You can also zoom in even closer for an *extreme close-up,* or ECU, for example, having just his face, or even one eye, fill the frame.

5   Select **surfer-two** and play it.

In this *two shot,* the frame gives equal importance to two subjects.

As you begin to review your material, think in terms of what shots will convey your message or story most effectively. You can use some of the shortcut references, such as CU for *close-up*, when labeling your footage or when making a list, or *log sheet*, of shots on your tape.

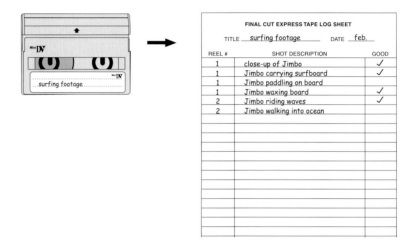

Creating a good labeling system for your source material is highly recommended for any type of project, especially larger editing projects. In Lesson 11, you will learn how Final Cut Express provides tools for keeping your clips organized.

Understanding Nonlinear Editing

There are an infinite number of ways to edit your shots together in Final Cut Express. What gives you so much flexibility is that Final Cut Express is a *nonlinear editing* program. Nonlinear editing allows you to change your mind about the placement or length of a shot over and over without affecting your original captured media.

Here's how it works. When you were viewing the QuickTime movies earlier in this lesson, you were screening the entire length of a captured clip of footage. When you are editing, you may choose to use only a portion of that clip. You will mark the portion you want to use and put it together with other marked clips to form a sequence of shots or edits. This sequence of edits will develop into your edited project.

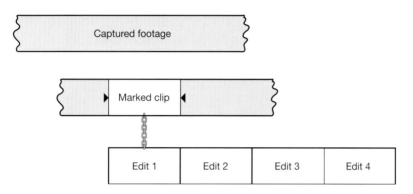

When you edit the sequence of shots together, you are not actually making any changes to your original QuickTime media files. You are only specifying what portions and in what order you wish Final Cut Express to show you the original media.

1   In the Lesson 1 Media folder, select and play the **man ab roller** clip.

    This clip is both audio and video, but not from the same sources. A CD music track was edited to the video of the man working out.

2   In the Lesson 2 Media folder, select and play the **jimbo surfs** clip.

    This is a QuickTime movie of edited portions of clips from your Media folder. The sequence includes only a few seconds of a specific action and does not include the material before or after that action, even though it is still available on the original captured clip.

3   Close the Finder window.

In a later lesson, you will work with the Cooking clips in Final Cut Express and begin to organize them as you prepare to edit.

Lesson Review

1. Final Cut Express 4 can edit in what two video standards?
2. What video formats can Final Cut Express 4 edit?
3. How is the aspect ratio of a video image determined?
4. Which format has a native 16:9 aspect ratio?
5. What kind of cable do you use to connect your camera to your computer?
6. True or false: When you edit in Final Cut Express 4, you don't change the original media files.

Answers

1. NTSC and PAL.
2. DV, HDV, and AVCHD formats.
3. The aspect ratio is a comparison of the width of an image (number of pixels across one line) to the height of the image (number of lines), such as 4:3 or 16:9.
4. The HD formats have a 16:9 aspect ratio.
5. A FireWire cable.
6. True. The clips you work with simply link back to the original media files but do not change them.

3

Lesson Files	Lesson 3 Project file
Media	Working Out folder, Music folder
Time	This lesson takes approximately 60 minutes to complete.
Goals	Launch Final Cut Express
	Open a project
	Work with the interface
	Work with menus, keyboard shortcuts, and the mouse
	Work with projects in the Browser
	Create a new bin
	Organize a project
	Quit and hide Final Cut Express

Lesson 3

Working with a Project

In this lesson, you will open the Final Cut Express 4 program, identify and work with the elements of your editing project, organize those elements, and begin working within the Final Cut Express editing interface.

Launching Final Cut Express

As with so many Apple programs, there are multiple ways to launch Final Cut Express. You might double-click the application icon in your Applications folder or double-click a Final Cut Express project file. For the purposes of this lesson, you will single-click the Final Cut Express icon you placed in the Dock in Lesson 1.

1   Single-click the Final Cut Express icon in the Dock.

After launching, Final Cut Express looks for any FireWire devices connected to the computer. If none are found, an External A/V window appears saying, "Unable to locate the following external devices."

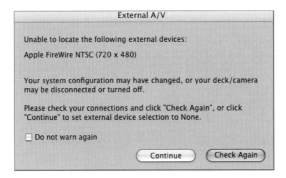

2   If an FCE 4 Book Files folder has been copied to your hard drive, select the "Do not warn again" box in this window and then click Continue. If you copied the lessons and media to an external hard drive, leave the box deselected and you will be reminded to connect the FireWire device every time you launch.

First-Time Use

If this is the first time you're opening the Final Cut Express software since installing it, a Choose Setup window will appear in which you can select the appropriate video format for your region and equipment. The options you select will create default settings within the program. You will also be prompted to choose your primary scratch disk. This is the hard drive where your captured media will be stored. You will learn about scratch disks in a later lesson. For now choose a secondary drive if you have one, or if not, leave it set on your Macintosh HD.

You can change these settings by choosing Final Cut Express > Easy Setup and choosing a different option. Whenever you change your Easy Setup selection, you will not change any of your past projects, only your future projects within Final Cut Express.

The Final Cut Express Interface

When a program opens, it presents a layout of menus, tools, and windows, known as the *interface*. Four primary windows make up the Final Cut Express editing interface: Browser, Viewer, Canvas, and Timeline. The window title appears in the title bar at the top of each window.

The basic functions of these windows fall into two categories: The Browser and Viewer windows are where you organize and view your uncut material. The Canvas and Timeline windows are where you view material as it's edited.

Two smaller windows, the Tool palette and the Audio Meters, allow you to choose editing tools and monitor audio levels.

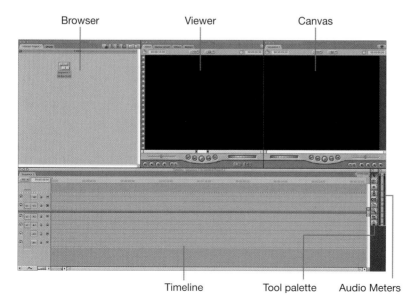

Browser   Viewer   Canvas

Timeline   Tool palette   Audio Meters

Manipulating Windows

The four windows in Final Cut Express can be individually resized, repositioned, and hidden in the Mac OS X Dock. The buttons to close, minimize,
and zoom a window in Final Cut Express do not appear in color, but
operate the same as they do in the Finder window. Practice controlling the
windows in the following steps:

1   In the Browser window, click the title bar and drag the window to
    another location. Restore it to its original place.

    The window seems to snap back into place.

2   Click the Zoom button in the upper-left corner of the window to see
    the window resized to accommodate all its contents. Click again to
    restore the window to its original size.

    NOTE ▶ Remember, the three upper-left window button symbols don't
    appear until you move the mouse over them.

3   Click the Minimize button (–) to see the window drift into the Dock.

4   Locate the Browser in the Dock, and click it once to restore it to the
    interface.

Exploring the Interface

As with all Apple windows, you click in a Final Cut Express window to select it, making it active.

NOTE ► An active window in the Final Cut Express interface has a dark gray title against a light gray title bar. Inactive windows have a dark gray title bar.

1   Click in the center of the Viewer window.

    The title bar changes to light gray with dark gray text.

2   Click in the center of the Canvas window, and note the change in the title bar.

3   Click in the Timeline window and note the change.

Browser

The Browser is where you organize all the material you will use in your editing project. The Browser has different ways of displaying your project elements. The following image shows the View as Medium Icon option.

►   Click in the Browser window to make it the active window.

Think of the Browser as a filing cabinet containing all of your clips and editing choices.

Viewer

The Viewer window is where you view your original source or unedited material.

▶   Click in the Viewer window to make it the active window.

The Viewer serves other purposes as well. Not only can you make editing choices or changes to your material in this window, but you can also edit audio, build titles, create effects, and view your transitions (such as dissolves and fade-outs).

Timeline

The Timeline window is a graphical representation of all the editing decisions you make.

▶   Click in the Timeline window to make it the active window.

This is your workbench area, where you place your material, trim it, move it, stack it, and adjust it. It's also where you can see all your material at a glance.

Canvas

The Canvas and Timeline windows are different sides of the same coin.

▶   Click in the Canvas window to make it the active window.

The Canvas, like the Timeline, shows you an edited sequence. But while the Timeline displays it graphically as bits of information, the Canvas shows it visually as a movie.

Tool Palette

The Tool palette is a collection of Final Cut Express editing tools that can be used throughout the editing process.

> **NOTE** ▶ Because of its small size, the Tool palette has only a Close button.

▶ Move the mouse pointer over any tool to display its name and keyboard shortcut. You can access all tools using their keyboard shortcuts.

Audio Meters

The Audio Meters window displays the audio volume level for whatever is playing, whether it is source material in the Viewer or the final edited sequence in the Canvas window.

Menus, Shortcuts, and the Mouse

Like most applications, Final Cut Express 4 has a main menu bar where editing functions are organized by category. Most of those functions have keyboard shortcuts.

Menu Categories

In many of the Final Cut Express menus, specific functions and commands are grouped together if they share a similar purpose. You can use these groupings as a way to locate similar editing options.

1   Click in the Browser window.

2   Choose the File menu from the main menu bar at the top of the Final Cut Express interface.

Notice how the New and Open commands are separated from the Save and Restore commands and the Import and Export commands.

NOTE ▸ Black menu commands can be applied in the current configuration. A dimmed command requires a different configuration, such as a selected window or item.

3   Choose the Effects menu.

4   Choose Video Transitions.

A submenu of video transition options appears.

5   Slide the mouse into the submenu and choose Dissolve.

Another submenu of dissolve options appears. These options are not available because there are currently no edits in the Timeline to which a dissolve might be applied.

Keyboard Shortcuts

Many Final Cut Express menu functions can be accessed using the keyboard. If a keyboard shortcut is available for a specific function, it will appear to the right of the listed function in the main menu area. Keyboard shortcuts also appear, as they do in the Tool palette, when you move the mouse pointer over certain buttons and tools within the Final Cut Express interface.

To make it easier to remember some of the keyboard shortcuts, similar functions in Final Cut Express are grouped around a single letter.

1   Choose the Effects menu again and look at the dimmed Default–Cross Dissolve shortcut.

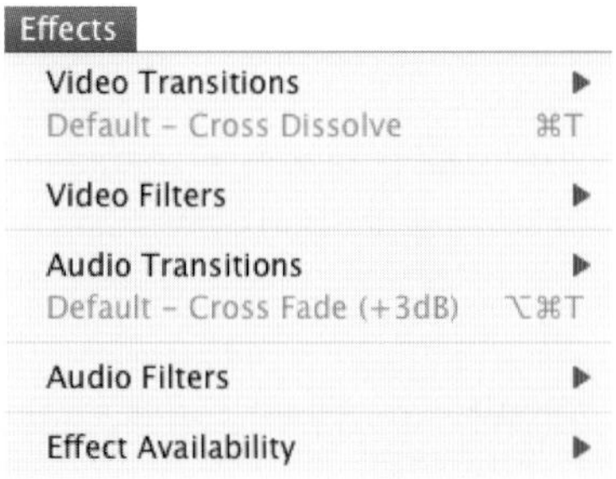

Effects	
Video Transitions	▶
Default – Cross Dissolve	⌘T
Video Filters	▶
Audio Transitions	▶
Default – Cross Fade (+3dB)	⌥⌘T
Audio Filters	▶
Effect Availability	▶

Both the Default–Cross Dissolve and the Default–Cross Fade (+3dB) shortcuts in this menu are associated with the letter *T*.

NOTE ▶ Keyboard shortcuts often use the first letter of the function, such as *T* for transition. When creating, removing, or viewing In or Out points for your edits, which will be discussed in a later lesson, many of those functions will have the letter *I* for In points or *O* for Out points in their shortcuts.

There are also shortcuts that combine a letter or number with one or more of the four modifier keys: Command, Option, Control, and Shift keys. The Command key is sometimes informally referred to as the Apple key.

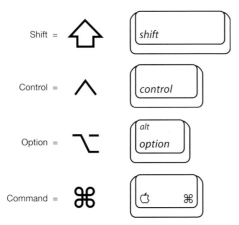

2   Choose the Window menu and choose Arrange.

For window arrangement shortcuts, the letter *U* is used along with several modifier keys.

Mouse

If you don't want to use keyboard shortcuts, you can do everything with your mouse. The mouse in Final Cut Express is position sensitive, meaning that when you move the mouse pointer over a button, a tool, or a certain area in the interface, the descriptive name of that item appears as a *tooltip*, along with its keyboard shortcut if one exists for that function.

1   Move the mouse into the lower portion of the Viewer window and position it over the big circular button with a triangle on it.

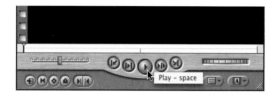

A tooltip appears that indicates this is the Play button and the keyboard shortcut is the spacebar.

2   Position the mouse over the first tool in the Tool palette.

The tooltip identifies this as the Selection tool. It is sometimes referred to as the pointer or arrow tool. But in Final Cut Express, you use it more to select things. There are several other selection tools, so we will refer to this one as the default Selection tool. Its shortcut letter is *A*. Make sure this is the tool selected for all your basic editing, unless otherwise directed.

Working with Projects in the Browser

Every time you begin to edit a new project, you create a new *project file* in which you organize all of its elements. These elements are displayed in the Browser window under a project tab.

Opening a Project

Depending on whether you have worked on other Final Cut Express projects or not, you will see in the Browser either a default Untitled Project tab or your most recent project. Let's open the project that was created for this lesson.

1   From the main menu, choose File > Open.

2   In the Choose a File window, click the FCE 4 Book Files folder in the first column.

3   Click the Lessons folder in the second column.

4   In the third column, click the **Lesson 3 Project** file icon.

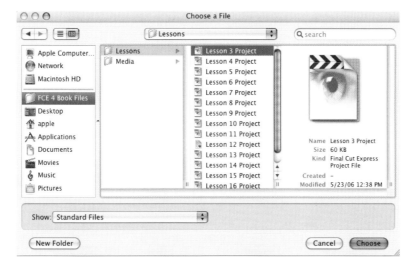

5   Click the Choose button in the lower-right corner of the window.

    NOTE ▶ If you had only a default Untitled Project file open, that project is replaced by the **Lesson 3 Project**. If you had other named projects open, they will remain open.

Selecting and Closing Projects

With the **Lesson 3 Project** open, the Browser window displays a new tab with that project's name on it. There is also an Effects tab and other possible project tabs. Let's close all open projects except the **Lesson 3 Project**.

1   Click the **Lesson 3 Project** tab in the Browser window.

2   Click the Effects tab in the Browser window.

    This is where you select effects such as video and audio transitions and filters. Effects will be covered in a later lesson.

3   Click any other project tab that may be open, besides the **Lesson 3 Project** tab.

4   From the main menu, choose File > Close Project. If you are prompted to save changes, click No.

    NOTE ▶ The use of tabs throughout Final Cut Express helps maximize space in the interface while keeping windows organized.

5   Click the **Lesson 3 Project** tab to make it active again.

Identifying Project Elements

The **Lesson 3 Project** file has four different types of project elements. Each is represented by a unique icon, which can appear larger or smaller depending on what view you select. In this section, you will see two views displayed for each icon.

> **NOTE ▶** Changing view options is discussed in the next exercise.

Clip

A *clip* is a digital file that serves as a link to the original captured media on your hard drive. When you previewed the QuickTime movies in Lessons 1 and 2, you were viewing media on your hard drive. The clip icons in this project represent and link back to the media in the Media folder. You can duplicate a clip icon and use it in a different project, but you will not be duplicating the media file. You will only be creating a second link back to it. The following icon can represent a video-only clip or a combined audio and video clip.

Audio Clip

Like video-clip icons, audio-clip icons link to the original QuickTime audio clips stored on your hard drive. The speaker icon can only represent an audio clip, such as a narration, a music track, or sound effects. The suffix .aif indicates a specific audio file format.

Sequence

The beauty of nonlinear editing in Final Cut Express is that you never corrupt or alter the original sound or video clip. Even as you edit, you do not change or cut the media file on your hard drive. Instead, you make a number of editing choices that result in a sequence of clips.

A *sequence* is a group of clips that have been edited and placed together to create your story. When you play the sequence, Final Cut Express links back to the original media to play just the edited portions of each clip.

Bin

In Final Cut Express, you use folders called bins to organize the project elements just described. The term "bin" comes from the days of film editing when pieces of cut film hung on hooks over large canvas containers called bins. These pieces of film, or film clips, would hang in a bin until the film editor selected them to use in a sequence.

Viewing Project Elements

There are different ways to view project elements, such as clips, sequences, and bins. You can view them as different-sized icons or as an alphabetized list. Viewing clips as icons gives you a visual reference to the content of that clip. But there are times when it's easier to organize your project if you view your elements as a list.

1   To see what view is currently selected, hold down the Control key and click in the empty gray space under the Name column of the Browser window.

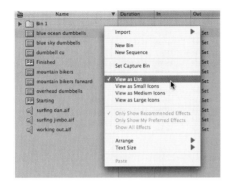

A menu with text options appears. This is called a shortcut menu, also referred to as a contextual menu.

NOTE ▶ Ctrl-click is a shortcut used throughout Final Cut Express. Different shortcut menus will appear, depending on where you click.

2   From the shortcut menu, choose View as Large Icons.

The sequence and audio project elements appear as large icons. The video clips appear as large thumbnail images of the first frame of the clip. You may have to use the blue vertical scroll bar to see all of them.

TIP ▶ To arrange the icons alphabetically, Ctrl-click again in the Browser gray area and choose Arrange > By Name from the shortcut menu. If you have a two-button mouse, you can access this menu, and other shortcut menus, by right-clicking the target—in this case, the gray space under the Name column of the Browser window.

Each of the four primary Final Cut Express windows contains an area in the upper-right corner of the window called a button bar. You can customize a window by placing function buttons in the button bar. The default layout of Final Cut Express includes four View buttons and two Arrange buttons in the Browser button bar.

3   Move your pointer over the first button in the button bar of the Browser. Once you see the tooltip confirm it is the button for View as List, click it to change the view back to list.

The list view is helpful when organizing a lot of elements because it alphabetizes the elements in a list and makes them small enough that you can see many items at once.

TIP ▶ To make the View as List text larger, you can Ctrl-click the empty gray area under the Name column and choose Text Size > Medium or Large from the shortcut menu.

Changing Window Layout

Another way you can change how you see your project is to reposition or rearrange the windows on the screen. Final Cut Express has a default Standard window layout. In addition, the interface can be adjusted dynamically. In a later lesson, you will create your own custom layout.

1   Choose Window > Arrange and then select Standard from the submenu.

   This is the default window layout and may be how your interface is
   currently configured. If it is, you will not see a change.

2   Move the mouse pointer over the boundary line between the Browser
   and Viewer windows.

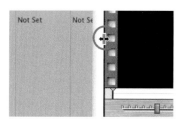

   The pointer changes to a resize pointer.

3   Drag right to make the Browser window larger. Then drag left to make
   the Browser as narrow as possible.

   The Viewer and Canvas windows dynamically change size to compensate for the new size of the Browser.

4   Move the pointer between the Viewer and Canvas windows. When
   you see the resize pointer, drag left to make the Canvas window larger.

5   Move the pointer between the Viewer and Timeline windows. When
   you see the resize pointer, drag up to create a larger Timeline window.

6   Choose Window > Arrange > Standard to return the interface to its
   standard configuration.

Working with Bins

Macintosh computers have always used folders to organize documents
on the hard drive. Within Final Cut Express, the same approach applies
to organizing your project elements. The only difference is that the folder
icons are referred to as bins, as described earlier.

Creating and Naming Bins

The first step in organizing your project is to create new bins to store your source clips, audio, and sequences. Generally, you organize a project by grouping similar elements together into specific bins. You will create three bins—one each for music, clips, and sequences.

In Final Cut Express, there are often several ways to perform the same task or access the same function. For example, you can create a bin in three different ways. You can choose a menu option, use a keyboard shortcut, or Ctrl-click to choose an option from a shortcut menu. You will create a bin using each approach. For this exercise, make sure your Browser is set to View as List rather than as icons, although you can also create and name bins in other views as well.

1   Click in the Browser window to make it active.

2   Choose File > New > Bin.

File		
New	▶	Sequence ⌘N
New Project	⇧⌘N	Bin ⌘B
Open...	⌘O	
Open Recent	▶	
Close Window	⌘W	
Close Tab	^W	
Close Project		
Save Project	⌘S	
Save Project As...	⇧⌘S	
Save All	⌥⌘S	
Revert Project		
Restore Project...		
Import	▶	
Export	▶	
Capture Project...	^C	
Capture...	⌘8	
Log and Transfer...	⇧⌘8	
Reconnect Media...		
Print to Video...	^M	

A new bin appears in the Browser with a default bin name and number.

3   Since the bin name is already highlighted within the text box, just type the word *Music*.

4   Press Return or Tab to accept the name. If you need to correct it, click in the text area of the name itself, not the bin icon, to select the name again.

> **TIP** If you want to change a bin name but it is not highlighted, click once to select the bin and once again to highlight the name.

5   To create the second new bin, press Cmd-B.

6   Type *Clips* in the name area.

7   To create the third bin, Ctrl-click a blank gray area under the Name column in the Browser window and choose New Bin from the short-cut menu.

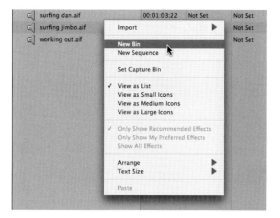

8   Type *Sequences* in the bin name area.

9   To delete Bin 1, the empty bin that was already in the project, click it once to select it and press Delete.

Putting Clips in Bins

Now that you've created your bins, it's time to move individual clips to their appropriate locations. Just as there are different ways to create new bins, there are different ways to select and move project elements.

1   Drag the **surfing jimbo.aif** speaker icon to the Music bin folder icon. When the folder becomes highlighted, let go.

> **TIP** ▶ Whenever dragging and dropping an item in Final Cut Express, you can drag from the item's icon or the name area. But remember, clicking the name area twice highlights it to change it.

2   Drag the **surfing dan.aif** and **working out.aif** music tracks to the Music bin icon the same way.

3   There are two sequence icons in the Browser. To select them both, click the *Starting* sequence, then Cmd-click the *Finished* sequence. Drag one of the selected sequence icons to the Sequence bin icon and let go.

4   Drag the remaining clips into the Clips bin.

> **TIP** ▶ You can select a group of clips by dragging a marquee around them. Create the marquee by clicking outside the clips and then dragging across one or more clips, or click the first clip and Shift-click the last of a continuous list. All the clips between the first and last become selected.

Viewing Bin Contents

Now that your project elements are organized, let's practice accessing and viewing them. There are several ways to do that.

1   Click the small disclosure triangle next to the Clips bin icon to display and view the bin's contents.

2   Click the triangle again to hide the contents of that bin.

3   Double-click the Clips bin icon.

This opens the bin as a separate window that can be moved anywhere in the interface.

4   Drag the window by its title bar, and position it next to the Browser.

In the Browser, the Clips bin icon appears as an open folder or bin, indicating that it is open as a separate window or tab.

5   In the Clips bin window, click the Close button.

6   Hold down the Option key and double-click the Clips bin icon.

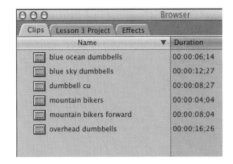

This opens the bin as a separate tab of items next to the project tab.

TIP ▸ Opening a bin as a separate tab is a helpful way to view and access clips without creating a separate window.

7   To change the view of the Clips bin, Ctrl-click in the gray area under the first column and choose View as Medium Icons from the shortcut-menu.

NOTE ▸ Each bin can be set to a different view option.

8   Ctrl-click the Clips tab, and choose Close Tab from the shortcut menu.

This returns the Clips bin to its original configuration in the **Lesson 3 Project** tab area.

9   Save these organizational changes by pressing Cmd-S.

Viewing Columns and Layouts

When the View as List option is selected, there are more than 40 columns of information in the Browser window. These columns reflect two types of information. First, Final Cut Express knows certain information about each clip or item, such as the number of audio tracks and the frame size, and automatically displays that information. Second, someone may have entered information about the clip, such as a log note or a scene or take number. You will work more with these columns in a later lesson.

1   Select the Browser window.

2   Click the Zoom button in the upper-left corner of the window.

The Browser window jumps to a wider view, allowing more columns to be displayed.

> **TIP** ▶ If you adjust an OS X window manually after clicking the Zoom button, clicking the Zoom button again will take you back to the most recent size, not the original size.

3   Click the Browser's Zoom button once again to return to the original Browser layout and size.

Quitting and Hiding Final Cut Express

You quit Final Cut Express just as you would any OS X program—from the main menu or by using the keyboard shortcut. You can also hide the Final Cut Express interface if you want to work on your Desktop or in another program.

1   To hide the interface, choose Final Cut Express > Hide Final Cut Express, or press Cmd-H.

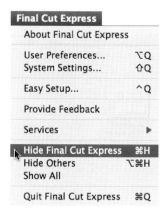

The Final Cut Express interface disappears, and you see your Desktop and any other programs you may have open.

2   Bring back the Final Cut Express interface by going to the Dock and clicking the Final Cut Express program icon once.

NOTE ▶ The small black triangle next to the program icon in the Dock is a reminder that the program is still open.

3   If you are ready to quit the program, choose Final Cut Express > Quit Final Cut Express, or press Cmd-Q. Or you can continue on to the next lesson.

Lesson Review

1.   What are three ways you can launch Final Cut Express?

2.   What are the four primary windows that make up the interface?

3.   What does it mean when a menu option is dimmed?

4.   What are the four modifier keys you use for keyboard shortcuts?

5.   What modifier key do you use to access a shortcut menu?

6.   What are three ways you can create a new bin?

7.   Which Browser view shows you a thumbnail image of the footage?

8.   How can you organize and group project elements together?

9.   How do you return your interface windows to the Standard layout?

10. How do you dynamically adjust a window size in the interface?

11. How can you hide the Final Cut Express interface? How do you restore it?

12. How do you quit Final Cut Express?

Answers

1. You can double-click the application in the Applications folder, click once on the icon in the Dock, or double-click a Final Cut Express project file.

2. The Browser, Viewer, Canvas, and Timeline windows.

3. The appropriate window may not be selected or active.

4. The Shift, Control, Option, and Command (Apple) keys.

5. The Control key. You can also right-click using a two-button mouse.

6. Choose File > New > Bin; press Cmd-B; or Ctrl-click in the gray area under the Name column in the Browser window and choose New Bin from the shortcut menu.

7. Any of the View as Icon views.

8. Create bins for different categories, such as Audio, Video, Sequences, and so on, then drag similar icons into the appropriate bins.

9. Choose Window > Arrange > Standard.

10. Move the pointer over a window boundary line. When the resize pointer appears, drag the line to the desired position.

11. To hide it, choose Final Cut Express > Hide Final Cut Express, or press Cmd-H. To restore it, click the application icon in the Dock.

12. Choose Final Cut Express > Quit Final Cut Express, or press Cmd-Q.

Keyboard Shortcuts

Cmd-B	Creates a new bin
Ctrl-click	Brings up different shortcut menus throughout Final Cut Express
Cmd-H	Hides the Final Cut Express interface
Cmd-Q	Quits Final Cut Express

4

Lesson Files	Lesson 4 Project file
Media	Cooking folder
Time	This lesson takes approximately 60 minutes to complete.
Goals	Open a project
	Work with the Timeline and Canvas
	Play a sequence in the Timeline
	Work with Timeline tracks
	Play a sequence in the Canvas

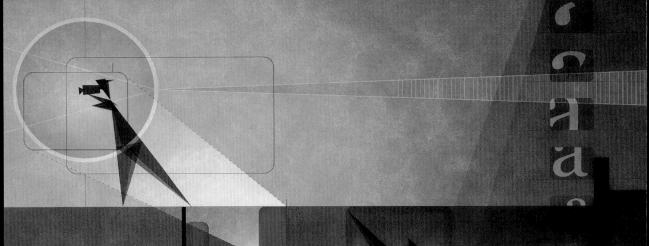

Working in the Timeline

In this lesson, you will begin to work within the Final Cut Express Timeline by playing a sequence and applying different settings to view the sequence in a variety of ways. You will also work with the Timeline track controls, and you will explore the Canvas, where you will view your sequence.

Preparing the Project

You will begin by clicking the Final Cut Express icon in the Dock to launch the application and then opening the **Lesson 4 Project** file. If you are continuing from the previous lesson, you can jump to step 2.

1   Single-click the Final Cut Express icon in the Dock.

2   From the main menu, choose File > Open and navigate to the Lessons folder as you did in Lesson 3.

3   Select the **Lesson 4 Project** file and click Choose.

4   In the Browser, select any other open project tabs, such as the **Lesson 3 Project** tab, and choose File > Close Project.

5   Take a moment to organize your project elements for Lesson 4 as you did in the previous lesson by dragging clips into their appropriate bins.

The Timeline and the Canvas

In the previous lesson, you learned that the Browser is a container for all your project elements. The Timeline is also a container. But unlike the Browser, which holds all your raw materials, the Timeline holds just the specific items you select to tell your story.

You choose only a few items of clothing to wear from a closet filled with all your clothes. In the same way, you will now take only selected portions of your clips to place in the Timeline to build a *sequence*. This sequence is what the Timeline displays graphically.

The Canvas is where you see the sequence. The name of the sequence appears at the top of both the Timeline and Canvas windows, along with the name of the project.

1   Click in the Timeline window and look at the title-bar information.

2   Click in the Canvas window and look at the title-bar information.

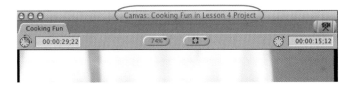

These two windows work in tandem, and many functions can be performed in either window. Let's look first at the Timeline and use the Canvas just as a viewing area.

Playing a Sequence in the Timeline

The first step in editing is screening your source material in the Viewer and marking the portions of the clip you want to use in your sequence. You will begin that part of the editing process in the next lesson. For now, you are going to focus on working with a sequence already in the Timeline.

Moving the Playhead

In the Timeline, you will see several clips placed one after the other, forming a sequence. In the middle of the sequence is a thin vertical bar with a yellow triangle on top. This is the playhead.

The playhead is like a pointer that indicates where you are in the sequence. If the playhead is standing still, you will see a still image in the Canvas.

If the playhead is moving, you will see moving footage in the Canvas. The playhead moves automatically when a sequence is played. The yellow triangular portion of the playhead is positioned in the Timeline ruler area.

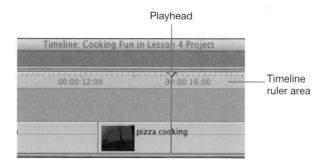

1   Click in several different places in the ruler area of the Timeline.

The playhead jumps to where you click, and you see the frame that represents that location displayed in the Canvas window.

2   Drag the yellow triangle of the playhead across the Timeline ruler area.

Dragging through the sequence this way is called *scrubbing*. Scrubbing is the term used in editing when you pass through your footage manually or not at normal play speed.

In the Canvas window under the image, there is a light-colored area called the scrubber bar. This bar represents the length of the entire sequence. Note that the small playhead in the Canvas scrubber bar tracks with the movement of the Timeline playhead to indicate where you are currently located within the sequence.

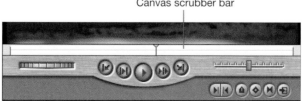

3   In the Timeline, drag the playhead through the **saute pan** clip and watch in the Canvas window until it looks as if the pan catches fire, then stop dragging and let go.

4   Now drag the playhead through the **strawberry cake** clip, and let go when the brush comes into view.

5   Drag the playhead through the **pizza cooking** clip, and stop when the pizza is centered in the screen.

> **NOTE** ▶ As you drag the playhead through the sequence, it snaps like a magnet to the beginning of each clip.

Using Playhead Shortcuts and Visual Clues

Moving the playhead to precise locations in the Timeline is an important part of the screening and editing process. In fact, these same movements can be applied to the playhead in the Canvas window as you view the sequence. They can also be applied to the playhead in the Viewer, but for slightly different purposes.

When you move the playhead, you will at times see visual clues to help you identify specific frames within the sequence. These visual clues appear in the Canvas window as an overlay on top of the video image. Some of the overlay clues represent first and last frames of a clip, the end of a sequence, and so on.

1   With the Timeline window active, press the End key to position the playhead at the end of the sequence.

> **NOTE** ▶ If you have a laptop, the End key may share a position with the right arrow key and require an additional key, such as the Fn (function) key in the lower left of the keyboard, to access it.

The blue vertical bar on the right side of the Canvas window indicates that you are looking at the very last frame of the sequence.

TIP ▶ These visual clues display by default, but if they do not appear, click the Canvas window and choose View > Show Overlays, or press Ctrl-Option-W.

2   Press the up arrow key to move the playhead back to the first frame of the clip in the Timeline.

In the Canvas window, the L-shaped mark in the lower-left corner of the image area is the visual clue that the playhead is positioned on the first frame of a clip in the sequence.

3   Press the up arrow key several times, and look for the L-shaped first-frame indicator in the Canvas window.

When moving from clip to clip using the up or down arrow keys, you are always moving to the first frame of the clip.

4   Press the down arrow key to move the playhead forward to the next clip.

There is a Location field in the upper left of the Timeline window and one in the upper right of the Canvas. Both of these fields reflect the playhead location in the sequence. The number in these Location fields gives you the precise location of the frame you are viewing in the sequence.

00:02:03;27

Think of this eight-digit number as a digital clock, only in this case, there are hours, minutes, seconds, and frames. The last two digits represent the exact frame location in the sequence. This eight-digit number is referred to as a *timecode number*. As you move the playhead through the sequence, that number updates to reflect your new location.

5   Press the left arrow key to move one frame backward.

In the Canvas window, the reverse L shape in the lower-right corner of the image area is the visual clue that you are on the last frame of that clip.

6   Press the right arrow key to move the playhead forward one frame to the first frame of the following clip.

7   Press Shift–left arrow or Shift–right arrow to move the playhead 1 second (30 frames) in either direction. Look at the Canvas Location field to see the time change.

8   Press the Home key to position the playhead at the beginning of the sequence.

Playing a Sequence

There are many ways to view clips in a sequence. You can use buttons in the Canvas, keyboard shortcuts, and even the spacebar.

1   Click in the Timeline window to make it active.

2   Press the spacebar to begin playing the sequence.

     In the Timeline, the playhead moves across the clips and ruler area, and the clips from the sequence play in the Canvas.

3   Press the spacebar again to stop playing the sequence. Practice playing and stopping this sequence by pressing the spacebar again and again.

     In the next steps, you'll use the J, K, and L keys to play the sequence forward and backward. These keys also offer additional play speeds.

4   Press L to play the sequence forward.

5   Press K to stop playing the sequence.

6   Press J to play the sequence backward, then K to stop.

7   To double the forward play speed, press L twice. Press it again to ramp up the speed even more. Press J, and the speed slows down a notch. Press K to stop. Press J twice to play in reverse double speed. Press K to stop.

Practicing with the J, K, and L keys when editing will help you
build speed as an editor. You will also be able to use the keys when
playing clips in the Viewer.

8   In the Canvas window, click the Play button once to play the
     sequence. Click it again to stop the sequence.

Working with Timeline Tracks

In the Timeline, video and audio clips sit on horizontal *tracks,* which are
linear representations of time. Time proceeds from left to right in the
Timeline. The blue clips on top represent video, and the green clips below
represent audio. To the left of the very first clips are track options and
controls used during the editing process.

In Final Cut Express, you can work with multiple tracks. You can have up to
99 separate video tracks and up to 99 separate audio tracks. You might wonder why you need more than one video track and a couple of audio tracks
since you can only see one thing at a time and hear one stereo sound track.

Think about this. What if you wanted to place a title over your original source
material? You would need two tracks, one for the source material and one
for the title. And if you wanted to create a complex opening sequence that
involved four different images moving about on your screen at the same time,

each of the four clips would require its own track in the Timeline. Think how many tracks they must use when editing the opening to any James Bond movie! In later lessons, you will add tracks for titles and motion effects. For now, you will work with one video track and two audio tracks.

Patching Source Tracks

Each track in the Timeline is given a level ID number, such as Video 1, or V1, and Audio 1 and Audio 2, or A1 and A2. As you begin to edit with more tracks, you will want to make sure you are placing your source clip on the right track level. The way to do this is to connect, or *patch,* a source audio or video track to a specific destination track. In many cases, this is done for you automatically when you open a clip. This is discussed more in Lesson 5.

The source and destination tracks appear in the Timeline track control area, with the source controls to the left of the destination tracks. The destination tracks are stationary and represent the tracks you see in the Timeline. The source tracks are indicated by a lowercase *v* for video and *a* for audio, while the destination tracks are indicated by an uppercase *V* or *A*. A DV audio/video clip has one video source track and two audio source tracks when there is stereo audio.

1   Move the pointer over the v1 source control in the Timeline track area.

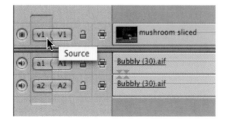

2   Click the v1 source control repeatedly to connect and disconnect, or patch and unpatch, it from the V1 destination track.

3   Click the a1 source control to unpatch it from the A1 destination track.

NOTE ▶ Assigning a source track to the appropriate destination track is only necessary during the editing process. It does not affect how the sequence plays in the Timeline.

4 Make sure the v1, a1 (left channel), and a2 (right channel) tracks are assigned and connected to the V1, A1, and A2 destination tracks, respectively.

Changing Track Visibility

There may be times during your editing process when you want to turn off the sound or picture of one of your tracks in order to focus on what you see or hear in the other tracks. For example, you may have used the original or background sound from one of your clips and added a narration and a music track. If you are trying to edit to the music beats, you may not want to hear the narration track. You can turn off a track by clicking the green Visible or Audible control on that track.

1 Click the green Audible control on the A1 track.

   The track turns dark in the Timeline to show it will not be heard.

2 Click the green A2 Audible control so that both tracks are dark.

3 Press the Home key to take the playhead to the top of the sequence. Play the sequence by pressing the spacebar.

   You see the video of the clips play in the Canvas but don't hear any audio.

   NOTE ▶ Whenever you toggle off the Visible or Audible control to a track, that track will not be seen or heard.

4   Click the A1 and A2 Audible controls again to turn them back on.

5   Turn off the visibility for the V1 track and play the sequence.

    Now you hear the sequence but don't see it.

6   Turn on visibility for the V1 track to view and hear all tracks.

Locking Tracks

Sometimes, you may need to make changes to some of the tracks in your
Timeline without affecting any of the other tracks. To do this, you *lock* the
tracks you do not want to affect.

1   On the V1 track, click the lock next to the track number. This is the
    Track Lock control.

    Diagonal lines appear across the track to indicate that track is locked.

2   Play the sequence.

    NOTE ▶ A locked track is visible and can play along with the other
    tracks, but it cannot be edited or changed.

3   Make the track active again by clicking the Track Lock control once more.

Adjusting Track Height

The vertical height of the Timeline tracks can be adjusted to suit your
personal preferences as well as the project requirements. If you are working
with a lot of tracks, you may want to make them all smaller to see more tracks
at one time. The Track Height control is at the lower left of the Timeline.

1   In the bottom of the Timeline, move your mouse pointer over any
    column in the Track Height control area.

    A tooltip appears, identifying this as the Track Height control.

2   Click the first column in the Track Height control.

    The first column turns blue when selected, and all the tracks in the
    Timeline become very small.

3   Click the second column to make the tracks taller. Then click the third
    and fourth track height.

    NOTE ▸ When changing track heights, you change all the tracks to be
    the same height.

4   Press Shift-T several times to cycle through the different track heights.

    As you cycle through using the keyboard shortcut, the active column
    height turns blue in the Timeline Track Height control area.

5   Move the pointer in the Timeline over the split double line dividing
    the video and audio tracks.

    The pointer turns into an up-down resize arrow.

    TIP ▸ In Final Cut Express, when you move the pointer over some-
    thing that can be adjusted, the pointer changes to a different tool.

6   With the resize pointer, click and drag the double line up and down.

This creates space for additional audio or video tracks you may add later.

7   Move the pointer over the boundary line between the A1 and A2 tracks in the track control area. When the pointer changes to a resize arrow, drag down to make just the A1 track taller.

TIP ▶ To manually adjust all the audio or all the video tracks to the same height, press Option and drag a single track. To manually adjust all the tracks using this method, press Shift as you drag.

8   In the Track Height control in the Timeline, click the third column to bring the tracks back to a uniform height.

NOTE ▶ The sequences created for all the exercises in this book were saved in the third column height, although they may appear smaller in this book than on your computer screen. Feel free to change the sequence track height to your preference throughout the exercises.

Changing the Thumbnail Display

There are three ways you can view clips in the Timeline. You can see just the name of the clip, the name plus a thumbnail image of the clip, or a filmstrip representation of the clip.

1   In the main menu, choose Sequence > Settings, or press Cmd-0 (zero).

TIP ▶ Make sure the Timeline or Canvas window is active so that this menu option can be selected.

The Sequence Settings window appears, containing a Timeline Options tab.

> **Sequence Settings**
>
> Name: Cooking Fun
>
> Timeline Options \ Render Control
>
> Track Size: Medium
> Thumbnail Display: Name Plus Thumbnail
>
> Track Display
> ☐ Show Keyframe Overlays
> ☐ Show Audio Waveforms
>
> Load Sequence Preset...   Cancel   OK

2   In the Thumbnail Display pop-up menu, choose Name, but don't click OK.

Clips appear in the Timeline with only clip names.

3   Click the Thumbnail Display pop-up menu again, and choose Name Plus Thumbnail.

A thumbnail image of the clip's first frame appears on each clip in the Timeline.

4   Click the Thumbnail Display pop-up menu again and choose Filmstrip.

The entire clip length has as many thumbnails as can fit in the clip area. Each thumbnail is different and represents a different portion of the clip. This is just a representation and is in no way subdividing your clip.

5 Click the Thumbnail Display pop-up menu again and choose Name Plus Thumbnail. Click OK.

Whether you use a single thumbnail display or a filmstrip of thumbnails is a personal choice. Depending on your computer, working with more thumbnail images can slow some operations down a bit. Since we will make references to specific names of clips throughout the lessons, it will be helpful to have the names of the clips visible in the Timeline. So a good compromise for these lessons is to choose Name Plus Thumbnail.

Scaling and Zooming the Timeline

In the lower-left portion of the Timeline are other controls for adjusting the horizontal scale and vertical height of the tracks within the Timeline, as well as the position of the sequence.

1 In the Zoom control box, drag the Zoom control to the far right to show more of the sequence in the Timeline.

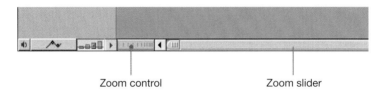

Zoom control   Zoom slider

> **NOTE ▸** Keep in mind that the lengths of the clips are not being changed, only how the clips appear in the Timeline.

2 Now click or drag the Zoom control to the left to expand the sequence.

The sequence is expanded around the playhead position.

3 Click the middle of the Zoom slider and drag to the left to see the beginning of the sequence.

4   Drag the Zoom slider to the far right to see the end of the sequence
    and back to the left again to the head of the sequence.

5   Click the tiny purple vertical line in the Zoom slider area.

NOTE ▶ The purple line may or may not be on the Zoom slider itself,
but it will be within the Zoom slider area.

This purple line represents the location of the playhead in reference to
the slider. Clicking it will take you to the playhead's parked position.

6   With the playhead visible, press Option-+ (plus) to zoom in to the
    playhead location. Press Option-– (minus) several times to zoom out.

7   Drag the right thumb tab, or scored-end portion of the slider, to the
    right to zoom out of the sequence a little.

    NOTE ▶ The size of the slider gets longer or shorter as you drag the
    scored tab on either end.

8   Press Shift-Z to make the entire sequence fit in the Timeline window.

Using Tools in the Timeline

There are tools in the Tool palette you can select to zoom or view the
sequence in the Timeline. These are the Zoom tool and the Hand tool. As
in other desktop media programs, the tools that look like a magnifying

glass are used to zoom in and out of something, and the tools that look like hands are used to reposition it.

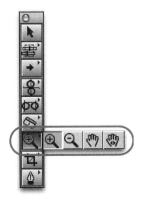

1   In the Tool palette, click the Zoom In tool (the magnifying glass icon with the plus sign in it), or press Z.

When you move the mouse pointer back into the Timeline, it turns into the Zoom In tool.

2   Click the Zoom In tool anywhere in the Timeline sequence to zoom in to that particular area.

TIP You can also drag the Zoom In tool to create a marquee around a portion of the sequence, and that section will fill the Timeline.

3   In the Tool palette, click and hold on the Zoom In tool to bring up additional tools. Select the Hand tool without any arrows.

NOTE ▸ You can also press the shortcut key, H, for the Hand tool.

4   In the Timeline, click and drag the Hand tool left or right across
    the screen.

> **NOTE ▶** As you drag left or right, you can view a different area of the
> Timeline. Using the Hand tool does not change the position of the
> sequence within the Timeline, only what portion you are viewing.

5   Change back to the Zoom In tool by pressing Z.

6   Hold down the Option key. The Zoom In tool changes to the Zoom
    Out tool (the plus inside the magnifying glass changes to a minus).
    Now click in the sequence to zoom out and display more of the
    sequence in the Timeline.

7   Press A to return your mouse pointer to its default Selection tool.

8   Press Shift-Z to make the entire sequence fit in the Timeline window.

Playing the Sequence from the Canvas

As you can see, the Canvas window is a visual display of your edited
sequence. You can also control the playing of the sequence from the
Canvas window, just as you do in the Timeline. In fact, many of the
Timeline shortcuts work here as well.

1   Click once in the Canvas window to make it active.

2   Click anywhere in the Canvas scrubber bar beneath the image area;
    the playhead jumps to the point where you clicked.

The Timeline playhead moves in tandem with the playhead in the Canvas.

NOTE ▶ In the Canvas window, the scrubber bar represents the full length of the sequence.

3   Drag the playhead to the beginning of the sequence on the far left and then toward the end of the sequence on the right.

The duration of the current sequence is always displayed in the Duration field in the upper-left corner of the Canvas window. The specific location of the playhead is displayed in the Location field in the upper-right corner.

Final Cut Express refers formally to these fields as the Timecode Duration field and the Current Timecode field. Throughout this book, we will use the shorter reference of Duration and Location fields.

4   Press the Home key to jump the playhead to the beginning of the sequence.

5   Play the sequence by pressing the spacebar. Stop it after a few seconds by pressing the spacebar again.

When you press the spacebar to start and stop the sequence, the Canvas Play button light goes on and off.

6   Play the sequence by pressing the L key. Double the speed by pressing L again.

7   Stop the sequence, and press the left arrow key to move backward a frame at a time.

8 Press the Home key to go to the beginning of the sequence, and then press the down arrow key to move forward to the first frame of the next clip. Continue moving forward through the sequence this way.

9 Go to the sequence location 00:00:10;04 by typing *1004* in the Location field in the upper-right corner and pressing Tab or Return.

TIP ▶ You can also click in the Location field in the Timeline, type a number there, and press Return to move the playhead to that location.

10 Under the image in the Canvas window are a shuttle slider and a jog wheel. Drag the shuttle slider left or right to go backward or forward through the sequence at a variable speed. Drag the jog wheel to move forward or backward a frame at a time.

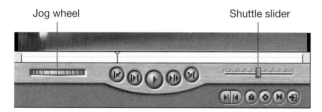

Saving and Quitting

Any changes you make to your Final Cut Express project can be saved. Even though you did not make any edits in this lesson, you changed how the Timeline was viewed. Saving the project at this point will save your current Timeline configuration and even the playhead position in the sequence.

1   Press Cmd-S to save the current project.

2   Choose File > Close Project if you want to close this project.

> **NOTE** ► If you want to keep working on this project the next time you open Final Cut Express, don't close the project prior to quitting the program. That way, it will open automatically the next time you launch the program. But if you are finished with the project, you can close it first and then quit the program.

3   Press Cmd-Q to quit Final Cut Express, or leave the program open and continue on to the next lesson.

Lesson Review

1. From what menu do you open and close a Final Cut Express project?

2. True or false: If the playhead in the Timeline is still, you may see moving images in the Canvas.

3. What is the white horizontal bar directly beneath the Canvas image area?

4. What do pressing the Home or End keys do?

5. True or false: Timecode is a six-digit number representing hours, minutes, and seconds.

6. How can you use the J, K, and L keys to play a sequence?

7. What does clicking a green Visible or Audible control in the Timeline track control area do?

8. What does clicking a video or audio source control do?

9. How can you change the height of the Timeline tracks?

10. How can you make an entire sequence fit in the Timeline window?

11. How can you tell how long the current sequence is?

Answers

1. The File menu.

2. False.

3. The scrubber bar.

4. Pressing the Home key moves the playhead to the beginning of the sequence; pressing the End key moves the playhead to the end of the sequence.

5. False. Timecode is an eight-digit number representing hours, minutes, seconds, and frames.

6. Press L to play forward, J to play backward, and K to stop playing. Press L or J repeatedly to ramp up speed forward or backward.

7. It turns off that track so you don't see or hear it.

8. It connects or disconnects a source track to a destination track.

9. By clicking the Track Height control in the Timeline, by pressing Shift-T repeatedly, or by choosing Sequence > Settings and choosing an option from the Track Size pop-up menu.

10. Click in the Timeline and press Shift-Z.

11. Look at the Canvas Duration field.

Keyboard Shortcuts

L	Plays the sequence forward
K	Stops playing
J	Plays the sequence backward
Home	Moves the playhead to the beginning of the sequence
End	Moves the playhead to the end of the sequence
Shift-T	Cycles through the different track heights
Cmd-0 (zero)	Opens the Sequence Settings window

Shift-Z	Places the entire sequence in the Timeline view
Z	Selects the Zoom In tool to zoom into the sequence
Option-Z	Converts the Zoom In tool to the Zoom Out tool to shrink the view
H	Selects the Hand tool
Up arrow	Moves the playhead backward to the first frame of the previous clip in the Timeline
Down arrow	Moves the playhead forward to the first frame of the next clip in the Timeline
Left arrow	Moves one frame to the left
Right arrow	Moves one frame to the right
Option-+ (plus)	In the Timeline, zooms in at the playhead location
Option-– (minus)	In the Timeline, zooms out at the playhead location
Shift–left arrow	Moves the playhead one second to the left
Shift–right arrow	Moves the playhead one second to the right

5

Lesson Files	Lesson 5 Project file
Media	Working Out folder
Time	This lesson takes approximately 60 minutes to complete.
Goals	Organize project elements into bins
	Open source clips in the Viewer
	Play clips in the Viewer
	Mark edit points
	Remove edit points
	View edit points
	Save and quit a project

Lesson 5

Working in the Viewer

Now the real fun of editing begins, as you look more closely at each clip and decide exactly which portion to use. This lesson will show you how to open and view source clips in the Viewer and mark edit points in preparation for editing these clips to the Timeline.

Opening Your Project File

You will begin by clicking the Final Cut Express icon in the Dock and then opening the **Lesson 5 Project** file. If you are continuing from the previous lesson, you can jump to step 2.

1   Single-click the Final Cut Express icon in the Dock.

2   From the main menu, choose File > Open and navigate to the Lessons folder as you did in Lesson 4.

3   Select the **Lesson 5 Project** file and click Choose.

4   In the Browser, select any other open projects by clicking their tabs, and choose File > Close Project.

Preparing the Project

To organize this project, you will create bins for clips and drag clips into those bins. After doing this several times, it will become a natural habit to look at your project elements and make sure they are organized or grouped together in an efficient, logical manner. Review Lesson 3 for additional details regarding these steps.

1   In the Browser, create two new bins.

2   Name one bin *Unmarked Clips* and the other *Viewing and Marking*.

3   Drag the following four clips into the Unmarked Clips bin: **blue ws dumbbells, golfer putts, skater ecu,** and **yoga mat**.

Unmarked Clips	
blue ws dumbbells	00:00:06;13
golfer putts	00:00:11;21
skater ecu	00:00:03;22
yoga mat	00:00:13;22

4   Drag the remaining video clips into the Viewing and Marking bin. Leave the music clip and sequence standing alone for this exercise.

5   For this exercise, choose Window > Arrange and choose Standard
    from the submenu to view the interface in the Standard layout.

6   Play the *Marking* sequence in the Timeline to see some of the clips
    you will be marking.

> **NOTE** ▶ In this lesson, you will focus on just playing and marking
> source clips. In the next lesson, you will learn to edit these clips.

Viewing Clips

The primary purpose of the Viewer is to provide a place to view the clips
you want to edit. The Viewer window has four tabs you can access during
your editing process. The default is the first tab, Video, where you can see,
hear, and mark your clips. There is a separate Stereo or Mono audio tab for
working more closely with the audio of a clip. Filters and Motion tabs will
be used when you start to create effects. If there is no audio present in the
clip, no audio tab will appear. These tabs will be covered in more detail in
later lessons.

The first use of the Viewer will be to view your original material or unedited source clips. To do this, you will use the Video tab.

Opening Clips in the Viewer

Opening a clip in the Viewer is the first step to screening your captured source clips. There are three different ways you can open a clip in the Viewer to screen it. You can double-click a clip, drag it into the Viewer, or select it and press Return. Let's practice opening clips all three ways.

1   Click in the Browser window.

2   Click the disclosure triangle next to the Viewing and Marking bin to reveal the contents of that bin.

3   To open the **ab roller** clip, double-click its clip icon.

     The clip appears in the Viewer.

4   To play this clip, click the Play button under the image area.

5   Double-click the **arm machine** clip to open it in the Viewer. Play it if you like.

6   Now drag the **overhead dumbbells** clip icon from the Browser into the Viewer image area and release.

7   Drag the **mountain bikers** clip into the Viewer.

8   Another way to open a clip is to select it and press Return. Click the **dumbbell cu** clip once in the Browser to select it, and then press Return to open it in the Viewer.

9   To access a clip that has recently been opened in the Viewer, click the Recent Clips pop-up menu button in the lower right of the Viewer window. Drag down and choose the **mountain bikers** clip.

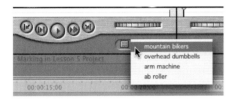

NOTE ▶ You can adjust the number of recent clips displayed in the Recent Clips menu in the User Preferences window (Option-Q).

Playing Clips in the Viewer

Once the clip is in the Viewer, you can play it. There are several ways to play the clip, similar to the ways you played the sequence in the Timeline and in the Canvas.

The Viewer has a scrubber bar and a playhead just like the Canvas window. But whereas the Canvas scrubber bar represents the entire length of the active sequence, the Viewer scrubber bar represents the entire length of only one clip, and the playhead indicates where you are located within that single clip.

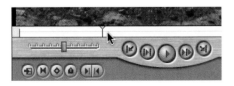

Practice different ways of playing a clip in the Viewer. Most of these are the same as playing a sequence in the Timeline or Canvas.

1   With the Viewer window active, press the spacebar to start and stop
    the **mountain bikers** clip. Let it play to the end of the clip.

2   Drag the playhead through the scrubber bar to scan, or *scrub*, the clip.

3   Click the Play button beneath the scrubber bar to start and stop play-
    ing the clip.

NOTE ▶ You will work with the other transport controls when you
begin marking your clips in this lesson.

4   Practice with the J-K-L keys. Press L to play the clip forward. Press
    K to stop. Press J to play the clip in reverse at normal speed. Press it
    again to increase the reverse speed. Press K to stop.

5   Press the up arrow key to move to the head of the clip and the down
    arrow key to move to the end of the clip.

    NOTE ▶ Notice the vertical filmlike strips signaling the head and tail,
    or first frame and last frame, of the clip.

6   Press the left or right arrow key to move backward or forward one frame.

7   Shuttle through the clip by dragging left or right on the shuttle slider.

Shuttle slider   Jog wheel

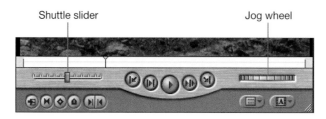

8   Drag the jog wheel to the right to move frame by frame through your clip.

Viewing Display Information

The Viewer displays information about the clip that is helpful during editing. Like the Canvas, there is a Duration field in the upper-left corner. While the Canvas Duration field displays sequence length, the Viewer Duration field displays the duration or length of the clip in the Viewer. In the upper-right corner is a Location field that indicates the playhead's current timecode position in the clip.

Each number has four sets of two numbers divided by colons. From the left, these are hours, minutes, seconds, and frames. The number 00:00:04;04 reads 0 hours, 0 minutes, 4 seconds, and 4 frames.

> **NOTE ▶** The semicolon separating the last two digits from the rest of the timecode number indicates that the Drop Frame option is selected. This type of timecode can be used to time your sequence in real time. If a colon appears in this location, the timecode is non-drop frame. You can read more about drop frame and non-drop frame timecode in the glossary.

1   Play the clip in the Viewer, and watch the number in the Location field change as the clip plays.

2   Drag the playhead through the scrubber bar and see the timecode number change in the Location field.

3   Press the left arrow key to move backward one frame and see the number in the Location field go down by one frame.

4   Press the right arrow key to move forward one frame and see the number in the Location field go up by one frame.

5   Hold down the Shift key and press the right or left arrow key to go forward or backward one second.

6   What is the duration of the mountain bikers clip?

7   From the Recent Clips pop-up menu, choose dumbbell cu. What is its duration?

8   Drag the playhead to 00:00:04;15 in the clip.

Marking Clips

Now that you have looked at your source clips in the Viewer, you are ready to make edit decisions. The editing process begins with deciding which portion of a clip you want to use in the sequence. Once you determine this, you mark the starting and ending points of the desired portion of the clip. These are your *edit points*.

You will draw from the clips you previously screened. They can be opened from the Recent Clips pop-up menu or from the Browser. As you screen a clip in the Viewer, you will mark starting and stopping points within the clip to identify only the portion you want to use in the sequence. The starting point is referred to as the *In point,* and the stopping point is the *Out point.* Occasionally, you may choose to use a clip in its entirety.

In the next lesson, you will edit your marked clips into a sequence. But for now, you will practice different ways to mark a clip. As with many Final

Cut Express operations, there are several ways to mark the edit points of a clip before editing.

Marking with Buttons

The Mark In and Mark Out buttons are located in the Viewer window below and to the left of the Play buttons. On the Mark In button is a triangle that faces in toward the material you want to use. On the Mark Out button is a reverse triangle that faces backward toward the material you want to use.

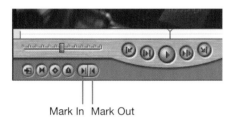

Mark In Mark Out

Clicking either button will place an edit point in the scrubber bar wherever the playhead is located.

1   From the Browser, open the **skater glasses on** clip into the Viewer and play the clip.

   NOTE ▶ The Duration field reflects the full length of the clip when there are no edit points present.

2   Drag the playhead to just before the woman puts the sunglasses on her face.

   TIP ▶ Scrubbing through a clip to find a specific point is sometimes a more efficient way of screening and marking than taking the time to play the full clip in real time.

3   Click the Mark In button in the Viewer to mark an In point at this
location.

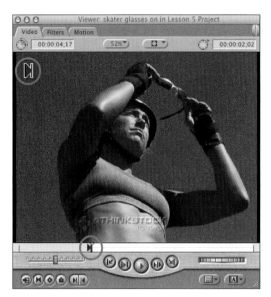

A new In point appears in the scrubber bar where the playhead is
located. Notice, too, the In point in the image area.

4   Play the clip to where the woman's right hand comes down and goes
out of the frame, and then stop the clip.

5   If necessary, drag the playhead to a different frame, or use the arrow
keys or jog wheel to adjust your location.

6   Click the Mark Out button to mark an Out point at this location.

A new Out point appears in the scrubber bar where the playhead is located. The Duration field reflects the length of the marked portion of the clip, and the scrubber bar dims the portion of the clip that will be unused.

7   Click the Play In to Out button to see only the marked portion of your clip.

> **NOTE** ▶ You will practice different ways to view the marked portion of clips later in this lesson.

At this point, you might normally edit the marked clip to the sequence. But you can also mark several clips at one time and then edit them to the sequence in a later step. Let's continue practicing marking clips.

Marking with Keyboard Shortcuts

Once you learn some of the keyboard shortcuts in Final Cut Express, you may find that using them speeds your editing process. When marking edit points, all the keyboard shortcuts that relate to the In point use the letter *I*. All the shortcuts that relate to the Out point use the letter *O*.

1   Open the **sword twirl** clip in the Viewer, and play it until the woman's body starts to come into the frame. Adjust with the right and left arrow keys to choose the precise frame you want.

2   Press the I key to mark an In point at this location.

TIP ▶ Choose the Mark menu to remind yourself of the keyboard shortcuts.

Mark	
Mark In	i
Mark Out	o
Mark Split	▶
Mark Clip	x
Mark to Markers	^A
Mark Selection	⇧A
Select In to Out	⌥A
Set Poster Frame	^P
DV Start/Stop Detect	
Clear In and Out	⌥X
Clear In	⌥I
Clear Out	⌥O
Clear Split	▶
Clear Poster Frame	
Markers	▶
Play	▶
Go to	▶
Previous	▶
Next	▶

3   Play the clip again, and press O to mark an Out point after the woman lands in her stance.

   NOTE ▶ In marking, you can play clips at normal speed and mark while the clip is playing. This is called marking *on the fly.* Or you can drag the playhead to the specific frame you want and then mark an edit point while the clip is stopped.

4   To play the marked portion of the clip, click the Play In to Out button or press Shift-\ (backslash).

5   To save the edit points you've created, choose File > Save Project, or press Cmd-S.

You may wonder what has happened to the skater glasses on clip you previously marked. Click the Recent Clips pop-up menu and choose the skater glasses on clip. All edit points are saved along with that clip in this project unless you remove them and resave.

Marking One Edit Point

When you are editing a clip to the sequence, Final Cut Express will default to using the first frame of the clip if no In point has been set and the last frame of the clip if no Out point has been set.

1   Open the mountain bikers forward clip and play it.

2   Mark an Out point about halfway through the clip.

With no In point marked, this clip will begin with the first frame.

3   Open the mountain bikers clip and play it.

4   Mark an In point about one second into the clip.

With no Out point marked, this clip will continue until the last frame.

Marking Durations from an In Point

Sometimes, rather than marking a specific action point to edit, you may choose to set a duration or an amount of time that you want to use that clip. For example, if there is a locked-down shot of some ongoing activity, such as a waterfall, the actual start or stop point may not be as critical as the amount of time you want to use the shot.

1   Open the **skater skates forward** clip and play it.

2   Press Home to move the playhead to the beginning of the clip.

> **NOTE ▶** If you press Home while the clip is still playing, the playhead will move to the Home position and then the clip will continue to play. To move to the head of the clip and stay there, press the spacebar to stop playing and then press the Home key again.

3   Mark an In point at the head of the clip by pressing the I key.

4   Click in the Viewer Duration field and type *200* for a 2-second dura-tion of the clip.

> **TIP ▶** You can also type this number with a period following the 2 to represent zero frames. Substituting a period for double zeros is acceptable throughout Final Cut Express.

5   Press Tab or Return to enter the amount.

> **NOTE ▶** An Out point is automatically created in the scrubber bar two seconds from the In point.

If you change your mind about the duration, just enter a new one in the Duration field and press Tab or Return. The Out point will adjust automatically.

Marking Durations from an Out Point

You can also use a duration from the end of a clip or from an Out point if, for example, you just want to use the last three seconds of a clip. In this situation, you are actually backing up the location of the playhead by a specific duration. At that point, you can enter an In point.

1   Open the **dumbbell cu** clip or choose it from the Recent Clips pop-up menu.

2   Press the End key or drag the playhead to the end or tail of the clip.

3   Press the O key to mark an Out point.

    NOTE ▶ It is not necessary to have an Out point at the end of this clip because the default Out is the end of the clip. But sometimes it's helpful to have an edit point as a visual reference.

4   With the mouse pointer in the image area, type *–300* or *–3.* (minus 3 period).

5   Press Tab or Return.

The playhead is backed up three seconds from the Out point.

6   Press I or click the Mark In button to set an In point at this location.

7   Click the Play In to Out button to play the marked portion.

Marking the Entire Clip

There are times when you want to use the full length of a clip in the sequence. Using the entire clip doesn't require any edit points at all. In fact, Final Cut Express defaults to using the entire clip if no edit points are present. But again, it can be helpful to have the edit points as a visual reference.

1 Open the **golfer hits ball** clip and play it.

2 Mark the entire length of the clip by clicking the Mark Clip button in the Viewer.

In one step, and regardless of where the playhead is located, this button marks an In point at the first frame and an Out point at the last frame of the clip.

3 Open the **blue ocean dumbbells** clip and play the whole clip.

4 To mark this entire clip using the shortcut, press the X key.

NOTE ▶ In and Out points remain unless changed or deleted.

Marking and Dragging Edit Points

Another way to mark your edit points is to mark the entire clip and then drag an edit point to where you want to begin or end the clip. As you drag an edit point in the scrubber, you can see the frames you are passing through in the Viewer image area. Dragging an edit point is another way of scrubbing through the clip.

1   Open the **blue sky dumbbells** clip and play it.

2   Drag the playhead to the center of the clip.

3   Press X to mark the entire length of the clip.

4   In the scrubber bar, drag the In point until the two dumbbells come into view, and release the In point.

NOTE ► As you drag either edit point, the Viewer displays the changing edit point, and the Duration field automatically updates to reflect the new distance between the In and Out points. However, when you stop dragging an edit point, the image in the Viewer reverts back to the frame where the playhead is located.

5 Drag the Out point from the right until the woman puts her arms down.

Using Location Numbers

There may be situations when you or someone else has screened clips and written down In and Out points for you to use in editing. When edit points have been selected through a separate screening process, you can go directly to those specific locations and set the edit points without having to scrub through the clip material.

1 Open the **overhead dumbbells** clip and play it.

The number in the Viewer Location field changes to reflect the current location of the playhead.

2 Click in the Location field and type *4:04*.

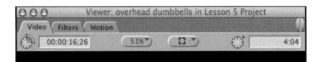

TIP ► When typing a timecode number, it is not necessary to type any preceding zeros before the first real digit or the colons or semicolons that separate the numbers. Final Cut Express will add those automatically. (However, it is helpful to use the colon in print so that the number can be read more easily.) You could simply type *404* in step 2 and get the same result.

3   Press Return.

The number is displayed in the Location field, and the playhead goes to this location.

4   Mark an In point at this location.

5   This time, with the Viewer window active and your pointer anywhere in the window, type *10:24*.

As you type, the numbers are automatically entered in the Location field.

TIP ▶ Typing a number in the Viewer, Canvas, or Timeline window automatically enters the number as a new location in that window's Location field.

6   Press Tab or Return.

7   Mark an Out point at this location.

8   Play the marked clip.

Removing Edit Points

Once you set edit points in a clip, they stay with the clip until you remove them. Removing unwanted edit points from a clip is a very easy process and uses the same keys that marking does—I, O, and X.

1   Click the Recent Clips pop-up menu and choose the **golfer hits ball** clip.

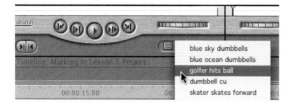

2   Press Option-I to clear the In point.

3 Press Option-O to clear the Out point.

4 Open the **blue sky dumbbells** clip.

5 Press Option-X to clear both the In and Out points at the same time.

Viewing Edit Points

Once you have marked a clip, there are several ways you can view the material at, around, or between those edit points. These options are available either by clicking one of the Viewer buttons or by using keyboard shortcuts. Let's use one clip and view its edit points in different ways.

Going to an Edit Point

Sometimes you want to go directly to the In or Out point you marked to see that specific frame. Is it where you want to begin the edit? Or should it be a frame earlier or later? Going to an edit point uses the keyboard shortcut keys I and O, along with the Shift key. To go to an edit point using buttons, use the Previous Edit and Next Edit buttons, located in the Viewer transport controls.

1 Open the **overhead dumbbells** clip from the Browser.

2 Press Shift-I to go to the In point of the clip.

3 Press Shift-O to go to the Out point of the clip.

4 Click the Go to Previous Edit button to go to the previous edit point, or in this case the In point.

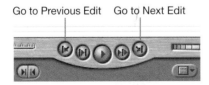

Go to Previous Edit   Go to Next Edit

NOTE ▶ The straight vertical line in the Play buttons represents an edit point. The arrows represent the direction you will move to go to the next edit point, backward or forward—that is, previous or next.

5   Click the Go to Previous Edit button again, and the playhead goes to the head of the clip.

6   Click the Go to Next Edit button to go to the next edit point, in this case the In point.

7   Click the Go to Next Edit button again to take you to the next edit point, or the Out point.

8   Click the Go to Next Edit button once again to go to the end of the clip.

Playing Between Edit Points

You have already been using the Play In to Out button to screen the marked area of your clips.

1   Click the Play In to Out button to see only the marked portion of the **overhead dumbbells** clip.

2   For the keyboard shortcut, press Shift-\ (backslash) to see the marked portion of your clip.

The clip plays from the In point to the Out point and stops.

3 To see the marked area play repeatedly, choose View > Loop Playback.

> **NOTE ▸** When active, this option applies to any play activity in the Viewer, Canvas, and Timeline windows.

4 Choose View > Loop Playback again to deselect this option.

Playing Around Edit Points

You have already practiced viewing the selected clip material between the In and Out points. But you might want to view the few frames around a specific edit point or location. Again, there are buttons and keyboard shortcuts that do this.

1 Press Shift-I to go directly to the In point.

2 Click the Play Around Current Frame button to play a little before the edit point and a little after.

Play Around Current Frame

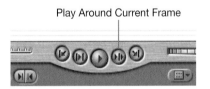

> **TIP** ▸ The Play Around Current Frame function is not tied to an edit point. It will play around the current location of the playhead, wherever that is in the clip. To play around an edit point, you must drag the playhead to that point first, and then click the Play Around Current Frame button.

3 Press Shift-O to go directly to the Out point.

4 Press the \ (backslash) key to play a little before and after the current playhead position, which happens to be on the Out point.

5   Drag the playhead to the middle of the clip.

6   Click the Play Around Current Frame button to play a little before and after the playhead's current position.

Project Tasks

Throughout this book, there will be project tasks that will give you an opportunity to practice what you have learned.

1   In the Browser, open each clip in the Unmarked Clips bin a different-way.

2   Mark a specific action within each shot. Some shots may not need two edit points.

Saving and Quitting

When you finish practicing viewing and marking clips, you can save your project and quit Final Cut Express. Saving your project at this point, although you haven't made any edits, will save your bin organization and your new edit points.

1   Press Cmd-S to save the current project.

2   Choose File > Close Project if you want to close this project.

> **NOTE ►** If you want to keep working on this project the next time you open Final Cut Express, don't close the project prior to quitting the program. It will open along with Final Cut Express the next time you launch the program.

3   Press Cmd-Q to quit Final Cut Express, or continue to the next lesson.

Lesson Review

1. What are three ways you can open a clip into the Viewer?

2. What are the different ways you can play or view a clip in the Viewer?

3. What are three ways you can mark an edit point in a clip in the Viewer?

4. When you create a duration for a clip, from what starting point is that duration calculated?

5. How do you change an existing edit point in the Viewer?

6. How do you move the playhead to an In or Out point?

7. How do you move the playhead to a specific timecode location?

8. How do you play only the marked portion of a clip in the Viewer?

9. When you save your project, are the marked edit points saved as well?

Answers

1. Double-click the clip, drag it into the Viewer, or select the clip in the Browser and press Return.

2. Press the spacebar or the Play button or use the J-K-L keys. You can also drag the playhead through the Viewer scrubber bar and use the shuttle and jog controls.

3. You can click the Mark In or Mark Out buttons, use the keyboard shortcuts I or O, or choose an appropriate option from the Mark menu.

4. The duration is calculated from either the In point or the beginning of the clip if no In point exists.

5. You can drag the edit point in the Viewer scrubber bar to a different location, or you can simply remark a new edit point.

6. Press Shift-I to move to the In point; press Shift-O to move to the Out point.

7. Click in the Location field and type the timecode number, then press Tab or Return.

8. Click the Play In to Out button in the Viewer transport control area, or press Shift-\ (backslash).

9. Yes, all marks are saved when you save the project.

Keyboard Shortcuts

I	Marks an In point
O	Marks an Out point
X	Marks the entire clip length
Option-I	Removes the In point
Option-O	Removes the Out point
Option-X	Removes both In and Out points together
Shift-I	Moves the playhead to the In point
Shift-O	Moves the playhead to the Out point
Shift-	Plays from the In to the Out point
****	Plays around the current playhead location

6

Lesson Files	Lesson 6 Project file
Media	Music folder, Working Out folder
Time	This lesson takes approximately 60 minutes to complete.
Goals	Prepare a sequence
	Mark edit points
	View edit points
	Make Overwrite and Insert edits
	Build a sequence

Making Edits

In this lesson, you will begin to edit by placing marked clips into a sequence in the Timeline. You will learn two types of edits, *Overwrites* and *Inserts*. To begin, you will open a project from within Final Cut Express; view a finished sequence to see what you will be creating; and open, close, and duplicate sequences.

Preparing the Project

You will start by clicking the Final Cut Express icon in the Dock and then opening the **Lesson 6 Project** file. If you are continuing from the previous lesson, you can jump to step 2.

1   Single-click the Final Cut Express icon in the Dock.

2   From the menu, choose File > Open and navigate to the Lessons folder as you did in Lesson 5.

3   Select the **Lesson 6 Project** file and click Choose.

4   Close any open projects by Ctrl-clicking the project's tab in the Browser and choosing Close Tab.

TIP ▶ To reopen a project you have recently worked with in Final Cut Express, choose File > Open Recent and choose the project.

5   The files in this lesson have been organized into bins for you. Click the disclosure triangles to display the contents of each bin.

Working with Sequences

Before you begin editing, you will open and play the finished sequence to see what your new sequence might look like. You will also duplicate an existing sequence and rename it so that you are ready to begin editing. The several ways to play a sequence were covered in detail in Lesson 4.

Opening and Playing a Sequence

You can work with several sequences open in the Timeline at the same time. In both the Timeline and the Canvas, each open sequence can be accessed by clicking its name tab. If you don't see a name tab for the sequence you want to view, it means that the sequence is not open.

1   Look at the tabs area in the Timeline and Canvas to see what sequences are currently open.

2   Play the *6-Finished w-Music* sequence in the Timeline.

3   In the Browser, click the triangle next to the Sequences bin to reveal the contents of that bin.

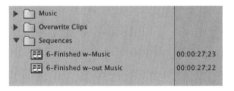

4   Double-click the *6-Finished w-out Music* icon in the Browser.

The sequence opens in the Timeline. There are now two open sequences.

You can click the two sequence tabs to see the different sequences. One version has music, and the other does not. Whatever sequence is active in the Timeline is also active in the Canvas window. The names of the sequences in the Timeline and Canvas window title bar will always match.

5   Play the *6-Finished w-out Music* sequence in the Timeline.

> **TIP** ▶ Different computer monitors will display different-sized Timelines. To make the entire sequence fit in the Timeline window, press Shift-Z.

Closing a Sequence

You close a sequence the same way you close a project or bin tab. Even though a sequence is closed and does not appear in the Timeline and Canvas, it is still available in the Browser.

1   Click the *6-Finished w-Music* tab in the Timeline.

2   Choose File > Close Tab.

The sequence is closed in the Timeline and Canvas windows but still remains in the Browser.

3   To close the other sequence a different way, Ctrl-click the *6-Finished w-out Music* tab in the Timeline and choose Close Tab from the short-cut menu.

> **NOTE** ▶ When no sequences are open, both the Canvas and Timeline windows close because their only purpose is to display open sequences. In the next exercise, you will bring those windows back by opening another sequence.

Creating a Sequence

When you create a new sequence in the Browser, it is given a default name and number, such as *Sequence 2* or *Sequence 3*, depending on how many sequences have been created in this project. It will also be given the current Timeline settings for number of tracks, track height, and type of thumbnail display. Those settings can be changed in the User Preferences window. In this exercise, you will change those settings, create a new sequence, and rename the new sequence to reflect the work you will be doing.

1   In the main menu, choose Final Cut Express > User Preferences.

    In the User Preferences window, you can make changes to the default Final Cut Express user settings.

2   Click the Timeline Options tab.

3   On the left side lower portion of the window, set the Default Number of Tracks to be 1 Video and 2 Audio, and choose Name Plus Thumbnail as the Thumbnail Display. Click OK.

NOTE ▶ Making changes to the Timeline preferences in this window will affect only the new sequences you create.

4   In the Browser, Ctrl-click the Sequences bin icon and, from the short-cut menu, choose New Sequence.

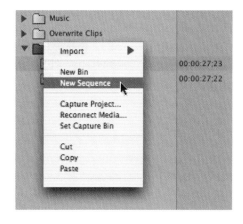

Creating a sequence this way automatically places the new sequence in the bin.

5   When the sequence name becomes highlighted, type *Overwrite Edits,* and press Return or Tab to accept the name change.

6   If the *Overwrite Edits* sequence icon is highlighted, you can press Return to open the sequence. If it's not, double-click the sequence icon to open it.

Even though there are no clips in the sequence, both the Timeline and Canvas windows open to display the *Overwrite Edits* sequence.

Making Overwrite Edits

There are different types of edits you can make in Final Cut Express, and each type places a clip in a sequence a little differently. Some edits place clips over whatever is on a Timeline track, and some insert them between other clips in a track. In this lesson, you will work first with the Overwrite type of edit.

Overwrite editing places a clip in the Timeline over whatever is currently at the playhead position. The Timeline may be empty at that point, or there may be another clip present. Either way, the new clip simply overwrites whatever space or material is in the Timeline track at the playhead position, as in the following graphic.

While there are different kinds of edits to choose from, the method of making different edits is similar. You will use the Overwrite edit to explore the different ways to make an edit in Final Cut Express. By trying each approach, you will find the one that suits you the best.

Preparing to Edit

Before you begin making edits, you position the playhead wherever you want the new clip to be placed in the Timeline. The playhead position determines the In point or edit location within the sequence. You will also need to make sure the source tracks are patched to the correct destination tracks for the edit. In these exercises, you will be editing just video clips.

1   In the Timeline, make sure the playhead is in the Home position at the beginning of the sequence.

> **NOTE ▶** Although the playhead determines the location of the new clip in the sequence, the clip's duration marked in the Viewer determines how much of the clip is used.

2   From the Additional Clips bin, double-click the **yoga mat** clip to open it in the Viewer. Look at the Viewer window tabs.

This clip has a Video tab but no audio tab, meaning there is no audio attached to this clip.

3   Look at the source control in the track area of the Timeline.

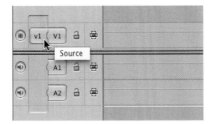

After opening a clip in the Viewer, any audio or video source tracks are represented by source controls in the Timeline track area. Since the V1 track is the only video destination track in the Timeline, the v1 source track is automatically patched to that track.

> **NOTE ▶** The process of assigning tracks is also referred to as *patching* tracks.

Dragging to the Edit Overlay

In the previous lesson, you practiced marking clips. Once a clip is marked and the project is saved, those edit points remain with the clips. To practice making edits in this lesson, you will open marked clips and drop them into the *Overwrite Edits* sequence in the Timeline.

Once your clip is marked in the Viewer and the playhead is in position in the Timeline, you are ready to make your first edit. To do this, you will drag the image of the clip from the Viewer into the Canvas window. When the pointer enters the Canvas window, the Edit Overlay appears in the Canvas. The Edit Overlay is like an editing palette offering you different edit options.

1   From the Overwrite Clips bin in the Browser, double-click the **dumbbell cu** clip to open it in the Viewer.

    NOTE ▸ All of the clips in this bin are already marked as they were in the previous lesson.

2   In the Viewer, click the image area and drag right.

    A thumbnail of your clip appears under the mouse pointer.

3   Drag the thumbnail image into the Canvas window, *but don't release the mouse!*

The Edit Overlay appears in the Canvas window, displaying a palette of different edit types. In the Edit Overlay, the red Overwrite section has a brighter border around it, indicating that it is the current default edit option. It also has a lighter downward arrow as part of its icon. This is a visual clue that you will be laying over or covering anything in its place in the Timeline.

4   Drop the **dumbbell cu** thumbnail image onto the Overwrite section in the Edit Overlay.

This clip is DV-NTSC format. If your sequence was set up for a different video format, this clip will not match the current sequence and a warning will appear. Final Cut Express can change the sequence settings automatically to match this clip.

Attention – This clip does not match this sequence's settings or any of your sequence presets.

For best performance your sequence and External Video should be set to the format of the clips you are editing.

Change sequence settings to match the clip settings?

No   Yes

5   If the above warning appears, click Yes to have Final Cut Express change the sequence settings to match the clip.

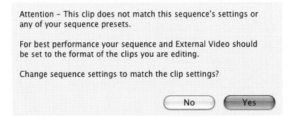

The marked portion of the clip is placed in the Timeline starting where the playhead was located. The playhead repositions to the end of the clip, awaiting the next edit.

6   Open the **overhead dumbbells** clip from the Browser.

This clip has already been marked, and the playhead is positioned where you want this edit to go, so you are ready to proceed to make another Overwrite edit.

7   In the Viewer, drag the thumbnail image to the Edit Overlay in the Canvas, and drop the image onto the Overwrite section.

8   Repeat the process with the **arm machine** clip. Open the clip and drag its thumbnail image onto the Overwrite section in the Canvas Edit Overlay.

> **TIP** ▶ If the Overwrite section is highlighted in the overlay, you can drop the clip anywhere in the Canvas image area to make an Overwrite edit.

Using the Keyboard Shortcut

You can also use a keyboard shortcut to make an Overwrite edit. This produces the same result as dragging to the overlay in the Canvas. The keyboard shortcut for Overwrite edit is F10. You will place the next edit at the end of the last one.

> **TIP** ▶ The Exposé function in Tiger (OS 10.4) uses the F10, F11, and F12 keys to change window layout on the Desktop. To use these keys for Final Cut Express editing functions, open your System Preferences window and select Dashboard and Exposé. Change the keyboard shortcuts from F10, F11, and F12, to F1, F2, and F3.

1   Open the **ab roller** clip in the Viewer.

2   View the marked portion of the clip by clicking the Play In to Out button to the left of the Viewer Play button.

3   Press F10 to edit this clip into the sequence as an Overwrite edit.

> **NOTE** ▶ To use the Fn keys on a laptop computer, you need to press the Fn key on the lower left of the keyboard.

4   Click in the Timeline and press Shift-Z to see the entire sequence fit
    in the window. Then press Home and the spacebar to view the new
    sequence.

Take a minute to view the edits you have put together in your sequence.
Which approach to making Overwrite edits did you enjoy the most? They
both get the same job done, so it really is a matter of personal preference.
Another approach, dragging a clip directly to the Timeline, will be covered
in the next lesson.

Project Tasks

1   Edit the following marked clips into the sequence by using the F10
    shortcut key or dragging to the Canvas Edit Overlay:

    ▶   **skater ecu**

    ▶   **mountain bikers**

    ▶   **golfer hits ball**

    TIP▶ If you get an unwanted result, remember that Cmd-Z will
    undo the damage.

2   In the Timeline, press Shift-Z if necessary to see the entire sequence.
    Press Home and then the spacebar to play the sequence.

3   When you finish playing, press the End key to ensure that the play-
    head is on the last frame of the last edit, in preparation for the next
    edit you make.

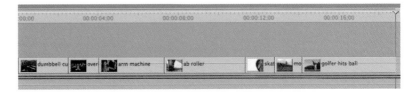

Backing Up Sequences

You created a sequence by making Overwrite edits. In the next set of exercises, you will insert new source clips between several of the clips in your
current sequence. Before you shift gears and start to make major editing
changes in a sequence, it's a good idea to back up your work by duplicating
the current sequence. That way you can always come back to this version if
you're not happy with subsequent changes.

Duplicating a Sequence

Duplicating a sequence makes an exact copy of it, just like duplicating a
document. After you've duplicated a sequence, you can then make new
edits or new changes and still have the original.

1   In the Browser, Ctrl-click the *Overwrite Edits* sequence icon.

    A shortcut menu appears with different options for that sequence.

2   Choose Duplicate.

A duplicate sequence is created under the original sequence in the
Browser. The original sequence name is used, along with the word *Copy*.

3 To rename the duplicate sequence, click in the name area to select it, and type *Insert Edits*. Press Tab or Return to accept it.

4 Double-click the *Insert Edits* icon to open this sequence in the Timeline.

NOTE ▶ When you open the sequence, it becomes the active sequence.

5 Take a moment to save the work you've done in your project by pressing Cmd-S.

As you edit, you can keep other sequences open in the Timeline for reference, or you can close them using the methods described earlier in this lesson. For now, let's close the *Overwrite Edits* sequence so that it won't be selected accidentally during editing.

6 In the Timeline, Ctrl-click the *Overwrite Edits* tab and choose Close Tab from the shortcut menu.

Inserting Clips

So far, you have laid clips end to end in the Timeline. When you want to drop clips between already existing clips and still preserve the old clips just as they are, you must use an Insert edit. When you insert a new clip into the sequence, all clips following the newly inserted clip are pushed down the exact length of the clip's duration to accommodate the new edit. The sequence is now longer by that amount.

As in Overwrite editing, the place where a clip will be inserted into the sequence is determined by the location of the playhead.

Dragging to the Edit Overlay

In the *Insert Edits* sequence, there are several shots of sports activities. Between some of these clips, you will insert additional clips of people working out. Because you will be inserting clips, you will continue to expand the length, or duration, of the sequence with every clip you insert.

As with Overwrite editing, you can also use the Canvas window's Edit Overlay to make an Insert edit. Since Overwrite is the default, you must drag and drop the image of the clip from the Viewer onto the Insert section of the Edit Overlay.

1   In the Browser, click the triangle to display the contents of the Insert Clips bin.

2   Click in the Timeline, and drag the playhead to the first frame of the **skater ecu** clip. You can also use the up or down arrow keys.

    NOTE ► You may want to zoom in to the Timeline to see the name on the clip revealed. Or you can look for the thumbnail of the extreme close-up of the skater with sunglasses.

3   Open the marked **sword twirl** clip into the Viewer.

4   As you did with the Overwrite edit, click and drag the image to the Canvas Edit Overlay, *but don't release the mouse.*

NOTE ▶ The Insert section is yellow, and its icon is of an arrow pointing to the right. That will remind you that all the following clips in the sequence will be moved forward to allow room for the new clip you are editing.

5   Place the clip on top of the yellow Insert section, and when the section is highlighted, release the mouse.

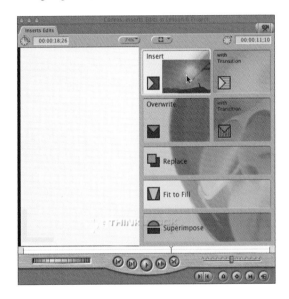

The playhead jumps to the end of this clip. Let's insert another clip at this point.

6   To review marking, open the **skater glasses on** clip, and mark an In point at 00:00:01;03 and an Out point at 00:00:04;15.

7   Drag the image from the Viewer to the Canvas window, and drop it on the yellow Insert section in the Edit Overlay.

8   Play the new clips in the sequence.

Using the Keyboard Shortcut

As with Overwrite editing, Insert edits have a keyboard shortcut (F9). Let's add one more skater clip to the sequence.

1   In the Viewer, open the **skater skates forward** clip.

2   Play the marked portion of the **skater skates forward** clip by clicking the Play In to Out button in the Viewer.

TIP ▶ You can also use the shortcut for this function, Shift-\ (backslash).

3   Click in the Timeline to make it active, and press the up or down arrow keys until you are on the first frame of the **mountain bikers** clip. Look for the first-frame indicator in the lower left of the Canvas image.

4   Press F9 to insert the **skater skates forward** clip into the sequence in front of the **mountain bikers** clip.

5   Move the playhead back to play a few of the new clips in the sequence.

Adding Music

What you have now is a video-only sequence with different clips. Throughout this book, you will learn numerous ways to work with audio in Final Cut Express. In this lesson, you will simply add an existing music track to the Timeline to spice up the sequence.

When you open a sound-only clip, the sound is displayed graphically in the Viewer. Actually, because this is a stereo music track, there are two audio tracks. The Video tab in the Viewer does not appear when there is no video to display. You will spend more time covering the details of the Stereo (or Mono) audio tab in another lesson. In this exercise, you will use the full length of the clip, so marking the clip will not be necessary.

1   In the Browser, click the disclosure triangle next to the Music bin.

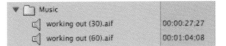

NOTE ▶ The .aif suffix at the end of the music clips denotes a type of audio file called *AIFF* (Audio Interchange File Format).

2   Double-click the **working out (30).aif** audio clip icon.

The clip opens in the Viewer in the Stereo (a1a2) audio tab. Since there is no video, only a waveform representation of the audio appears.

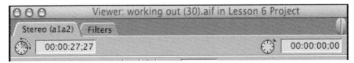

In the Timeline, the a1 and a2 source tracks are automatically patched to the A1 and A2 destination tracks. You will work with other audio options in a later lesson.

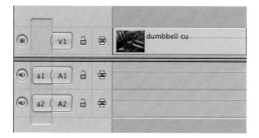

3   Move the playhead to the beginning of the sequence in the Timeline.

4   If you zoomed in to the Timeline, press Shift-Z to see the entire sequence again.

5   Press F10 to drop the music clip in as an Overwrite edit.

The entire stereo music track is laid in the Timeline on the A1 and A2 tracks from the beginning of the sequence.

6   Press the Home key and play the sequence with the music.

In a later lesson, you will learn how to make adjustments to clips to improve the timing of the action to the music.

NOTE ▶ Make sure the sound level on your computer is at an audible level.

Project Tasks

1   Create a new sequence and name it *Practice Edits*.

2   Open five different clips from any of the three clips bins, mark them, and edit them into the sequence as Overwrite edits.

NOTE ► Remember, inserting new edit points replaces the old. But if you want to delete an edit point in the Viewer, press Option-I to delete the In point, Option-O to delete the Out point, or Option-X to delete both.

3 Open five additional clips, mark them, and insert them between the existing clips.

4 Add either the 30- or 60-second music track to the sequence.

Saving and Quitting

If you are finished with this lesson, you can save your project and quit Final Cut Express or continue to the next lesson.

1 Press Cmd-S to save the current project.

2 Press Cmd-Q to quit Final Cut Express, or continue to the next lesson.

Lesson Review

1. How do you open a sequence into the Timeline?

2. When you open a clip in the Viewer, where do the source track controls appear?

3. What two ways can you make an Overwrite edit?

4. What happens to the remaining clips in a sequence when you make an Insert edit?

5. How do you duplicate a sequence?

6. How do you change the number of tracks a new sequence will have?

7. When you open a music or audio clip in the Viewer, does a Video tab appear in the window?

Answers

1. You can double-click it, or select it and press Return.

2. In the Timeline track control area.

3. You can drag the clip from the Viewer into the Canvas and drop it on the Overwrite section of the Edit Overlay, or you can press F10.

4. All the remaining clips are pushed down the length of the clip you are inserting.

5. Ctrl-click the sequence in the Browser and choose Duplicate from the shortcut menu.

6. Choose Final Cut Express > User Preferences. In the User Preferences window, click the Timeline Options tab and make the changes in the appropriate area.

7. No Video tab appears in the Viewer when you open an audio-only clip.

Keyboard Shortcuts

Cmd-O	Opens a project
Ctrl-click	Brings up a shortcut menu
Shift-Z	Fits the entire sequence in the Timeline window
Cmd-S	Saves the current status of a project
Cmd-Z	Undoes the last action
F10	Edits a clip to the Timeline as an Overwrite edit
F9	Edits a clip to the Timeline as an Insert edit

7

Lesson Files	Lesson 7 Project file
Media	Music folder, Vacation Fun folder
Time	This lesson takes approximately 60 minutes to complete.
Goals	Move clips in the Timeline
	Copy and paste clips
	Move and delete clips
	Overwrite clips directly to the Timeline
	Insert clips directly to the Timeline

Editing to the Timeline

The flexibility of Final Cut Express allows you to edit clips in different ways. You can drag a clip to the Edit Overlay in the Canvas or press a shortcut key, such as F9 or F10. These editing approaches automatically place the clip in the Timeline at the playhead location. A more "manual" approach is drag-and-drop editing, where you can drag a clip from the Viewer and drop it directly into the Timeline to make an edit. Once a clip is in the Timeline, you can select it, move it, or copy and paste it directly in the Timeline. Drag-and-drop editing is an easy yet powerful way to edit your sequence.

Preparing the Project

To get started, you will launch Final Cut Express and open the project file for this lesson. In the **Lesson 7 Project** file is a finished sequence of what you will accomplish. You will also create a new sequence to begin editing.

1   Launch Final Cut Express and choose File > Open, or use the keyboard shortcut, Cmd-O.

2   Select the **Lesson 7 Project** file from the Lessons folder on your hard drive.

> **NOTE ▶** The Timeline and Canvas windows do not open because there are no open sequences. These windows open only to display an active sequence.

3   In the Browser, display the contents of the Sequences bin and double-click the *7-Finished* sequence. Play it to see what you will accomplish in this lesson.

4   To create a new sequence to begin editing, Ctrl-click the Sequences bin in the Browser and choose New Sequence from the shortcut menu.

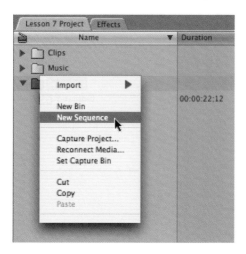

TIP ▶ Remember, to change your Timeline preferences before creating a new sequence, choose Final Cut Express > User Preferences, or press Option-Q. Select the Timeline Options tab, set your preferences, and click OK.

5   Name the new sequence *Moving Edits* and double-click it to open it in the Timeline.

▼ 🗀 Sequences	
🎞 7-Finished	00:00:22;12
🎞 Moving Edits	00:00:00;00

6   In the Timeline, Ctrl-click the *7-Finished* sequence tab and choose Close Tab to close it. Close any other open sequences (besides *Moving Edits*) the same way.

Manipulating Clips in the Timeline

There will be times during editing when you will simply want to reach in, grab a clip, and do something with it. But before you start editing a lot of clips in the Timeline, let's take another moment to work with a single clip, to get a feel for how to select it, move it, copy and paste it, and even delete it from the Timeline.

Selecting and Deselecting a Clip

As you have seen, you can make edits quite easily by marking your clips and dragging them to the Edit Overlay or using a keyboard shortcut and never touching the Timeline. The first step to drag-and-drop editing is learning how to select and deselect a clip. As with all Apple applications, clicking an icon once selects it; clicking twice opens it. For this exercise, you will select a clip by just clicking once.

1   In the Browser, display the contents of the Clips bin, and then double-click the **horseshoe island** clip to open it in the Viewer. This clip has already been marked. To view the marked area, click the Play In to Out button.

2   In the Timeline, move the playhead toward the middle of the empty sequence.

3   To edit the **horseshoe island** clip into the sequence at this location, use the Overwrite shortcut, F10.

> **TIP** If the clip appears too short or too long to work with in the Timeline, press Option-+ (plus) to magnify the view and make the clip appear longer or press Option-− (minus) to make it appear shorter.

4   Single-click the **horseshoe island** clip in the Timeline.

The clip becomes brown to indicate that it is the selected clip.

5   To deselect it, click in the gray space above the clip.

Repeat steps 4 and 5 for practice.

6   Hover the mouse pointer over the very end of the clip. When the pointer changes to the left-right resize arrow, click once.

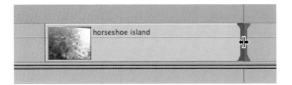

You have selected the Out point of this clip.

7   To select the clip itself and not the edit point, click in the middle away from the ends of the clip.

8   To deselect the clip, click in the empty gray space above it. You can also choose Edit > Deselect All, or use the keyboard shortcut, Shift-Cmd-A.

Dragging Clips

Clips can be dragged left or right and up or down in the Timeline. Dragging clips left or right repositions them in the sequence. Dragging a video clip up or an audio clip down will automatically create an additional track for that clip. For now, let's concentrate on just moving the clip left and right to reposition it in the Timeline.

1   Click the **horseshoe island** clip again to select it.

When you move the mouse through the clip, the pointer changes to a Move pointer.

2   Click and drag the **horseshoe island** clip to the right, *but don't release the mouse.*

An information box appears that displays a plus sign and a number. This is how far in time you have moved the clip forward from its original position.

3   Release the mouse.

> **NOTE ▶** Wherever you let go of the clip, this is the clip's new position, and any movement from that point will be displayed as a new measurement in the information box.

4   Now drag the clip to the left past its original location.

A minus or plus sign appears, indicating how far you have moved from that position.

5   Drag the clip to the right a few seconds and let go. Then drag to the left a few seconds and let go.

6   Position the playhead on the left and away from the clip, but not at the beginning of the sequence.

7   Drag the clip toward the playhead. When you get close, let the clip *snap* to the playhead.

8   Now drag the clip to the beginning, or head, of the sequence and release it.

Copying and Pasting Clips

You may have edited a beautiful shot into your sequence and now want to use that as both the opening and closing shots. Since you already marked and edited this clip to your desired length, and since it's already in the Timeline, copying and pasting it wherever you want to use it is very easy.

Copying and pasting in Final Cut Express is similar to copying and pasting in a word-processing program. Let's say you want to copy and paste a word. First you select it. Next you copy it. Then you click at the point where you want to paste it, and you paste the word. In Final Cut Express, you even use the same Apple shortcut commands for copy and paste: Cmd-C and Cmd-V.

1   Open the **island twirl** clip in the Viewer.

2   In the Timeline, move the playhead past the end of the first clip a second or two, and press F10.

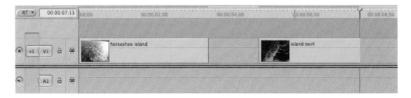

3   Select the new clip and choose Edit > Copy, or press Cmd-C.

NOTE ▶ The copy of the clip is stored in your computer's Clipboard, just as the word you copy in a document would be.

4   With the playhead still at the end of the **island twirl** clip, choose Edit > Paste from the menu, or press Cmd-V.

A copy of the **island twirl** clip is placed at the playhead position in the Timeline, and the playhead moves to the end of that new clip.

5   With the playhead at its current position at the end of the second **island twirl** clip, press Cmd-V again, and then one more time.

NOTE ▶ You can keep pasting the clip again and again because it remains in the Clipboard until something else replaces it.

6   Press Cmd-Z to undo the most recent pasting.

The number of times you can undo an action can be set in the User Preferences window.

7   In the main menu, choose Final Cut Express > User Preferences. In the General tab, change the number in the Levels of Undo box to *15* and click OK.

User Preferences

General \ Editing \ Timeline Options \ Render Control

Levels of Undo: 15 actions
List Recent Clips: 10 entries

Real-time Audio Mixing: 8 tracks
Audio Playback Quality: Low (faster)
☐ Limit real–time video to: 20 MB/s

☐ Prompt for settings on New Project
☐ Prompt for settings on New Sequence

☑ Report dropped frames during playback
☑ Abort capture on dropped frames
☑ Do not show A/V Device Warning on launch

NOTE ► Although you can have up to 32 levels of Undo, the higher the number, the more computer memory is required.

8   In the Timeline, drag the clip on the far right over a few seconds and let go.

9   Drag it back to its original position and let it snap to the clip.

island twirl
↓
–00:00:23

NOTE ► Just before you let go, note that the clips display triangular-snapping indicators around the edit point where the two clips meet.

Viewing Canvas Edit Frames

The Canvas window usually displays whatever frame the playhead is parked on or playing over in the Timeline. But when you drag a clip left or right in the Timeline, the Canvas window displays two small edit frames in a *two-up display*.

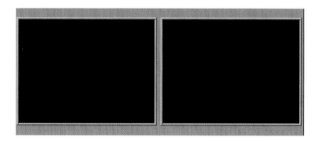

The two edit frames, or windows, in the Canvas display the frames adjacent to or bordering the current clip in the Timeline. The left window displays the frame in the sequence immediately in front of or before the clip you are dragging. The right window displays the first frame in the sequence after the clip you are dragging. If there are no clips on one or both sides of the selected clip, the windows remain black.

1   Make sure the playhead is at the end of the last **island twirl** clip in the Timeline.

2   Open the **boy surf casts** clip and press F10 to place it in the sequence at the end of the last **island twirl** clip.

3   Open the **rockscape surf** clip and place it at the end of the sequence.

NOTE ▶ If you can't see all your clips at this point, select the Timeline and press Shift-Z to bring the sequence into full view.

4   Start dragging the first clip, **horseshoe island**.

The two-up display appears in the Canvas window. If there are no clips on either side of the **horseshoe island** clip, both frames will be black.

5   Now snap the current clip to the first **island twirl** clip, *but don't release the mouse.*

There are no clips to the left of the clip you are dragging, so the left edit frame is black. But the right frame displays the *next frame* after the **horseshoe island** clip, which is the first frame of the **island twirl** clip.

TIP ▶ If you don't see an image in the right edit frame as you drag, move the pointer closer to the clip's edit point on the right.

6   Drag the **horseshoe island** clip farther to the right in the sequence until it covers parts of the third **island twirl** clip and the **boy surf casts** clip. Drag left and right in this area, *but don't release the mouse.*

In the Canvas, you see the two frames that will border this clip if you release this clip at this location.

7 Now drag the **horseshoe island** clip into the last clip, **rockscape surf**, *but don't release the mouse.*

The **boy surf casts** clip appears in the left Canvas edit frame because now it's on the left side of the clip. The frames in the Canvas continue to update as you drag.

8 Drag the **horseshoe island** clip left back to the head of the Timeline and release.

Moving a Clip by Duration

If you know how far you want to move a clip in the Timeline, you can type a specific amount of time, or duration, to move it earlier or later in the sequence.

1 If it's not already there, drag the playhead to the end of the sequence.

2 Select the last clip in the Timeline, **rockscape surf**.

3 Type the number *2* followed by a period (*2.*) to represent 2 seconds.

In the middle of the Timeline, above the video clips, a Move box automatically appears, indicating the amount you typed. Like all things numerical, it assumes a positive direction unless you type a minus (−) sign before the number.

4   Press Tab or Return to execute the move.

The clip moves forward in the Timeline two seconds.

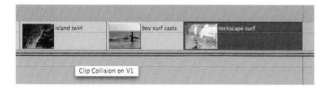

5   Now type −*1.* (minus 1 period) and press Return to move the clip backward in the Timeline one second.

The Move box appears in the same place in the Timeline no matter where the clip you're moving is located.

6   Type −*2.* (minus 2 period) and then press Return to *try* to move the clip back another two seconds.

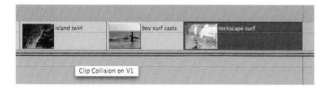

The clip moves back up against the last clip in the sequence, but a note appears in the center of the Timeline, indicating that there is a clip collision on V1. This type of move command will not allow you to move a clip into an adjacent clip.

Selecting and Moving Multiple Clips

You can also select and move a group of clips together in the Timeline. There are several ways you can select a group of clips. You can use a menu option to select all the clips in the sequence, you can use a keyboard shortcut and select the clips you want, or you can drag a marquee around a group of clips. Dragging a marquee in the Timeline is the same Apple concept as dragging a marquee, or rectangular outline, around items on your Desktop.

In the following exercise, you will practice these methods. There are additional selection tools in the Tool palette, which you will explore in another lesson.

1   In the Timeline, select all the clips by choosing Edit > Select All from the main menu. The shortcut for Select All is Cmd-A.

Edit	
Undo	⌘Z
Redo	⇧⌘Z
Cut	⌘X
Copy	⌘C
Paste	⌘V
Clear	⌫
Duplicate	⌥D
Paste Insert	⇧V
Paste Attributes...	⌥V
Remove Attributes...	⌥⌘V
Select All	⌘A
Deselect All	⇧⌘A
✓ Linked Selection	⇧L
Find...	⌘F
Find Next	F3
Item Properties	▶
Project Properties...	

NOTE ▶ The Cmd-A shortcut is used in many other Macintosh applications as a way to select all of something. For example, Cmd-A selects all the text in a document or all the contents of a folder.

2   With all the clips selected, click any one of the selected clips and drag right a few seconds, then release the clips.

3   Deselect the clips by clicking in the gray space above the clips in the sequence.

4   To drag a marquee around the last two clips, click in the gray space above the **boy surf casts** clip and drag down and to the right into the **rockscape surf** clip. When they are both selected, let go.

As you drag the marquee, each clip your pointer tip touches is selected.

5   Type *2.* (2 period) in the Timeline and press Return to move these two clips forward two seconds.

6   Deselect all the clips using the shortcut Shift-Cmd-A.

7   There is another way to select a group of adjacent clips: Click the first clip in the sequence and Shift-click the last clip.

These two clips and all clips in-between are selected.

You can also select and make changes to a group of clips that are not next to each other in the Timeline.

8   Press Shift-Cmd-A to deselect the clips.

9   Click the first clip in the sequence, hold down the Command key, and click the last clip in the sequence.

NOTE ▶ As in other Macintosh applications, using the Command key allows you to select nonadjacent clips. Cmd-clicking a selected clip a second time will deselect it.

Project Tasks

1   Practice selecting and deselecting groups of clips in different ways.

2   Practice moving single clips and groups of clips by dragging or by typing a Move amount.

3   Finish by moving the first clip to the head of the sequence and dragging the other clips up to snap together so that there are no spaces between them.

4   Save your project by pressing Cmd-S.

Drag-and-Drop Editing Basics

Drag-and-drop editing is the process of dragging a clip from the Viewer directly to the Timeline. This type of editing creates the same result as any of the other approaches you used when making Overwrite or Insert edits. Drag-and-drop editing is fun and direct and opens the door to many other Timeline editing functions.

Although this editing approach is not hard, you need to be aware of some of the *automatic* functions and responses so that you can control the process. You have already become familiar with selecting and moving clips in the Timeline. Before you start dragging clips directly to the Timeline, let's focus on a few important aspects of this editing process.

Positioning the Pointer

As you have seen, Final Cut Express has a position-sensitive mouse pointer. When it is positioned over certain parts of a clip in the Timeline, or in the Timeline itself, the pointer automatically changes to a different tool to help you with a particular editing option or Timeline adjustment. For example, when you positioned the pointer over the end of a clip earlier in this lesson, it changed to the left-right resize pointer so that you could select the edit point and not the whole clip.

When you drag a clip to the Timeline, the position of your pointer will determine the type of edit you make, either Overwrite or Insert. Each Timeline audio and video track has a thin gray line running across the upper third of the empty track. This is the line you will focus on when making edits directly to the Timeline.

> **TIP** ▶ The key to dragging clips to the Timeline is to position the pointer correctly in the track.

1   Ctrl-click the Sequences bin in the Browser and choose New Sequence.

2   Name the sequence *Timeline Edits* and double-click it to open the sequence in the Timeline.

3   Pause the tip of your pointer over the thin gray line in the V1 or A1 track.

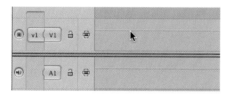

> **NOTE** ▶ Nothing happens now, but this is the point where edit options change when you have a clip in hand.

4   Open the **horseshoe island** clip into the Viewer and use the current edit points.

5   Click in the Viewer image area and drag the **horseshoe island** clip to the Timeline, *but don't release the mouse*.

6 With clip in hand, drag the tip of your pointer up and down over the thin gray line in the V1 track as you did before.

When the tip of the pointer is positioned below the thin gray line, the overwrite arrow, which has a downward arrow, appears with a solid box behind it representing the clip's length.

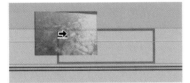

When you move the tip of the pointer above the thin gray line, a forward insert arrow appears with a hollow clip box representing the clip's length.

7 Now drag the clip back into the Viewer and release it.

> **TIP** ▶ You can always drag a clip back into the Viewer if you change your mind about working with it.

Snapping to the Playhead

When you made Overwrite and Insert edits in previous lessons, you always moved the playhead in the Timeline to where you wanted to place the new clip. This is not required in drag-and-drop editing. A new clip can be placed wherever you choose to release it, regardless of the playhead position.

However, when you drag a clip to the Timeline, it will snap to the play-head when you move past it, as long as the snapping option is active. The Snapping control is located in the upper-right corner of the Timeline in the

Timeline button bar. The snapping icon appears as left and right opposing arrows, indicating the magnetic interaction of clips in the Timeline.

> **NOTE ▶** Each main Final Cut Express window has a button bar, which acts like a well that can hold several shortcut buttons. Customizing these button bars is covered in more detail in Lesson 11.

Snapping can be toggled off or on during the editing process and even as you drag a clip or move the playhead. When snapping is active, the icon appears concave, or sunken looking, and the arrows are green. When snapping is inactive, the icon appears convex, and the arrows are gray.

Snapping on   Snapping off

In order to fully observe all the aspects of drag-and-drop editing, follow the "don't release the mouse" suggestions in the following steps.

1   Drag the playhead to the center of the Timeline.

2   Drag the **horseshoe island** clip from the Viewer to the Timeline again and position it on the track to be an Overwrite edit—*but don't release the mouse.*

3   Drag the clip sideways left and right—*but don't release it.*

4   Drag the clip's In point and Out point across the playhead.

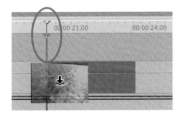

The In point or Out point of the clip snaps to the playhead. Brown snapping icons appear beneath the yellow playhead, and the playhead stem is darker.

NOTE ▸ Keep an eye on the body of the clip, not the image thumbnail.

5   Now return the clip to the Viewer.

6   Click the Snapping control in the upper-right corner of the Timeline to turn snapping off.

7   Now drag the **horseshoe island** clip from the Viewer over the playhead in the Timeline.

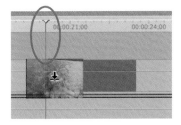

The clip passes over the playhead without snapping to it.

8   Drag the clip back to the Viewer and release it.

9   Make snapping active again by pressing the shortcut key N.

10 Drag the clip to the head of the Timeline. Make sure the downward, Overwrite edit arrow is showing, and release the **horseshoe island** clip as the first Overwrite edit of this sequence.

The playhead jumps to the end of the newly placed clip, just as it did when you made Overwrite edits in the previous lesson.

Dragging to the Timeline

So far, you have worked with clips to select, move, copy, and paste them within the Timeline. You've also practiced some drag-and-drop editing basics. This is really in preparation for editing directly to the Timeline, sort of like warming up your fingers by doing scales on a piano before playing a piece. Now that you're warmed up, it's time to play a piece—or rather, build a sequence. The sequence you build will include some vacation shots of people and scenery. You will first lay down some scenery shots as Overwrite edits and then insert some people shots in-between.

Making Overwrite Edits

Let's make some Overwrite edits to build the sequence using drag-and-drop editing.

1 Open the **island twirl** clip from the Browser and use the current edit points.

2 Drag the clip from the Viewer to the Timeline as an Overwrite edit and snap it up against the end of the first edit, paying attention to the pointer to select the correct type of edit.

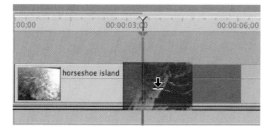

TIP If you release the clip in the Timeline before placing it where you want it to go, you can drag the clip into place in a separate step as you did earlier in this lesson, but be careful that you don't overwrite part of the first clip.

3 Open the **mountain surf** clip, and drop it in as the third Overwrite edit at the end of the previous clip.

4 Open the **rockscape surf** clip, mark the last six seconds of the clip, and drop it in as the fourth Overwrite edit at the end.

TIP Don't forget to save (Cmd-S) frequently throughout your editing sessions.

Overwriting an Existing Edit

So far, you have been making Overwrite edits end to end, laying one clip down where the previous edit left off. Occasionally you may find that the previous edit is too long, and you want to overwrite the tail end of it with a new source clip. You can back the playhead into the previous clip where you want to start overwriting with new clip material and press F10 or use the Edit Overlay to make this edit. But you can also drag a clip and slide it on top of the previous one, dropping it wherever you want.

1 Drag the **rockscape surf** clip you just dropped in the Timeline to the left into the **mountain surf** clip, *but don't let go.*

The left window of the Canvas two-up display updates to reflect the last frame you will see should you drop the clip at that position.

2   Using the offset information box as a guide, drag the clip –10 frames
    to the left, and drop the clip there.

    TIP ▶ If the clip keeps snapping to the Out point, press N to turn
    snapping off as you make the adjustment, and then press it again
    afterward to turn snapping back on. You can turn snapping off and
    on as you drag.

3   Now move the **rockscape surf** clip to the right.

    When you drag and drop a clip over another one in the Timeline, you
    overwrite the original clip with the current one wherever they overlap.
    It's as though you deleted that unwanted portion of the **mountain
    surf** clip in the Timeline.

4   Make sure that snapping is on, and snap the last clip back to the end
    of the sequence.

Making Audio Edits

When you drag and drop a clip directly to the Timeline, you drag from the
image area of a clip in the Viewer to the Timeline. But when you open a
music clip, there is no video display. Instead, you drag from a Drag Hand
icon as though that were the clip's image.

1   In the Browser, click the triangle to display the contents of the
    Music bin.

2   Open the **Latin.aif** music track into the Viewer.

3   Move your pointer over the Drag Hand icon (which looks like a hand on a speaker).

The mouse pointer becomes a Hand tool you can use to drag the clip to the Timeline.

4   With the Hand tool, drag the Drag Hand icon directly to the Timeline to the A1 and A2 audio tracks. Drop it at the head of the sequence as an Overwrite edit.

5   Play the sequence.

Inserting Between Clips

With Insert editing in the Timeline, you want to place the tip of the pointer just above the thin gray line in the track. The visual clue of having done this successfully is the sideways insert arrow along with the hollow clip representation.

1   For this exercise, make sure that snapping is active. Also, lock the A1 and A2 tracks to keep the music track from being affected.

2   Open the **kayakers tracking** clip in the Viewer, and mark a 3-second duration wherever you like. (Type *3.*—3 period—in the Duration field once the In point is set.)

3   Drag this clip into the Timeline as an Insert edit between the **horseshoe island** and **island twirl** clips, *but don't release the mouse.*

In the Timeline, you should see the forward insert arrow and hollow clip representation. In the Canvas window, you see the last frame of the previous clip and the next frame, which is the first frame of the following clip.

4   Release the **kayakers tracking** clip.

The sequence opens up to allow for the new Insert edit.

5   Open the **boy surf casts** clip, and mark an In point at 2:07 and an Out point at 5:25.

6   Drag and drop the clip as an Insert edit between the **island twirl** and **mountain surf** clips.

NOTE ▶ As your sequence expands, you may need to slide the Zoom slider at the bottom of the Timeline to view the rest of your sequence or use the Option-+ and Option-– (minus) shortcuts.

7   Open the **frolicking in ocean** clip and mark a three-second duration from 4:02.

8   Drag and drop this clip as an Insert edit between the **mountain surf** and **rockscape surf** clips.

9   Click in the Timeline, and press Shift-Z to see the entire sequence.

10 Press Cmd-S to save these edits.

Inserting Within a Clip

So far, you have inserted a clip between two other existing clips in the sequence. You can also insert a clip right in the middle of another clip. For example, you might decide to break up the action of a long clip by inserting a different image for a few seconds in the middle. The long clip will be split into two parts, and the second part will be pushed down the length of the newly inserted clip. In either situation, no frames are ever lost in Insert editing.

1   Open the **kid underwater** clip and mark the first two seconds.

2   Drag it into the **horseshoe island** clip as an Insert edit (with the forward arrow and hollow clip appearing), and slide it left and right, *but don't release the mouse.*

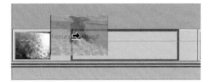

In the Canvas, you see the frame before the new clip's position and the frame after it. They look very much the same because one follows the other in the current clip.

3   Drop the clip into the middle of the **horseshoe island** clip and play these clips.

   NOTE ▸ Unlike what happens with Overwrite editing, inserting the new clip at this point does not erase or cover up any of the original clip. It literally splits it into two parts and pushes the second part down to make room for the new clip.

4   Press Cmd-Z to undo this last step.

Project Tasks

1   Create a new sequence, and lay down the people shots first as Overwrite edits.

2   Place the scenery shots between them as Insert edits.

Saving and Quitting

Always save your project before you close it or quit Final Cut Express.

1   Save the current project one last time by pressing Cmd-S.

2   If you are finished working in Final Cut Express, quit the program by pressing Cmd-Q. If not, continue with the next lesson.

Lesson Review

1.   How do you select a specific clip in the Timeline? How do you deselect that clip?

2.   How can you select a group of adjacent clips? All clips?

3.   How do you copy and paste a clip?

4.   In what ways can you move a clip or group of clips in the Timeline?

5.   Can snapping be turned off and on while you're moving a clip?

6.   When you drag a clip directly into the Timeline, how do you determine whether it will be an Overwrite or Insert edit?

7.   How do you drag an audio clip directly to the Timeline?

8.   If you're making video Insert edits into a sequence with a music track, what must you do so the music track won't be split by the Insert edit?

Answers

1. Click once on the clip to select it. Click in the gray empty space above the Timeline track to deselect it, or press Shift-Cmd-A.

2. Click the first clip and Shift-click the last clip in the group, or drag a marquee around those clips. To select all clips, press Cmd-A.

3. Select the clip and press Cmd-C to copy it. Move the playhead to the desired clip location and press Cmd-V to paste it.

4. By dragging them, or by selecting them, typing the amount of the move, and then pressing Return.

5. Yes, by pressing the N key.

6. Drag the tip of the pointer beneath the thin gray line to make it an Overwrite edit (solid box/downward arrow). Drag the tip of the pointer above the thin gray line to make it an Insert edit (hollow box/forward arrow).

7. By dragging the Drag Hand icon in the Audio tab of the Viewer.

8. Lock the music tracks.

Keyboard Shortcuts

Cmd-A	Selects all clips in the sequence
Shift-Cmd-A	Deselects all clips
Cmd-C	Copies a selected clip
Cmd-V	Pastes a copied clip
Option-Q	Brings up the User Preferences window
N	Toggles snapping on and off

8

Lesson 8
Other Editing Options

Now that you are comfortable working and making edits in the Timeline, let's expand the possibilities by introducing some additional editing options. These options include building a sound track, adding cutaways, marking in the Timeline, deleting clips and gaps, editing from the Browser, and storyboard editing. In addition, we'll take a look at a new type of edit, the *Replace edit*.

Preparing the Project

To get started in Lesson 8, you will launch Final Cut Express by clicking the program icon in the Dock and then opening the project for this lesson.

1   Within Final Cut Express choose File > Open or press Cmd-O, and choose the **Lesson 8 Project** file from the Lessons folder on your hard drive.

2   Close any other projects that may be open from a previous session by Ctrl-clicking their name tabs in the Browser and choosing Close Tab from the shortcut menu.

3   In the Timeline, play the *Jimbo Finished* sequence. This is the first sequence you will create in this lesson. It is not a finished sequence but the first stage of one.

4   In the Browser, display the contents of the Sequences bin. To create a new sequence in the Sequences bin, Ctrl-click the Sequences bin and choose New Sequence. Name the new sequence *Jimbo Tracks*.

5   Double-click to open the new *Jimbo Tracks* sequence in the Timeline.

6   Ctrl-click the *Jimbo Finished* tab in the Timeline and choose Close Tab to close that sequence.

7 Click the disclosure triangle to display the contents of the Surfing Clips bin.

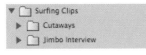

The clips in this bin have been organized into two separate bins.

TIP ▸ Putting bins in other bins is a way to further organize your material in a project.

Building a Sound Track

So far, you have been working with music clips and video-only clips where the audio was never recorded or has been stripped away. However, when you shoot video, you usually record both audio and video together. When you capture this material, the audio and video are linked together as one clip. Any edit point you create on the video also applies to the audio and vice versa.

You will be marking and editing sound bites in this sequence to create a sound track. A sound bite is the portion of a clip where someone states something on camera. It's generally a complete thought or sentence. In this exercise, a young surfer named Jimbo is interviewed. You will cut together some of his sound bites on surfing. Together these sound bites will form a sound track you will use in the next exercise.

1 In the Surfing Clips bin, click the disclosure triangle to display the contents of the Jimbo Interview bin.

2 Open the **name** clip into the Viewer, and mark the beginning and end of his sound bite.

NOTE ▸ There may be some "off-camera" sound from a director, but it is clear where the subject (Jimbo) starts and stops talking.

3 In the Timeline, make sure the v1, a1, and a2 source controls are patched to the V1, A1, and A2 destination tracks.

4 Place the playhead at the head of the sequence and edit the clip as an Overwrite edit.

TIP If the clip settings warning appears, click Yes. To change the preset so all new sequences will match this footage, choose Final Cut Express > Easy Setup then choose to use DV-NTSC.

In the Timeline, the clip appears on the V1, A1, and A2 tracks. There are two audio tracks because this footage was shot with a DV camera that records stereo audio.

5 Click the V1 portion of the clip in the Timeline once.

All three tracks of this clip become selected because the audio and video are linked together.

6 Deselect the clip. Click in either one of the audio tracks and notice that, again, all tracks become selected.

7 Open the **carry head** clip. Mark the sound bite and place it in the Timeline at the end of the first clip.

NOTE ▶ You will be editing seven clips in the Timeline end to end just to create the sound track. You can drag them to the Timeline, use the F10 key, or use the Canvas Edit Overlay.

8 Open the following clips and mark the sound bites tight to Jimbo's comments. Place each clip in the Timeline one at a time as Overwrite edits in the following order:

▶ **wax every time**

▶ **catch a wave**

▶ **nose ride**

▶ **leash**

▶ **surfing feels good**

NOTE ▶ In preparation for another exercise, make sure the **wax every time** clip's duration is no longer than 5:11.

TIP ▶ Subjects often need to repeat or rephrase what they are saying on camera, so as you are marking, be prepared to update your In point.

9 Press Cmd-S to save the project and play the sequence.

Three-Point Editing

In this lesson, you just edited clips using In and Out points marked in the Viewer and a location determined by the playhead position in the Timeline. In other words, you used three edit points to make your edit. Professionals call this *three-point editing*. Three-point editing refers to any combination of three edit points to determine duration, location, and content of a clip. The following exercises continue to explore three-point editing.

Marking in the Timeline

In the *Jimbo Tracks* sequence you just created, the sound track begins to tell a story. But you also need pictures to complete the job, and the current combination of Jimbo clips is not pleasing. When a clip jumps from one person to the same person in a similar camera framing, in this case a medium close-up, it's called a *jump cut*. In this exercise, you will cover some of the Jimbo video with other video shots that help tell the story, while keeping the sound track intact. These other shots are referred to as *cutaways* because you literally cut away to something else. Sometimes cutaway material is referred to as *B-roll footage*.

To edit video clips or cutaways over existing material, you will need to mark edit points directly in the Timeline to identify just the portion of material you want to replace or overwrite. Marking in the Timeline uses all the same shortcuts as marking in the Viewer, but the mark buttons for the Timeline appear in the Canvas window.

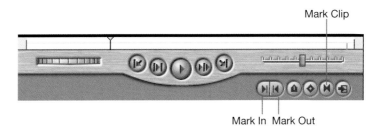

Mark Clip

Mark In Mark Out

Editing with One Timeline Edit Point

For this exercise, you will set In and Out points in the Viewer to determine what portion of the cutaway clip you want to see. You will also mark an In point in the Timeline where you want to place the cutaway. Actually, this will give you the same result as parking the playhead where you want the edit to be placed.

1   In the Browser, locate the *Jimbo Tracks* sequence. Ctrl-click it and choose Duplicate from the shortcut menu. Name it *Jimbo Tracks Cutaways* and double-click to open it.

> **TIP** ▶ It's a good idea to duplicate a sequence and work on the duplicate when you are making major editing changes.

2 Park the playhead on the first frame of the fourth clip, **catch a wave,**
and mark an In point by clicking the Canvas Mark In button or pressing the I key.

An In point appears in the Canvas scrubber bar and in the Canvas
image area. An In point also appears in the ruler area of the Timeline.

NOTE ▶ When you mark in the Timeline, the marked portion appears
lighter than the other clips in the sequence.

3 To edit just the video of this clip, click the a1 and a2 source controls to disconnect them from the destination tracks. You can also click the destination track controls to get the same result.

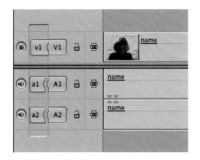

4 In the Surfing Clips bin, display the contents of the Cutaways bin and double-click to open the **out to sea** clip.

5 In the Viewer, position the playhead one second into the clip and mark an In point. Mark an Out point one second before the end of the clip.

TIP ▶ Press Shift–right arrow to move forward one second and Shift–left arrow to move backward one second.

6 Drag the clip from the Viewer to the Canvas Edit Overlay and drop it into the Overwrite section.

The new video-only cutaway is placed on V1 at the Timeline In point. It continues for the length it was marked in the Viewer.

NOTE ▶ In order to show the clips more clearly, the playhead in the preceding image has been moved away from the clips.

7   Play the clip in the sequence.

Editing with Two Timeline Edit Points

An alternate method is to make two edit points in the Timeline and one in the Viewer. You mark an In and an Out point in the Timeline to identify the clip placement *and* length. When you do this, you only need to mark an In point on the source clip in the Viewer to identify where you will start using the clip. The source clip will automatically stop at the Out point in the Timeline.

1   In the Timeline, play from the beginning of the sequence and mark an In point just after Jimbo says "… since I was 5 years old." This time press the I key to mark an In point.

2   Continue playing into the next clip, and mark an Out point after Jimbo says, "… putting it on my head."

The Timeline In and Out points define the placement and duration of the new clip.

The marked Timeline duration appears in the Canvas Duration field.

3   From the Browser, open the **board on head** clip, and mark an In point
at 4:11.

4   Edit this clip into the sequence by dragging it into the Overwrite section of the Canvas Edit Overlay.

In the Timeline, the first frame of the new source clip is placed at the
In point. The Out point in the Timeline determines where the clip
stops, or how much of the clip is used.

Backtiming a Clip

There are occasions when the *last* frame you want to use of a source clip
is more important than the first. In this case, you mark In and Out points
in the Timeline to create the edit placement and duration, and mark an
Out point in the Viewer on what you want to be the last frame of the clip.
Final Cut Express aligns the source clip's Out point to the Out point in
the Timeline and uses whatever portion of the clip it needs to fill the distance back to the Timeline In point.

This is referred to in editing as *backtiming* a clip. You are literally backing
it into an edit slot.

1   In the Timeline, park the playhead on the first frame of the **nose ride**
clip, and mark an In point.

2   Play the sequence, and mark an Out point on the last frame of the **leash** clip.

The new video cutaway will cover the video from both of these Jimbo clips, from the In point to the Out point.

TIP ▶ By looking at the marked duration in the Canvas Duration field, you can see how much source material you will need to cover this edit.

3   From the Browser, open the **nose riding** clip, and mark just an Out point where Jimbo falls behind the waves, which is at about 14:27 in the clip. Make sure the Viewer duration is as long or longer than the Canvas duration.

TIP ▶ It is very important when backtiming clips to remove any In points in the Viewer. Otherwise the clip will line up In point to In point and not Out to Out.

4   Edit this clip into the sequence as an Overwrite edit.

The Out point of the source clip is aligned with the Out point in the sequence.

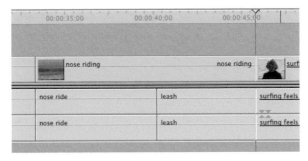

5   Press Cmd-S to save your project and edit decisions.

Three-Point Editing Summary

To put it all together, three-point edits can be created as follows:

▶ In point and Out point marked in the Viewer plus a start point in the Timeline determined by playhead location or a Timeline In point

▶ In point and Out point marked in the Viewer plus a stop point in the Timeline determined by a Timeline Out point

▶ In point and Out point marked in the Timeline and just an In point marked in the Viewer

▶ In point and Out point marked in the Timeline and just an Out point marked in the Viewer

Project Tasks

Let's cover the first three seconds of the **wax every time** sound-bite clip in the Timeline with the cutaway, **waxing board med**. Using three-point editing, you have some choices:

▶ You can mark the first three seconds of the **wax every time** clip with an In point and Out point in the Timeline. Then mark either an In point or Out point in the Viewer.

▶   You can mark just an In point in the wax every time clip in the
     Timeline. Then in the Viewer, mark an In point and Out point with a
     three-second duration in the waxing board med clip.

Replacing Edits

In the previous exercise, you marked the Timeline to replace portions of
clips already in the sequence. But you can also replace the full length of one
clip with another. You do this with the Replace edit function in the Edit
Overlay. In the following exercises, you will duplicate the original *Jimbo
Tracks* sequence and replace all but two of the original Jimbo video clips.

Replace edit replaces any clip in the sequence with a new source clip from
the Viewer. The clip length and position in the sequence remain the same.
So whatever new source clip you replace it with must be at least the same
duration as the clip that is being replaced. If you don't select a clip that's
long enough to replace the Timeline clip completely, a message appears
saying "Insufficient content for edit."

An important consideration in replacing edits is where the playhead is located
in both the source clip in the Viewer and the original clip in the Timeline. In
fact, the Replace edit function is dependent on the alignment between the two
playhead positions. Replacing edits in the Timeline is a very fast, easy process
but requires a little thought and preparation to get the desired effect.

Replacing from the Head of a Clip

For the first Replace edit you perform, let's park both the Viewer and
Timeline playheads on the first frame of the two clips that are involved in
the Replace edit. Here, the Replace function will fill the duration forward
from the playhead position.

1   In the Browser, locate the original *Jimbo Tracks* sequence and dupli-
     cate it. Name the duplicate *Jimbo Tracks Replace* and double-click it to
     open it in the Timeline.

2   Since you want to edit only the video portion of this clip, make sure
     the v1 source control is patched to the V1 destination control and dis-
     connect the a1 and a2 source controls.

3   Park the playhead on the first frame of the **wax every time** clip.

4   To find the duration of this clip, press X to mark the clip where the playhead is located. Note the duration in the Canvas Duration field, then press Option-X to remove the edit points.

5   From the Cutaways clips bin, open the **waxing board med** clip into the Viewer and make sure the playhead is parked at the beginning of this clip. Check the clip duration to make sure it's long enough to replace the sequence clip.

NOTE ▶ Replace editing responds to the playhead position in the Viewer and Timeline and ignores any In and Out points when you make the edit.

6 Drag the source clip to the Canvas, drop it on the blue Replace section of the Canvas Edit Overlay, and play the edit.

The entire video portion of the sequence clip is replaced by footage starting at the source playhead position.

Replacing from the Tail of a Clip

You can also use the Replace edit function to backtime a replacement clip into position. This is similar to the backtiming exercise, except you are replacing an entire clip. You will place the Timeline playhead on the last frame of a clip in the sequence. Then choose the corresponding frame on a source clip in the Viewer. Final Cut Express will line up the two clips and fill in, or backtime, the duration from that point.

1 In the Timeline, place the playhead on the last frame of the **carry head** clip.

> **TIP** Be careful that you don't accidentally park on the first frame of the next clip. If you do, use the left arrow key to move one frame back.

2   Open the **board on head** clip in the Viewer, and position the playhead after Jimbo leaves the frame, toward the end of the clip.

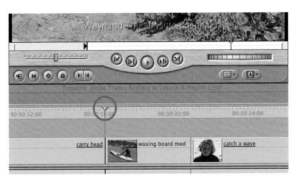

If there are any In or Out marks in the source clip, as there is in this clip, it will be ignored when you make a Replace type edit. Only the playhead location determines the edit point.

3   Drag the source clip to the Canvas and drop it on the Replace section in the Edit Overlay. You can also use the Replace shortcut, F11.

4   Play the new edit.

The last frame you parked the Viewer playhead on appears as the last frame of the new sequence edit. All earlier material is filled in automatically to cover the duration of the sequence clip.

NOTE ▶ If you want to replace both the audio and video of a clip in the Timeline with the audio and video of a different source clip, or replace an audio-only or video-only clip, you do not have to unlink the tracks.

Replacing from a Specific Point

The most fun you can have with Replace edit is replacing a specific action point with another one. Maybe it's a certain action move, where the baby spits up or where the touchdown pass was caught. You select a replacement source clip and position the playhead in the Viewer on the frame that you want to align with the frame in the Timeline. Once again, Final Cut Express will align the frame at the Viewer playhead with the frame at the Timeline playhead.

The question to ask yourself as you begin this type of Replace edit is: What frame from the new source clip do I want to be placed at the playhead location in the Timeline? This time, rather than filling from first frame forward (the first exercise) or last frame backward (the second exercise), Final Cut Express will fill out the frames before and after the playhead to fill the existing duration.

In this example, you will find a spot in Jimbo's sound track to match with a different video clip.

1   In the Timeline, play the **nose ride** clip, and park the playhead before he says, "… walk up to the nose of the board." This is the point you want to match with new video.

2   From the Browser, open the **nose riding** clip into the Viewer, and park the playhead where Jimbo actually begins to walk up to the nose of the board.

This is the point that will line up with the place in the sequence clip where Jimbo refers to walking up to the nose of the board.

3   Drag the source clip to the Canvas, and drop it on the Replace section of the Edit Overlay.

4   Play the sequence.

    TIP▶ You can change your mind and undo what you did by pressing Cmd-Z, or simply readjust your playhead positions and perform another Replace edit.

5   Press Cmd-S to save project changes.

Deleting Clips and Gaps

Deleting clips is an important part of the editing process. When you remove or delete material from a sequence, you create a space called a *gap*. When the playhead plays over a gap in the sequence, you see black in the Canvas and hear no sound. There are different ways to delete clips and gaps in a sequence.

Deleting Clips

When you delete a clip in a Timeline, you have two choices. You can delete the clip and leave a gap the length of the clip behind. Or you can delete a clip along with the space it occupied, which leaves no gap. Deleting a clip this way creates a rippling effect and pulls up all the following clips in the sequence to the point where the deleted clip originally began. Let's delete a clip you no longer need for this sequence.

1   In the current *Jimbo Tracks Replace* sequence, click the **leash** clip to select it.

2   Choose Sequence > Lift, or just press Delete.

The clip is removed, or lifted, from the sequence, but the space it occupied remains, creating a gap.

3   Move the playhead to before the gap and play through the gap.

You see black in the Canvas for the duration of the gap.

4   Press Cmd-Z to undo the delete.

5   Now delete this clip by choosing Sequence > Ripple Delete, or pressing Shift-Delete.

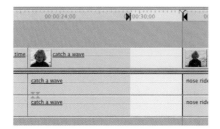

The clip, along with the gap, is removed, and all the clips that follow are moved up in its place, creating a "rippling" effect.

As a general editing rule, when you decide against a shot, you will usually want to remove the clip along with its gap by using Shift-Delete. But if you need to hold the place for sequence timing purposes, you lift the clip by using just Delete.

Deleting Between Edit Points

You can apply the same deleting techniques described in the preceding section to a group of clips or a marked portion of the sequence. In this exercise, you will delete just a portion of a clip.

1   In the current *Jimbo Tracks Replace* sequence, play the **catch a wave** clip and mark an In point after Jimbo says, "… too fast or too slow."

2   Mark an Out point at the end of this clip.

3 Press Delete to lift the material and leave a gap.

4 Press Cmd-Z to undo the delete.

5 Press Shift-Delete to remove the material along with the gap.

This pulls the following clip up to the new last frame of the clip you changed.

6 Play this area of the sequence.

Selecting and Deleting Gaps

Gaps are not clips, but they can be selected and deleted as you would a clip. For this exercise, you will duplicate the original *Jimbo Tracks* sequence and create a shorter version by deleting certain clips and gaps. As you have seen already, you can delete clips and gaps at one time, but leaving the gaps here will create an opportunity to learn more about them in the next exercise.

1 In the Browser, locate and duplicate the *Jimbo Tracks* sequence, and name the copy *Jimbo Tracks Short*. Double-click to open the new sequence in the Timeline.

NOTE ▶ As you continue to open new sequences in the Timeline, additional sequence tabs appear. To go to any open sequence, select its tab. To close any of the open sequences you've already worked with, Ctrl-click their tabs and choose Close Tab from the shortcut menu.

2 In the *Jimbo Tracks Short* sequence, press Option-X to remove any edit points that may be left over from previous exercises.

3 Click the **carry head** clip and press Delete.

4   Click in the gap area to select the gap. Deselect it the way you deselect a clip, and select it again.

5   Press Delete.

NOTE ▸ Unlike what happens when you delete a clip, pressing Delete alone will remove the gap and pull up the following clips.

6   Press Cmd-Z to undo that delete, then Cmd-click the **catch a wave** and **leash** clips to select them both.

7   Press Delete to delete them and leave gaps in their places.

Moving to Gaps

Wherever you are parked in the sequence, you can always find a gap by moving to it. You may think you will always notice a gap, but sometimes you may be zoomed in to a clip and not be aware of a gap elsewhere in your sequence. Checking for gaps before you output to tape is a good idea so you don't accidentally leave any black spaces in your sequence. There are menu selections and shortcuts to help you locate sequence gaps.

1   Park your playhead at the head of your sequence.

2   Choose Mark > Next > Gap, or press Shift-G.

Mark	
Mark In	i
Mark Out	o
Mark Split	▶
Mark Clip	x
Mark to Markers	^A
Mark Selection	⇧A
Select In to Out	⌥A
Set Poster Frame	^P
DV Start/Stop Detect	
Clear In and Out	⌥X
Clear In	⌥I
Clear Out	⌥O
Clear Split	▶
Clear Poster Frame	
Markers	▶
Play	▶
Go to	▶
Previous	▶
Next	▶

Edit	'
2 Edits	^9
Marker	⇧↓
Frame	→
Keyframe	⇧K
Gap	⇧G
Track Gap	

The playhead jumps to the first frame of the next gap in the sequence.

3 Continue to press Shift-G until you reach the end of the sequence.

4 Choose Mark > Previous > Gap, or press Option-G, to go back to the previous gap in the sequence. Press Option-G again and again until the playhead is on the first gap.

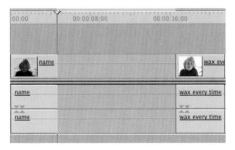

TIP In Final Cut Express, the Shift key is often used to move forward to a specific point in the sequence, and the Option key is used to move backward.

5   To remove this gap, you can use a menu option, Sequence > Close
    Gap, or a keyboard shortcut, Ctrl-G. Or you can just select the gap
    and press Delete as you did before.

6   Remove the other gaps in the sequence.

    TIP ▶ Remember that the fastest way to delete clips along with their
    gaps is to use Shift-Delete.

7   Play this shorter version of the sound track.

8   Press Cmd-S to save project changes.

9   Close all open Jimbo sequences in the Timeline, and remember that
    the Timeline and Canvas windows will disappear.

Storyboard Editing

Moviemakers use *storyboards* whenever they need to explain something
with pictures. For example, to explain how a scene will look when it's cut
together, an artist sketches potential camera shots and places them side by
side in individual frames. This allows the director and crew to imagine more
clearly what the film will look like. It also helps them anticipate what prob-
lems may arise during the shoot.

In Final Cut Express, you can also arrange clips or storyboard them
according to how you would like to see them in the sequence. You work
with thumbnail images of your clips as though you were working on a
jigsaw puzzle of your story, and then you drag them to the Timeline as a
group. Storyboard editing begins in the Browser. You select clips you want
to use in your sequence and place them in a new bin. Then you arrange
the clips' thumbnail images, or storyboard them, according to how you
would like to see them in the sequence.

Although storyboard editing is a simple process that takes only a few steps,
the following exercises incorporate additional information about organizing clips in the Browser.

Preparing for Storyboard Editing

For this exercise, you will work with the clips in the Vacation Fun bin, which are the same clips you used in the previous lesson. Before you begin storyboarding, let's take a moment to organize this part of the project.

1   In the Browser, Ctrl-click the Sequences bin. From the shortcut menu, choose New Sequence and name it *Storyboard Edits*. Double-click it to open it in the Timeline.

2   In the Browser, collapse all open bins by clicking the disclosure triangles next to them.

3   Double-click the Vacation Fun clips bin icon to open it as a separate bin window. Drag the lower-right corner to make the window larger.

> **TIP** ▶ If you do not want to use all of the clips in a bin for your storyboard, copy the clips you want to use and paste them into a new bin, and work with that bin of clips. Copying and pasting icons like this doesn't make new copies of your media, just new links to the media files.

4   With the Browser in list view, look at the In and Out columns next to the Duration column of the Vacation Fun clips. No edit points have been set.

If a clip has not been marked, Not Set appears in the In and Out columns, and the full clip's duration appears in the Duration column.

Name	Duration	In	Out	Tracks
boy surf casts	00:00:06;18	Not Set	Not Set	1V
frolicking in ocean	00:00:10;16	Not Set	Not Set	1V
horseshoe island	00:00:22;13	Not Set	Not Set	1V
island twirl	00:00:15;01	Not Set	Not Set	1V
kayakers tracking	00:00:20;04	Not Set	Not Set	1V
kid underwater	00:00:04;04	Not Set	Not Set	1V
Latin.aif	00:00:22;12	Not Set	Not Set	2A
mountain surf	00:00:07;13	Not Set	Not Set	1V
rockscape surf	00:00:10;25	Not Set	Not Set	1V

5 Take a moment and mark In and Out points for a few of these clips. You may need to reposition the Vacation Fun window so that you can see the Viewer.

Name		Duration	In	Out	Tracks	C
boy surf casts		00:00:03;08	00:00:01;09	00:00:04:16	1V	
frolicking in ocean		00:00:03;25	00:00:03;03	00:00:06;27	1V	
horseshoe island		00:00:22;13	Not Set	Not Set	1V	
island twirl		00:00:05;15	00:00:03;25	00:00:09;09	1V	
kayakers tracking		00:00:20;04	Not Set	Not Set	1V	
kid underwater		00:00:00;29	00:00:01;02	00:00:02;00	1V	
Latin.aif		00:00:22;12	Not Set	Not Set	2A	
mountain surf		00:00:02;17	00:00:01;21	00:00:04;07	1V	
rockscape surf		00:00:10;25	Not Set	Not Set	1V	

When a clip has been marked, the Duration time in the Browser reflects the marked duration, and In and Out points appear in the In and Out columns.

TIP ▶ If a clip is marked, the marked portion will be used in storyboard editing, but don't forget that you can mark and delete portions of clips in the Timeline as well.

6 To prepare for storyboard editing, change the bin view in the Vacation Fun bin by Ctrl-clicking in the gray area under the Name column. Choose View as Large Icons from the shortcut menu.

7 If the thumbnail images are not all in view, click the Zoom button in the upper left of the window. To arrange the icons alphabetically, Ctrl-click the bin gray area and choose Arrange > by Name.

8 Position the window so that it doesn't cover the Timeline.

Scrubbing Clips in the Browser

You have scrubbed clips in the Viewer window to view clip content manually. You did this by dragging the playhead through the scrubber bar. But you can also scrub a clip in the Browser when it is in one of the icon views. You can scrub through a clip slowly or quickly and go backward or forward.

Scrubbing a thumbnail clip in the Browser involves the Scrub tool, which shares the same row in the Tool palette as the Zoom In, Zoom Out, and Hand tools.

1   In the Tool palette, click and hold the Zoom In tool, and select the Scrub tool.

The Scrub tool has left and right (forward and backward) arrows on the hand icon.

2   With the Scrub tool, click the **boy surf casts** clip and drag across the image to the right to scrub through the clip content.

Dragging right on the clip with the Scrub tool moves you forward in the clip; dragging left moves you backward in the clip.

TIP ▶ When you scrub through a thumbnail clip, you can drag way outside the thumbnail image area.

3   Click the `kid underwater` image in the same bin, and drag it left and right.

NOTE ▶ When you release the clip after scrubbing through it, the thumbnail image reverts back to the first frame of the clip. The thumbnail image remains dark because the image is still selected.

4   To see a clear thumbnail image, deselect the clip by clicking in the gray area with the Scrub tool.

5   Scrub through a few other clips in this bin.

NOTE ▶ When you scrub through a thumbnail clip, you can scrub through the full length of the clip, whether or not there are any edit points attached to the clip.

Changing a Thumbnail Image

When you capture media from your original source tapes, you often begin a few seconds before a specific action begins. This extra footage gives you additional material or handles for adding dissolves or fade-ups in the editing process. It also ensures that the start of action is clear and complete.

In a thumbnail image, a clip is always represented by the image of the first captured frame. This is called the *poster frame* because it represents a clip visually the way a poster represents a movie. But sometimes the poster frame of the captured clip is not a good indicator of the action that follows. For example, you may have a clip of someone skating. But because you included a few seconds of scenery at the head of the clip before the action begins, you don't see the skater in the thumbnail image. There are several ways a clip's poster frame can be changed so that you can better identify the content of the clip.

1   With the Scrub tool, scrub through the **boy surf casts** clip until you see the boy, *but don't release the mouse.* This is the frame you will use to represent this clip.

NOTE ▶ When you drag the Scrub tool, it disappears from view so that your thumbnail image is not covered.

2   While still holding on to this frame, press and hold down the Control key.

3   Release the Scrub tool.

4   Release the Control key.

5   Deselect the clip to see a clearer image of the new thumbnail image.

6   Repeat steps 1–5 to create new poster frames for each of the clips except **frolicking in ocean**.

7   Double-click the **frolicking in ocean** clip to open it in the Viewer, and move the Vacation Fun bin if necessary.

8   In the Viewer, move the playhead to where the man reaches out to touch the boy.

9 From the menu, choose Mark > Set Poster Frame, or press Ctrl-P.

Mark	
Mark In	i
Mark Out	o
Mark Split	▶
Mark Clip	x
Mark to Markers	^ A
Mark Selection	⇧ A
Select In to Out	⌥ A
Set Poster Frame	^ P
DV Start/Stop Detect	
Clear In and Out	⌥ X
Clear In	⌥ I
Clear Out	⌥ O
Clear Split	▶
Clear Poster Frame	
Markers	▶
Play	▶
Go to	▶
Previous	▶
Next	▶

The thumbnail image updates in the Vacation Fun bin window.

TIP ▶ If changing the poster frame in a clip is important to your editing, add it as a step when you initially view your clips in the Viewer.

Storyboarding Clips

You're now ready to have some fun with storyboard editing. This is the step where you put together a picture puzzle of your sequence—only you don't have a puzzle box top to follow. You make it up as you go. What shot do you want to start with? Which one should follow? Maybe you know the ending clip but not the beginning just yet. Going through the following steps will help you get a feel for one way you might storyboard this sequence.

How you place the images in the Vacation Fun bin will determine how they eventually appear in the sequence. Final Cut Express will begin placing the clips from the top-left corner, move across as though it were reading a book, then drop down to the next line, read across, and so on. If a clip is higher than the other clips on its row, it will be read or placed before the others, as though it were on its own separate row.

1   To convert your pointer back to the default Selection tool, either click the Selection tool in the Tool palette or click in the Timeline and then press A.

2   In the Vacation Fun bin, drag the audio clip off to the side and position the thumbnail clips by dragging them into the following order:

NOTE ▶ You may have to move some clips out of the way to allow room to position others. They don't have to be perfectly aligned but they do have to follow in a slightly downward direction to the right.

First row:	**horseshoe island**	**frolicking in ocean**	**island twirl**
Second row:	**boy surf casts**	**rockscape surf**	**kayakers tracking**
Third row:	**kid underwater**	**mountain surf**	

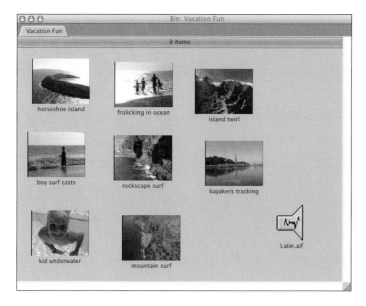

Dragging Clips to the Timeline

In an earlier lesson, you dragged clips from the Viewer directly to the Timeline one at a time. You can drag a clip from the Browser directly to the Timeline as well. But in editing from the Browser, you can also drag a group of clips into the Timeline, as you will do with your storyboard edits. First, let's drag the music clip into the sequence.

1   From the Vacation Fun bin window, drag the **Latin.aif** clip into the Timeline and release it at the head of the sequence on tracks A1 and A2 as an Overwrite edit.

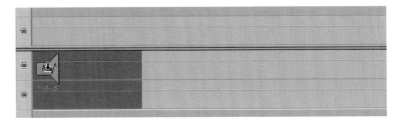

2   In the Vacation Fun window, select all the clips except the music clip.

3   Drag one of the selected clip icons down into the Timeline, *but don't release the mouse.*

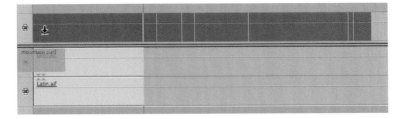

The entire group of selected clips moves together. If the Timeline view has been made smaller, you can see all the clips you are dragging. But whether or not you see all the clips in your view, you are dragging them all at the same time.

4   Position the clips at the head of the sequence on the V1 track as an
    Overwrite (downward arrow/solid clip box) edit and release the mouse.

> **NOTE ▶** These clips are longer than the current music track. You can
> fix this in the following project.

5   Close the Vacation Fun bin window by clicking the Close button.

6   Play the sequence.

    All the Vacation Fun clips are positioned in the Timeline just as they
    were in the Vacation Fun bin. If you marked a clip, only the marked
    portion is edited.

Project Tasks

1   Undo the last step and rearrange the clips in a different order. Then
    drag them to the Timeline.

2   Lock the A1 and A2 audio tracks (so that the music won't be affected
    by the next step).

3   Delete unwanted portions of clips so that the video clips match the
    length of the music track.

Saving and Quitting

Always save your project before you close it or quit Final Cut Express.

1   Save the current project one last time by pressing Cmd-S.

2   Quit Final Cut Express by pressing Cmd-Q, or continue on with the
    next lesson.

Lesson Review

1. True or false: When you edit sound bites of several clips together, you create a narrative sound track.

2. When you mark edit points in the Timeline, do the same shortcuts apply that you used in the Viewer to mark clips?

3. How many edit points are required to make an edit, three or four?

4. How can you remove a clip in the Timeline and remove the gap at the same time?

5. What edit function can you use to exchange one clip in the Timeline with another clip?

6. How can you tell whether the video track of a clip is linked to the audio tracks beneath it?

7. When in icon view, if you want to scrub through a thumbnail image in a bin, what tool must you use?

8. How do you set a new poster frame for a clip in the Browser? How do you set it for a clip in the Viewer?

9. How do you align clips in a bin when you want to practice storyboard editing?

Answers

1. True.

2. Yes.

3. Only three points, often referred to as three-point editing.

4. Select the clip and press Shift-Delete.

5. The Replace edit function.

6. A line appears under the clip name on the video track.

7. The Scrub tool.

8. In the Browser, scrub to a new frame, press Control, release the mouse, then release the Control key. In the Viewer, move the playhead to the desired frame and choose Mark > Set Poster Frame.

9. Place clips in a row from left to right, but make sure each clip is slightly lower than the previous one, creating a downward slant.

Keyboard Shortcuts

Shift-Delete	Deletes a clip and the gap it creates in the Timeline
Delete	Deletes the selected clip and leaves a gap
F11	Replaces edit
Shift-G	Moves the playhead forward to the next gap
Option-G	Moves the playhead backward to the most recent gap
Ctrl-G	Closes a gap in the Timeline
Cmd-L	Unlinks the tracks of a selected, linked clip
Ctrl-P	Sets a new poster frame

9

Lesson Files	Lesson 9 Project file
Media	Surfing folder
Time	This lesson takes approximately 60 minutes to complete.
Goals	Trim one edit point at a time
	Trim an edit point by dragging
	Work with the Ripple tool
	Extend an edit point
	Trim edit points in the Viewer

Trimming an Edit Point

After you've put your sequence of clips together, you will want to refine some of your edit points. You may want to subtract a few frames from the end of one clip or add a few frames to the beginning of another. Trimming one edit point at a time in this way lengthens or shortens a clip, and therefore the entire sequence. As always, there are different ways to approach trimming one edit point at a time, including a special trimming tool, called the Ripple tool.

Preparing the Project

To get started in Lesson 9, you will launch Final Cut Express and then open the project for this lesson.

1   In the menu, choose File > Open, or press Cmd-O, and select the **Lesson 9 Project** file from the Lessons folder on your hard drive.

2   Close any other projects that may be open from a previous session by Ctrl-clicking their name tabs in the Browser and choosing Close Tab from the shortcut menu.

3   In the Timeline, click the *Dad Finished* sequence and play the sequence.

    This is the first sequence you will create in this lesson. It is not a finished sequence but the first stage of one.

4   Look in the Canvas Duration field to see the duration of this sequence.

5   Click the *Dad Sound Bites* sequence in the Timeline. What is the duration of this sequence?

    Even though the two sequences look the same length in the Timeline, they do not represent the same length of time. Whenever you press Shift-Z, the entire sequence is resized to fit in the Timeline window, no matter how long the sequence actually is.

    You will be trimming about one minute off the length of this sequence to make it look more like the *Dad Finished* sequence.

    Let's make another copy of the *Dad Sound Bites* sequence so that you can use it for a second trimming method later in this lesson.

6   In the Browser, duplicate the *Dad Sound Bites* sequence and name the copy *Dad Sound Bites 2*.

7   Leave the *Dad Finished* sequence open for reference.

Trimming

Trimming is a basic part of the editing process. It allows you to change your mind about where you want a clip to start or stop *after* you've placed the clip in the Timeline. In this lesson, you will work with different approaches to trimming an edit point.

When you trim an edit point, the In and Out points of the edit can be trimmed to the left or right, making the clip either shorter or longer.

Consider the In point at the head of the clip and the Out point at the tail of the clip:

▶ Trim the In point to the left and the clip will begin on an earlier frame, making the edited clip longer.

▶ Trim the In point to the right and the clip will begin on a later frame, making the edited clip shorter.

▶ Trim the Out point to the left and the clip will end on an earlier frame, making the clip shorter.

▶ Trim the Out point to the right and the clip will end on a later frame, making the clip longer.

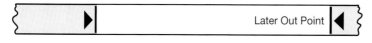

In each of the following trimming methods you will work with sound bites again, as you did in the previous lesson. This time, they are sound bites of Jimbo's dad, Jim. You will shave about a minute off of the longer *Dad Sound Bites* sequence by trimming the clips. Remember, the maximum amount you can trim an edit point in an outer direction (head or tail) depends on how much material is available in the original source clip. Also, when you trim clips whose audio and video are linked together, you are trimming both the audio and video edit points at the same time.

Dragging Edit Points

One way to trim a clip in the Timeline is simply to drag its edit point left or right. Keep in mind that the clip in the Timeline is linked to the original clip in the Browser. Even though you are seeing only the marked portion of your clip in the Timeline, when you trim, you have access to all the frames from the original clip.

Dragging an Edit Point

Dragging edit points is a direct and easy way to trim in the Timeline. Depending on what clip you are trimming, the process may require a few additional steps to complete.

1   In the *Dad Sound Bites* sequence, select the last clip, proud of kids, and drag the entire clip to the right a few seconds so that you have some room to experiment. If necessary, you can create additional blank Timeline space at the end of the sequence by pressing Option-– (minus) or adjusting the Zoom control.

2   Park the playhead in the middle of the clip after Jim says, "… really good so far also."

    This is where you want the new Out point to be.

3   Click just the Out edit point to highlight it.

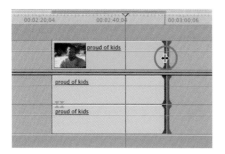

Just the edge of the clip is selected, not the body of the clip. If the
entire clip were selected, you would end up moving the whole clip,
not trimming the Out point.

4   Drag the Out point left. As you drag, look at the trim amount and
new duration as they are being updated in the information box.

5   Drag the Out point to the left until you see it snap to the playhead.
Release the mouse and play the clip to see the new edit point.

6   To trim the In point, play the clip from the head, and park the playhead just before Jim says, "So naturally." This is close to the In point,
so you might want to zoom in on the Timeline by pressing Option-+.

7   Click and hold the In point of the clip.

In the Canvas, the end-of-clip filmstrip overlay on the left indicates that the current In point is at the very first frame of the media file. You can't trim any farther to the left.

8   Drag the edit point to the right until it snaps to the playhead.

The new In frame is displayed in the Canvas.

9   Press Shift-Z to see the entire sequence. Select the whole clip, not just the edit point, drag the clip you trimmed back to the end of the sequence, and play the new trimmed version of the clip.

Dragging Edit Points Between Clips

When you want to trim clips that are between other clips in the sequence, the dragging option has a different impact. For example, when two clips are side by side, Final Cut Express won't allow you to drag the edit point of one clip into its neighboring clip. You can drag away from the neighboring clip but not into it.

Generally, trimming a clip to be longer or shorter changes the overall length of the sequence. When you trim or shorten a clip by dragging an edit point, it leaves a gap in the sequence, and the sequence length remains unchanged. You can delete the gap as you did in the previous lesson, but there is a way to trim without leaving a gap in the sequence. You will work with that method in the next exercise.

1   In the current sequence, play the **support Jimbo** clip, and stop the play-head after Jim says, "… only thing I wanted to do was support him."

    If you can't see the clip, press Shift-Z to see the entire sequence, or drag the Zoom slider left.

2   You won't be able to, but click the Out point of this clip and try to drag it to the right into the following clip.

    NOTE ▶ You can't drag an edit point over another clip without a special trim tool. You will work with that tool later in this lesson.

3   Now drag it left until it snaps to the playhead, and release.

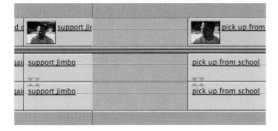

    Dragging this clip's Out point to the left creates a gap in the Timeline.

4   Delete this gap by selecting it and pressing Delete.

    When you delete the gap, the following clips are pulled up the dura-tion of the gap. This is called *rippling* because deleting the gap ripples the locations of the rest of the sequence clips.

5   Repeat the process for the In point of this clip. Park the playhead just before Jim starts speaking, and drag the In point to that location.

6   Select and delete the gap to ripple the remaining clips.

7   Play the trimmed clip.

NOTE ▸ When you drag a clip's edit point, you see the updated frame in the Canvas. But when you stop dragging and let go, the Canvas image reverts to wherever the playhead is parked in the Timeline.

Project Tasks

1   Continue dragging edit points to trim the length of this sequence.

2   You can make your own editorial decisions, or you can trim to the following sound-bite suggestions: Drag the new In points to just before the beginning of the quote, and drag or trim the new Out points to just after the end of the quote.

Clip	Quote
name and start	"My name's Jim Borland … Jimbo's dad."
obvious to surf	"Where I grew up … couldn't wait for the day."
over and over again	"Jimbo was about … learning how to surf."
support Jimbo	Already edited.
pick up from school	"What I do … we'll go to the beach."
proud of kids	Already edited.

NOTE ▶ Not all current edit points will need trimming.

3   Press Cmd-S to save your work.

Rippling Edits

Dragging edit points and deleting gaps is one way you can trim a clip in the Timeline. Another way is to drag the edit point and ripple the remaining edits in the sequence at the same time without having to delete. You do this by using the Ripple tool. The Ripple tool shares the fourth position in the Tool palette.

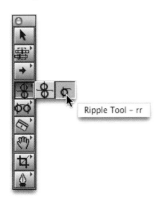

When you use the Ripple tool to trim an edit point, you can drag the edit point past a neighboring clip. Also, when you drag, all the clips that follow are automatically pushed down or pulled up the length of the trim, lengthening or shortening the sequence. In these exercises, you will make the same trim adjustments you made in the *Dad Sound Bites* sequence, but you will do them using the Ripple tool.

Using the Ripple Tool

Using the Ripple tool adjusts either the head or tail of a clip in a sequence in either a forward or backward direction. Any change you make with the Ripple tool will cause a change in the overall length of the sequence.

1   In the Sequences bin in the Browser, double-click the *Dad Sound Bites 2* sequence to open it in the Timeline.

Look at the Canvas Duration field. This sequence duplicate was created before any adjustments were made on the original. It is the same length as the first *Dad Sound Bites* sequence was before you started working on it.

2   Park the playhead on the **proud of kids** clip, and press Option-+ to zoom in to that clip.

3   In the Tool palette, click and hold the fourth tool. Slide over and stay on the single roller icon for a moment until the tool's name, Ripple, appears, and then let go. You can also press RR as the keyboard shortcut to select this tool.

4   In the **proud of kids** clip, park the playhead after Jim says, "… good so far also."

5   With the Ripple tool selected, don't click or drag but just move your pointer over the middle of this clip.

The Ripple tool icon appears over a clip. In the middle of the clip, the icon has an X on it, indicating that you can't use it in this area. You can only use the tool on an edit point.

6   Move the tool toward the clip's Out point. When you get close to the
     Out point, the X disappears, and the tail of the Ripple icon points
     toward the inside of the clip you will be trimming.

7   Drag this edit point left until it snaps to the playhead position.

8   In this same clip, park the playhead just before Jim starts speaking,
     and zoom in to this location by pressing Option-+.

     NOTE ▶ When you move the playhead in the Timeline ruler area, the
     default Selection tool appears. Final Cut Express knows you can't trim
     here, so it reverts to the Selection tool to allow you to do other things,
     such as moving the playhead. When you move the pointer back into a
     clip, it changes back to the currently selected tool.

9   Click the inside edge of the **proud of kids** clip to select its In point.

     When the edit point is correctly selected, just the right side, or In
     point of this clip, is highlighted. The horizontal tail of the Ripple tool
     icon points inward toward the clip it's adjusting. If you select the Out
     point of the previous clip, the tail of the Ripple tool will point toward
     that clip.

10   Drag this edit point to the right until it snaps to the playhead.

     As you drag, the yellow information box appears with just the trim
     amount. In the Canvas, you see the fixed Out frame of the previous clip
     and the updated In frame of the current clip. There is no gap left over.

Trimming with Durations and Shortcuts

Sometimes you may have a trim amount in mind. Perhaps it's one second or a few frames. Just as you typed a move duration in the Timeline to move a clip, you can also type a trim amount to trim a clip. For keyboard enthusiasts, there are also a few keyboard shortcuts you can use to trim your edit point.

1   With the Ripple tool still selected, click the inner edge of the In point of the last clip in the sequence, **proud of kids**. Play the beginning of this clip. You will trim the In point so that it begins later, just before Jim says, "… I'm proud to …" This is about a three-second duration.

2   In the Timeline, type *3.00* or *3.* (3 period).

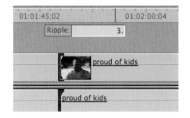

A Ripple trim box appears in the center of the Timeline with the amount of the trim.

3   Press Return to enter that trim amount.

That edit point is trimmed forward by that amount, and no gap is created.

In the **pick up from school** clip, Jim says, "Uhhh," before he begins speaking. Let's apply some keyboard shortcuts to trim away the "Uhhh."

4   With the Ripple tool, click the In point of the **pick up from school** clip to select it.

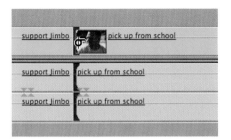

5   To move the In point later, press the] (right bracket) key. Each time you press it, the In point is trimmed by one frame.

> **TIP** ▶ You can also press Shift-] to trim a default number of frames, such as 5, 10, or 20. To change this number, press Option-Q to open the User Preferences window and enter the desired Multi-Frame Trim Size on the Editing tab.

6   Press Shift-] a few times to get closer to where Jim speaks.

> **TIP** ▶ You can also use the < and > keys to adjust an edit point in one-frame increments, and Shift-< or Shift-> for the multi-frame trim amount.

Any change you make using these keyboard shortcuts ripples the following clips in the sequence. With such minor adjustments, it may be difficult to see the clips shifting, but they are. You can see the thumbnail image in the Timeline clip update every time you change the In point.

Project Tasks

1 Practice selecting individual clip edit points with the Ripple tool and making the following trims.

Clip	In and Out Points
name and start	"My name's Jim Borland … Jimbo's dad."
obvious to surf	"Where I grew up … couldn't wait for the day."
over and over again	"Jimbo was about … learning how to surf."
support Jimbo	"Since Jimbo … wanted to do was support him."
pick up from school	"What I do is… we'll go to the beach." (first one)
proud of kids	Already edited.

Make sure you are selecting the inside edge of the clip's edit point you want to trim.

2 Press Cmd-S to save your work.

Extending an Edit

A third way to trim a clip is to *extend* a selected edit point to a new location. Extending an edit always works in conjunction with the playhead location and the default Selection tool. The selected edit point snaps to the location of the playhead in the sequence. As with all trim options, extending an edit can make a clip longer or shorter. You can use this method to adjust two edit points at once, but that will be covered in the next lesson.

Extending an edit point takes only a few steps. The first step is to make sure your pointer is the default Selection tool.

1 Press A, or click the default Selection tool in the Tool palette.

2   Let's say you want to extend the end of the **proud of kids** clip 10 seconds. Move the playhead 10 seconds past the end of this clip. Use the Canvas or Timeline Location field or Timeline ruler as a guide.

3   Select the Out point of this clip.

Both sides of the edit point become selected.

4   In the main menu, choose Sequence > Extend Edit, or press E.

The Out point is extended to the right 10 seconds.

NOTE ▶ Not all edits have this much material to use in trimming. Sometimes you will trim just a few frames or a second at a time. It all depends on how long your original clips are.

5   Let's go back the other way. Park the playhead earlier in this clip, where you trimmed it before, right after Jim says, "… really good so far also."

6   With the Out point still selected, press E to extend the edit point back to the playhead location.

You can continue adjusting your edit point this way until you get it the way you want it.

Keep in mind that you can only extend an edit if you have enough clip material to support the move. If you have placed the playhead too far out of the clip's range of material, it won't be able to extend the edit to that location.

Trimming in the Viewer

The Viewer is where you have screened and marked your clips before editing them into the sequence. But you can also use the Viewer to make adjustments to clips already in the Timeline. You can drag edit points as you did earlier in this lesson. You can also select the Ripple tool and use that in the Viewer as well.

1   In the Browser, open the *Dad with Cutaways* sequence and play it.

This is the same sequence as *Dad Finished* but with the second clip deleted. You should already have the default Selection tool as your pointer.

2   To open a clip into the Viewer from this sequence, double-click the **over and over again** clip in the Timeline. As with clips in the

Browser, you can also select a clip in the Timeline and press Return to open it.

The clip opens in the Viewer, and the In and Out points used for this clip in the sequence appear in the scrubber bar. The scrubber bar now displays two lines of dots like film sprocket holes. This is the visual indication that you are working with a clip that has already been edited into the sequence.

3   Play the clip, and stop the playhead after Jim says, "… I first took him down to the beach."

4   Move the pointer over the Out point in the scrubber bar. Look for the pointer to change to the left-right resize arrow you saw when you dragged the edit point in the Timeline.

5   Drag the Out point of this clip to the left, to the playhead location.

    As you drag the Out point, you scrub through the clip's audio; you'll hear a digital version of the audio, which might be helpful in trimming.

In the Timeline, a gap is left by the trim amount, just as it is when you drag the clip's edit point directly in the Timeline.

6   Now drag the Out point back to the right as far as you can.

A Media Limit note appears to let you know you are up against
another clip in the Timeline. You couldn't drag over another clip in
the Timeline, and you can't do it from the Viewer, either.

7   Select the Ripple tool in the Tool palette, or use the keyboard shortcut
RR to select it.

8   Now move the pointer into the Viewer scrubber bar and then over the
Out point.

When the pointer is moved over the Out point, it changes to the
Ripple tool.

9   Drag the Out point to the same playhead location you used before.

In the Timeline, after you complete the trim and release the mouse,
the following edits are rippled and pull up to cover the gap.

Project Tasks

In order to set up for the next exercise, you will edit two video cutaways to cover the video jump cuts in the following sequence. To do this, you will use the Replace edit function.

1   In the Timeline, make sure the *Dad with Cutaways* sequence is still open, and close all other sequences. Press A to change to the default Selection tool.

2   From the Cutaways bin, open the high 5 clip into the Viewer, and place the playhead 25 frames from the head of the clip.

3   Place the playhead on the first frame of the second clip in the sequence, over and over again.

4   To replace just the video portion of this linked clip, select the over and over again clip and press Cmd-L to unlink the tracks. Then deselect the clip.

5   In the Viewer, drag the high 5 clip into the Canvas and drop it on the Replace section in the Edit Overlay. Play the edit.

6   Open the back up again clip from the Cutaways bin into the Viewer, and park the playhead at 8:17.

    Since this source clip has audio attached, and you only want to edit video, you will have to disconnect the a1 and a2 source controls in the Timeline.

7   In the Timeline, disconnect the a1 and a2 source controls. Then move the playhead to the first frame of the fourth clip, pick up from school.

8   Select the pick up from school clip and press Cmd-L to unlink the tracks. Then deselect the clip.

9   Drag the clip from the Viewer to the Canvas, and drop it on the Replace section. Play the clip, and then press Cmd-S to save your project.

NOTE ▶ The DVD that comes with this book includes an Advanced Trimming PDF that covers additional trimming methods.

Lesson Review

1.   What is one way to trim an edit point with the Selection tool?

2.   True or false: You can never drag an edit point into or over an existing clip in the sequence using the Selection tool.

3.   What tool can you use to trim an edit without leaving a gap?

4.   What are some ways you can trim with the Ripple tool besides dragging an edit point?

5.   How can you change the Multi-Frame Trim Size amount?

6.   What are the three steps to extend an edit?

7.   How do you open a sequence clip into the Viewer?

Answers

1.   You can drag an edit point using the Selection tool.

2.   True.

3.   The Ripple tool.

4.   You can select the edit point with the Ripple tool and type a trim amount; you can select the edit point and press the left or right bracket key to trim one frame at a time; or you can press Shift–left bracket or Shift–right bracket to trim the Multi-Frame Trim Size amount.

5. Press Option-Q to open the User Preferences window, click the Editing tab, and enter the amount in the appropriate field.

6. Move the playhead to where you want to extend the clip, select the clip's edit point, and press E.

7. Double-click the clip in the Timeline.

Keyboard Shortcuts

E	Extend an edit
RR	Ripple tool

10

Lesson Files	Lesson 10 Project file
Media	Working Out folder, Vacation Fun folder, Surfing folder
Time	This lesson takes approximately 75 minutes to complete.
Goals	Trim two edit points at the same time
	Slip In and Out points
	Work with the Roll tool
	Slide clip placement
	Drag a clip to a new location
	Extend edit points

Fine-Tuning Edit Points

You now have different approaches under your belt for trimming a single edit point by adding and subtracting frames to a clip in the Timeline. But once you have the length of the sequence set, other editing tools will allow you to finesse or fine-tune your edit points without changing the overall length of the sequence. There are three tools that allow you to do this: the Slip, Roll, and Slide tools. Each of these tools allows you to make fine-tuning adjustments to the edit points in your sequence.

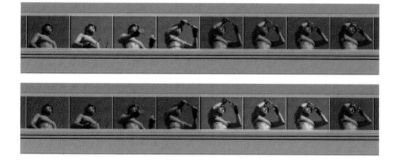

Preparing the Project

To get started in Lesson 10, you will launch Final Cut Express and then open the project for this lesson.

1 Launch Final Cut Express, choose File > Open or press Cmd-O, and choose the **Lesson 10 Project** file from the Lessons folder on your hard drive.

2 Close any other projects that may be open from a previous session by Ctrl-clicking their name tabs in the Browser and choosing Close Tab from the shortcut menu.

The Browser does not contain any clips but does have four sequences open in the Timeline. These sequences will be familiar because they were copied from four earlier lessons. In each case, there are some ways in which adjusting the edit points will improve or polish the sequences. The lesson number has been added to the sequence name so you have a reference to its origin.

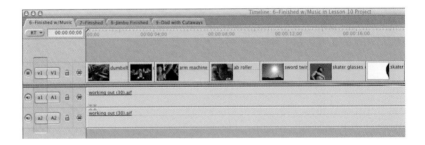

Trimming Two Edit Points

Once you have trimmed your clips and your sequence length is set, you will want to finesse clip content and placement. For example, you may want a specific action in a clip to fall on a beat of music. Or you may want to shift a clip's placement slightly in the sequence. There are three ways to adjust and fine-tune edit points, and each method uses a tool from the

Tool palette. The three methods are *slipping*, *rolling*, and *sliding*. Each of these options will trim two edit points at the same time without changing the overall length of the sequence.

> **NOTE ▶** In editing, the term *edit point* can refer either to an individual In or Out point, or to the juncture at which two individual edit points meet.

Slipping

Slipping trims both the In point and Out point in a single clip the same amount in the same direction at the same time, moving both edit points either to the left or to the right. This process is called *slipping* because you keep the clip length and location in the Timeline the same but slip the content earlier or later to adjust the selection of material.

Rolling

Rolling involves two adjacent clips. You can trim the Out point of the first clip and the In point of the following clip at the same time. This *rolls* the two clips' edit points earlier or later. One clip becomes shorter while the other becomes longer, still keeping the overall sequence length the same.

Sliding

Sliding adjusts two edit points but involves three adjacent clips. You can *slide* or shift the middle clip to the left, changing the Out point of the first clip and making it shorter. But the In point of the third clip adjusts to compensate, making it longer. This changes the position of the middle clip in the sequence but does not change the middle clip's duration or content.

Slipping Clip Content

Slipping a clip shifts both the In and Out points the same amount as you select slightly different content for that clip. It's like trimming both edit points the same amount in the same direction at the same time. You can only slip a clip if there is additional source material, or *handles*, on either side of the current edit points. If you used the entire clip length when you made the edit, there will be no additional frames to shift or slip the clip.

> **NOTE ▶** In the following images, the darker frames represent the additional source material, or handles, available to use when slipping a clip.

Current clip content

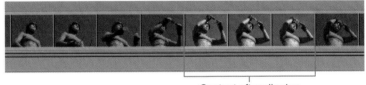

Content after slipping

Working with the Slip Tool

The Slip tool is the fifth tool in the Tool palette. Its shortcut key is S.

1   Click the *6-Finished w/Music* sequence tab in the Timeline and play it.

There are several clips in this sequence that could be improved by slipping the source selection slightly.

2   Play the **ab roller** clip. This will be the first clip you adjust.

3   Click the Slip tool in the Tool palette.

4   With the Slip tool, click and hold the **ab roller** clip in the Timeline.

When you select the clip with the Slip tool, a brown outline appears past the area of the clip box. This outline indicates graphically how much original source material is available for you to draw from on either side while making your adjustment.

> **TIP** ▶ Think of the clip space as the windshield of a car. There's more scenery on either side of the windshield even though your focus is on the windshield viewing area. If you want to use material that's before the current first frame of the clip, or to the left of the windshield, you drag it right, bringing it into view.

5   With the Slip tool, drag right until you see the man in the up position in the left frame of the Canvas's two-up display, then release the mouse.

NOTE ▶ When snapping is on, it is sometimes difficult to drag just a few frames. Press N to turn snapping off or on as you slip the clip. Leave it on after you've made the adjustment.

As you drag, the two frames in the Canvas two-up display visually update your new In and Out points.

In point   Out point

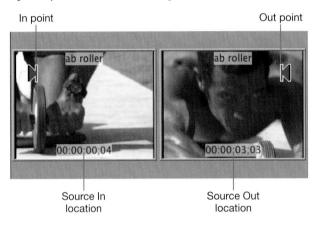

Source In   Source Out
location   location

6   Play the **skater glasses on** clip. With the Slip tool, click and hold the clip.

In the Canvas, the end-of-clip filmstrip symbol appears in the left frame to indicate that you are currently on the first frame of the clip. Therefore, you cannot slip to the right. If you drag all the way to the left, you will see the end-of-clip symbol on the right frame.

7   Drag until you see the woman's hand start to come up to put on her glasses in the left Canvas frame, and in the right Canvas frame look for where she has lowered her hand, then release the mouse.

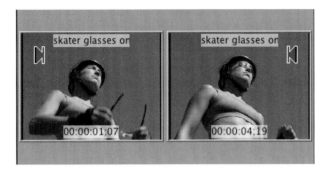

As in any move, when you slip a clip in the Timeline, a duration box appears that shows the amount you have adjusted the clip forward or backward.

Project Tasks

Now that you see how the slip function works, practice making slipping adjustments to the following clips. During all these adjustments, the original clip durations remain the same. Don't forget to view the two image frames in the Canvas two-up display to locate a specific action in the clip.

1   With the Slip tool selected, click the first clip, **dumbbell cu**, and drag right until just before the hand first appears in the left Canvas frame.

2   Slip the **mountain bikers** clip left until you see the last biker leave the right Canvas frame.

3   Slip the **skater ecu** clip right until the face is just out of sight in the left Canvas frame.

You will slip other clips in the following exercises.

Slipping by Numbers

Another way to slip a clip is by typing in the number of frames or even seconds you want to slip the clip, as you did to move or trim a clip.

1   Press A to select the default Selection tool. Select the **sword twirl** clip in the sequence and play it.

    You will adjust or slip this clip so that the person lands on the strong beat of the music, about 20 frames earlier.

2   Now select the Slip tool from the Tool palette, or press S.

3   Type *–20*.

4   Press Return and play the new clip selection.

5   With the Slip tool still selected, type additional frames backward or forward to slip the clip until the action is just right.

6   Play the **golfer hits ball** clip at the end of the sequence. If you wanted the hitting of the ball to coincide with the strong beat of the music, how far would you slip this clip and in which direction?

    The ball hit happens about one second before the strong accent in the music, so you would want to slip the ball hit forward one second.

7   Use steps 1–5 as a guide to slip this clip one second forward.

    TIP ▶ Instead of pressing A to switch to the default Selection tool just to select a clip, you can hold down the Shift key while the Slip tool is still active. This temporarily changes the Slip tool to the default Selection tool. After selecting a clip, release the Shift key, and the pointer changes back to the Slip tool.

Slipping in the Viewer

You can also use the Slip tool to adjust a clip in the Viewer, as you did with the Ripple tool in the previous lesson. First, of course, you must open the clip from the Timeline.

1   Make sure you still have the Slip tool selected.

2   In the current sequence, double-click the **skater skates forward** clip and hover the pointer over one of the edit points in the scrubber bar.

Several things happen. The clip opens in the Viewer, and the two rows of dots appear in the scrubber bar to indicate that this clip is already in the sequence. Also, the pointer changes to the Slip tool when you move it over an edit point.

3   In the Viewer scrubber bar, reposition the playhead between the edit points. Then drag one of the edit points left or right.

As you drag, both edit points move together because slipping maintains the original edit duration. Also, you now view the first frame of the adjusted clip in the Viewer and the last frame in the Canvas.

4   Slip the clip to get an earlier portion of the woman skating.

Look at the clip in the Timeline. The thumbnail image for the clip has been updated to reflect the new In point. When you open clips from the Timeline into the Viewer, any changes you make are also made directly to the clip in the Timeline.

> **TIP** ▶ For keyboard enthusiasts, you can slip an opened sequence clip in the Viewer another way. Select the default Selection tool, and hold down Shift as you drag an edit point.

Rolling Edit Points

The Roll tool also adjusts two edit points at the same time. But unlike the Slip tool, which adjusts two edits points in a single clip, the Roll tool adjusts two edit points in two adjacent clips. It will adjust the Out point of one clip the same amount it adjusts the In point of the following clip. This allows you to move edit points in tandem earlier or later in the sequence without changing the overall sequence duration.

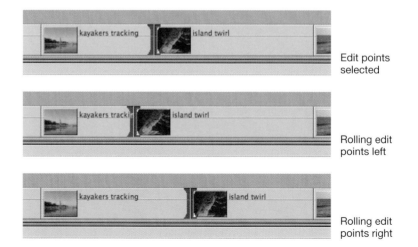

Edit points selected

Rolling edit points left

Rolling edit points right

1   In the Timeline, select the *9-Dad with Cutaways* sequence and
play it.

This is the sequence you added cutaways to in the previous lesson.
In this sequence, the cutaways were placed directly on the edit points.
In review, the sequence could be improved by making the cutaways
come in a little earlier or stay a little later to cover some of Jim's head
moves and to make the dialogue seem more natural.

2   Select the Roll tool in the Tool palette, or press R.

3   Play from the end of the **high 5** clip into the following **support Jimbo**
clip. Park the playhead after the first two words in the clip and just
before Jim says, "Jimbo started surfing…."

Moving the **high 5** Out point to this location could improve this edit
point. But you want to move only the video portion of this edit, not the
audio track. Since the video and audio of this clip are linked together,
you have to lock the audio tracks so that they won't be affected.

4   Click the A1 and A2 Lock Track controls in the Timeline to lock the current audio tracks.

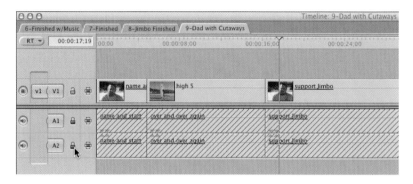

5   With the Roll tool selected, click the edit point between the **high 5** and **support Jimbo** clips. Both sides of the edit point become highlighted.

6   Drag the edit point until it snaps to the playhead location, and note the following two things before you release the mouse:

In the Timeline, look at the brown outline that surrounds both clips. It indicates that these two clips are involved in this adjustment. You also see the yellow information box indicating the amount of the adjustment or roll.

Now look at the two frames in the Canvas. The left frame is the outgoing clip and displays an Out point in its upper-right corner. The right frame is the incoming clip and displays an In point in its upper-left corner. The clip names and source locations also appear on the clip frames.

7 Release the mouse button and play the edit.

8 Now play through the edit point between the **back up again** and **proud of kids** clips. As in the previous example, this edit point might be improved if you carry the cutaway a little farther.

   If you are rolling an edit point to a specific playhead location, you can also use the Extend Edit shortcut to move both edit points at the same time.

9 Park the playhead just after Jim says, "proud to have a…" and click the edit point between the two clips before this location. This time press E, the Extend Edit shortcut key, to extend the edit point to the playhead location.

   Since the playhead was parked where you wanted the new edit point to be, pressing E extends or rolls the selected edit point to that location.

10 Play the new edit.

   Remember, if a clip does not have any more frames to use in your adjustment, an end-of-clip filmstrip symbol will appear on one of the Canvas frames, and you won't be able to roll the edit point any farther.

Project Tasks

1   Roll the edit point between the **support Jimbo** and **back up again** clips so that the cutaway appears right after Jim says, "talented at the sport and uh…."

2   At the end of the first clip, Jim looks down after he introduces himself. To cover that head move with some of the following cutaway, roll the **high 5** cutaway back into the first clip. Select the edit point with the Roll tool, then use the number-typing approach to do this. Try –10 frames.

> **TIP** You can also apply the same bracket-key shortcuts you used earlier to make roll adjustments. Select the edit point with the Roll tool and press the left or right bracket key ([or]), or press Shift-[or Shift-] for the multi-frame trim duration.

Sliding Clips

The third way you can adjust two edit points is to slide one clip that sits between two others. Sliding the middle clip maintains its content and duration but adjusts its placement between its bordering clips. As the middle clip is repositioned, the Out point of the first clip and the In point of the third clip are trimmed by complementary amounts to allow for the change. Again, the overall sequence length does not change when you slide a clip in the sequence.

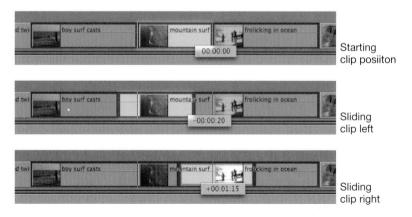

Starting
clip posiiton

Sliding
clip left

Sliding
clip right

Using the Slide Tool

The Slide tool is used when you want to reposition a clip slightly to the left or right between two other clips. The clip you are moving does not change duration or content. But the previous clip's Out point and following clip's In point change. The Slide tool shares the same square as the Slip tool in the Tool palette.

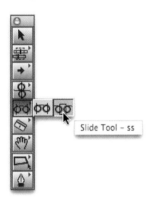

1   In the Timeline, click the *7-Finished* sequence and play it.

In this sequence, some of the edit points could be improved if they were placed on one of the strong music beats. To do this, you will slide a clip left or right into the previous or following clip. You will automatically be changing the length of the adjacent clips but not that of the overall sequence.

2   To select the Slide tool in the Tool palette, click and hold the Slip tool until the Slide icon appears to the side, and then select it. You can also press its shortcut, SS.

NOTE ▶ In this sequence, the video clips are not linked to the music, so you do not need to lock the audio tracks before adjusting the edits.

3   In the Timeline, move the playhead to 5:15, where a beat of music occurs.

4   Drag the **kayakers tracking** clip to the right until the right edge of its clip box snaps to the playhead. Take note of the bounding box and the Canvas frames before releasing the mouse.

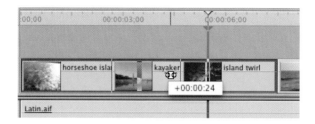

When you slide a clip, the brown clip outline now includes the three clips involved: the preceding clip, the current clip you are sliding, and the following clip. As you slide the middle clip, the outer two edges of the adjacent clips do not move; only the inner edges that border the middle clip move to compensate for the adjustment.

In the Canvas, the two new edit points on either side of the clip you are sliding appear. The left frame displays the new Out point of the first clip, and the right frame displays the new In point of the third clip. These are the two frames that will now border the clip you are sliding.

5   Play the new edit and then park the playhead at the next strong beat of music at 9:02.

6   Slide the **boy surf casts** clip to the right until its left edge snaps to the playhead. This extends the **island twirl** clip to this point. Play the edit.

7 Park the playhead after eight beats of music at 12:22, and slide the **mountain surf** clip left to this point.

Project Tasks

1 With the Slide tool (SS), slide the **frolicking in ocean** clip to the right so that it begins on the first drum rat-tat-tat at 14:14.

> **NOTE** ▸ If you want to use the numbers approach on this edit, press A to select the default Selection tool and select the clip. Then press SS to select the Slide tool. Type *20* and press Return to slide the clip 20 frames forward. You can adjust the slide amount by pressing the left or right bracket keys ([or]). You can also press Shift to temporarily revert to the default Selection tool.

2 To adjust the final edit point in the sequence, between **frolicking in ocean** and **rockscape surf**, you can use the Roll tool, since the adjustment involves only two clips. Park the playhead at 19:27, select the Roll tool (R), and roll the edit point to the playhead location.

Now that the edit points are where you want them against the music beats, are there clips whose content you would like to slip? Remember, slipping content does not change the placement of a clip in the sequence.

3 Play the sequence. Use the Slip tool (S) to slip the contents of the **horseshoe island** clip to the left to see more of the island from overhead.

4 Experiment with adjusting clip content in this sequence by applying the Slip tool to the **boy surf casts** and **frolicking in ocean** clips.

Dragging to Reposition a Clip

Another way to change the position of a clip in the sequence is to drag it completely away from its current position to a new location and insert it there. This will not change any of the clips prior to the insertion point, but all clips following will be pushed down the length of the inserted clip. Since no new clips are added to the sequence, the overall sequence length remains the same.

Dragging and dropping a clip to a new location in your sequence does not require any editing tool other than the default Selection tool. In this exercise, you will work with the Jimbo interview clips and rearrange their order.

1   Click the *8-Jimbo Finished* sequence and play it.

2   Press A to select the default Selection tool.

3   To get right to the surfing dialogue after Jimbo introduces himself, drag the **catch a wave** clip left toward the **name** clip and let it snap to the end of that clip, *but don't release the mouse.*

As you drag, the Overwrite edit tool (a downward arrow) appears. If you were to release the mouse at this point, you would overwrite the material beneath the new clip and also leave a gap from the clip you are moving.

In the Canvas, look at the names of the clips in the two frames. These are the frames that would appear on either side of this clip if you dropped it in as an Overwrite edit.

4   Now press and hold the Option key.

When you press Option, the pointer changes to a hooked downward arrow, indicating that you will be inserting this clip at this point.

The two Canvas frames display the frame before the current clip and the frame after it, as though you were inserting this clip.

5   This is important: To complete this move, first let go of the mouse and then let go of the Option key.

6   Drag the **nose ride** clip left, and snap the head of that clip to the end of the **catch a wave** clip. Hold down the Option key to make sure you are inserting this clip at this location. When you see the hooked arrow, let go of the mouse and then let go of the Option key.

Project Tasks

1   Drag the **leash** clip to follow the **nose ride** clip.

> **TIP** ▶ Don't forget that you can use Cmd-Z to undo any mistakes.

2   Drag the **carry head** clip to follow the **wax every time** clip.

3   Play the new configuration of clips in this sequence.

You may notice that a few of Jimbo's clips are very bright. You will learn how to correct this in Lesson 16.

> **NOTE** ▶ The DVD that comes with this book includes an exercise on the Trim Edit window. In this window, you can either ripple or roll edit points by previewing them. You can find this exercise in "Advanced Trimming."

Saving and Quitting

Remember to save your project before you close it or quit Final Cut Express. This time, you will quit Final Cut Express first so you can see the Save dialog that appears.

1   Quit Final Cut Express by pressing Cmd-Q.

A window appears, letting you know your project has been changed or modified since you last saved it. You have the choice of canceling, which stops the quitting process; saving the project using a different name or location; not saving the most recent changes; or saving changes.

The project 'Lesson 10 Project' has been modified. Do you want to save it?

Cancel   Save As...   No   Yes

2   Click Save to save your most recent changes, close this project, and quit Final Cut Express all at the same time.

Lesson Review

1. Which two edit points does the Slip tool adjust?

2. How can you slip a clip in the Viewer?

3. What two edit points does the Roll toll adjust?

4. How do you use shortcut keys to roll an edit point one frame at a time?

5. What modifier key can you use to slip, roll, or slide the multi-frame trim amount?

6. How many clips does the Slide tool involve?

7. How do you reposition a clip in the sequence to an entirely different location?

Answers

1. The In and Out points of a single clip.

2. In the Timeline, double-click the clip to open it into the Viewer. With the Slip tool, drag either edit point left or right. With the default Selection tool, hold down Shift and drag an edit point left or right.

3. One clip's Out point and the following clip's In point.

4. With an edit point selected, you press the left bracket to roll back one frame, the right bracket to roll forward one frame.

5. The Shift key.

6. Three adjacent clips.

7. Drag the clip to the new location and hold down the Option key before releasing the clip.

Keyboard Shortcuts

E	Extends an edit
S	Slip tool
R	Roll tool
SS	Slide tool
[(Left bracket)	Applies a single-frame change backward to the selected edit point, based on the current tool
] (Right bracket)	Applies a single-frame change forward to the selected edit point, based on the current tool
Shift-[	Applies a multi-frame change backward to the selected edit point, based on the current tool
Shift-]	Applies a multi-frame change forward to the selected edit point, based on the current tool

11

Customizing Your Project

In this lesson, you will begin to organize your clips in a different way. You will work more with Browser columns, adding labels and notes to clips, and changing, removing, and adding columns to customize your Browser layout. You will also learn to customize the Final Cut Express interface, as well as work with the button bars in each window. In the process, you will learn what makes a clip a master clip, how to subdivide master clips into subclips, and how to add markers to clips and sequences to identify specific locations.

Preparing the Project

This time, to launch Final Cut Express and get started in Lesson 11, you will open that project from the Lessons folder.

1   Navigate to the Lessons folder on your hard drive and double-click **Lesson 11 Project**.

2   Close any other projects that may be open from a previous session by Ctrl-clicking their name tabs in the Browser and choosing Close Tab from the shortcut menu.

   NOTE ▶ For this exercise, make sure you view the items in the Browser as a list.

3   There are two open sequences in this project. In the Timeline, click the *Starting* sequence tab.

   At the moment, this sequence is empty.

Organizing Browser Information

Using the View as List mode in the Browser, you have access to more than 40 columns of information. Each column has a heading, such as Name, Duration, In, and Out. Any information you may have entered about a clip while you were editing or capturing it, or anything else that Final Cut Express knows about the clip, will be organized under these column headings. As you have also seen, it's not necessary to focus on or even refer to this information during the editing process. But it's always there if you need it. Organizing Browser information is a way for you to begin to customize the Final Cut Express interface to your personal preferences.

Sorting Browser Columns

When the Browser is viewed as a list of items, clips are sorted according to their names because the Name column is the default sort mode. But it may be helpful occasionally to sort the information a different way. It takes just a moment to change the sort order to look for particular information and then change back to the default Name sorting mode.

1   Click the Browser Zoom button in the upper left to expand the window to a wider view. Then click the Zoom button again to return the Browser to its original size.

2   Display the contents of all bins, and click the Zoom button again.

The Zoom button expands the Browser over the Viewer and Canvas windows to show all the items displayed in the window, but only as many columns as can fit across the interface. In the Name column, all clips and sequences are arranged alphabetically by name within a bin, and all bins are arranged alphabetically as well.

3   At the bottom of the Browser window, drag the horizontal scroll bar to the right to see the other column heads.

4   Drag the scroll bar left and notice that the Name column heading remains stationary as you scroll through the other columns.

The Name column heading is lighter than the other column heads. This indicates that it is the primary sort column. There is a downward triangle indicating that sorting is going down from A to Z.

5   Click the Name column heading to reverse the current sort order so the items are sorted upward, from Z to A.

All the elements in the window reverse order, including the order in which the bins themselves appear.

6   Click the Duration column heading to sort the clips by duration.

Name	Duration ▼	In	Out
▼ ☐ Relaxing Weekend			
☐ couple at beach	00:01:10;09	Not Set	Not Set
▼ ☐ Sequences			
⊞ Starting	00:00:00;00	Not Set	Not Set
⊞ Marking	00:00:29;13	Not Set	Not Set
▼ ☐ Surfing Clips			
☐ waxing board med	00:00:05;12	Not Set	Not Set
☐ support Jimbo	00:00:05;25	00:00:16;16	00:00:22;10
☐ out to sea	00:00:05;27	Not Set	Not Set
☐ high 5	00:00:06;17	00:00:06;16	00:00:13;02
☐ board on head	00:00:15;26	Not Set	Not Set
☐ nose riding	00:00:16;29	Not Set	Not Set
☐ back up again	00:00:26;19	Not Set	Not Set
◁ surfing voices.aif	00:01:03;02	Not Set	Not Set

The default sort order is always from low to high, such as A to Z, or in this case, short durations to long durations.

7   Click the Name column heading again. To expand the Name column, drag the column boundary line to the right.

Name	▼◀▶Duration	In
▼ ☐ Relaxing Weekend		

Moving, Showing, and Hiding Browser Columns

To customize your Browser, you can move a column or hide it from
view. You can also show additional columns that do not appear in the
default layout.

1 In the Browser, find the Good column and drag it left. Release it when
   it is just to the right of the Duration column.

   When you drag a column heading, a bounding box appears representing that column.

2 Scroll the Browser window contents until you see the Reel column
   heading, and then drag it to follow the Out column.

   If after scrolling you can't see a column because it is hidden from
   view, drag a column left across the column headings, and hold the
   pointer against the stationary Name heading to move all the earlier
   columns back into view.

3 Drag the Browser scroll bar to the right until you see the Comment
   2 column. To hide this column, Ctrl-click the column heading and
   choose Hide Column from the shortcut menu.

4   To make Comment 2 active again, Ctrl-click the column heading that
     you want the Comment 2 to appear *before*, and choose Show Comment
     2 from the shortcut menu.

     The shortcut menu contains additional columns you can show in the
     Browser layout. Keep in mind that as you make changes to the Browser
     column layout, those changes are saved as part of your project settings.

5   Ctrl-click the Duration column heading and choose Show Length
     from the shortcut menu.

     The Length column appears before the Duration column.

6   In the Name column, select the **high 5** clip in the Surfing Clips bin.
     Look at the Length, Duration, In, and Out columns.

Name	Length	Duration	Good	In	Out
▼ ☐ Relaxing Weekend					
🎞 couple at beach	00:01:10;09	00:01:10;09		Not Set	Not Set
▼ ☐ Sequences					
🎞 Marking	00:00:29;13	00:00:29;13		Not Set	Not Set
🎞 Starting	00:00:00;00	00:00:00;00		Not Set	Not Set
▼ ☐ Surfing Clips					
🎞 back up again	00:00:26;19	00:00:26;19		Not Set	Not Set
🎞 board on head	00:00:15;26	00:00:15;26		Not Set	Not Set
🎞 high 5	00:00:14;20	00:00:06;17		00:00:06;16	00:00:13;02
🎞 nose riding	00:00:16;29	00:00:16;29		Not Set	Not Set

Lesson 11 Project / Effects

If a clip has marked In and Out points, they appear in the In and Out
columns, and the marked duration appears in the Duration column.
The Length column displays the full length of the clip.

TIP ▶ When you move your pointer over a clip in the Name column, a highlight line appears across the other Browser columns so
that you can easily find the information for that clip.

There is also a Thumbnail column that provides a visual reference to your clips. Unlike the thumbnail icons in the View as Icons option, the thumbnails in the Thumbnail column are organized according to the alphabetized clips in the Name column.

7   Ctrl-click the Length column heading and choose Show Thumbnail. Scroll down until you see the **nose riding** clip.

8   To scrub through the **nose riding** clip, click the thumbnail image in the Thumbnail column. Drag right and then left.

high 5		00:00:06;17	00:00:06;16
nose riding		00:00:16;29	Not Set
out to sea		00:00:05;27	Not Set
support Jimbo		00:00:05;25	00:00:16;16

In this column, you don't have to change the pointer to scrub the thumbnail clip. You can also set a new poster frame for a clip.

9   In the **nose riding** clip, scrub to a new poster frame, hold down the Control key, release the mouse, then release Control.

10 To hide the Thumbnail column, Ctrl-click its column heading and choose Hide Column from the menu. Hide the Length column as well.

▼ Length	Hide Column
	Edit Heading
00:01:10;0	Show Type

Adding Column Information

Having information about a clip can help you find it when you organize larger projects. You can enter information about a clip when you first capture the clip or at any time during the editing process. Some information columns allow you to simply click in the column; others allow you to enter text.

1   Find the **couple at beach** clip in the Relaxing Weekend bin, and click its line in the Good column. A checkmark appears.

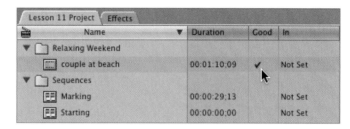

   NOTE ▶ "Good" might suggest that you particularly like this clip and may want to use it in your sequence.

2   Click in the Good column for these clips: **back up again**, **nose riding**, and **high 5**.

3   Now click the Good column heading to sort the clips labeled Good. Click it again to reverse the order so that all the checked clips appear at the top of the bin.

4   Find and drag the Log Note column to appear next to the Good column.

5   In the Name column, select the **nose riding** clip and click in the Log Note column on the clip's highlighted line.

   A text box with a blinking insertion point appears.

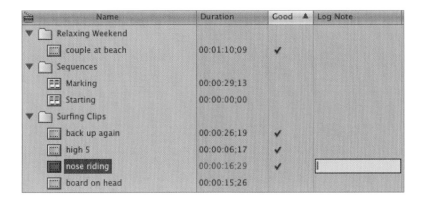

6   In the Log Note text box, type *surfing action* and press Enter. (Pressing Return will open the clip into the Viewer.)

7   Select the **high 5** clip, click in the Log Note text box area, and then enter *cutaway* in the Log Note text box.

8   Move to the row where the **back up again** clip sits. This time, Ctrl-click in the Log Note area and choose "surfing action" from the shortcut menu of previously entered options.

NOTE ▶ In this option, you don't have to preselect the clip before bringing up the Log Note options.

9   Ctrl-click the **waxing board med** line under the Log Note column, and choose "cutaway" from the shortcut menu.

TIP ▶ To delete a log note, select the clip or the line the clip occupies, click in the Log Note area to select the text, and press Delete.

Finding Items in the Browser and Timeline

Macintosh computers have a Find function that allows you to locate a specific document anywhere in your computer's hard drive. Final Cut Express has a similar Find function, which helps you locate a specific clip or item anywhere in a project or sequence.

1   Deselect any selected clips in the Browser by clicking in the empty gray area under the Name column. Then close all the Browser bins.

2   With the Browser window active, choose Edit > Find, or press Cmd-F.

A Find dialog appears in which you can enter the name of the clip or item you wish to locate and the name of the project where you want to look for it.

3   In the Search pop-up menu, choose Project > Lesson 11 Project and enter *nose riding* in the lower-right text field. Click Find Next or press Return to find this clip in this project.

In the Browser, the bin with the **nose riding** clip opens, and the clip is highlighted.

4   Click the *Marking* sequence tab in the Timeline, and make sure the playhead is at the beginning of the sequence.

NOTE ▸ If the Browser window is blocking the Timeline, you may need to click the Zoom button to return it to its original position and size, or simply drag it away from the Timeline. Don't forget to click the Timeline window to make it the active window again.

5   Press Cmd-F to open a Find dialog for this sequence, and enter *high 5* in the Find text field.

6   Click Find or press Return.

The playhead jumps to the first frame of that clip, and the clip becomes highlighted.

Saving and Recalling Window Layouts

When you perform different types of functions within Final Cut Express, you may need to resize or rearrange the interface windows, as you did with the Browser columns in the previous exercises. Once you create a custom layout, you can recall it using a keyboard shortcut.

Since you currently have a wider Browser layout displayed that might be useful for adding additional clip information, let's save this as Custom Layout 2, and then save another layout you might use more frequently for editing as Custom Layout 1.

1 Choose Window > Arrange and look at the options at the top of the menu.

Window	
Minimize	⌘M
Send Behind	
Arrange ▶	Custom Layout 1 ⇧U
	Custom Layout 2 ⌥U
✓ Tool Palette	
✓ Viewer ⌘1	Compositing
✓ Canvas ⌘2	Small Windows
✓ Timeline ⌘3	Standard ^U
✓ Audio Meters ⌥4	Voice Over Recording
✓ Browser ⌘4	
Effects ⌘5	
Viewer: Slug	
Canvas: Sequence 1 in Untitled Project 1	
Timeline: Sequence 1 in Untitled Project 1	
Browser	

Unless you have already saved a layout on your own, the Custom Layout 1 and Custom Layout 2 options are dimmed because no custom layouts have been saved.

2 With the Browser still in its wide layout, press Option and choose Window > Arrange.

Window	
Minimize	⌘M
Send Behind	
Arrange ▶	Set Custom Layout 1 ⇧U
	Set Custom Layout 2 ⌥U
✓ Tool Palette	
✓ Viewer ⌘1	Compositing
✓ Canvas ⌘2	Small Windows
✓ Timeline ⌘3	Standard ^U
✓ Audio Meters ⌥4	Voice Over Recording
✓ Browser ⌘4	
Effects ⌘5	
Viewer: Slug	
Canvas: Sequence 1 in Untitled Project 1	
Timeline: Sequence 1 in Untitled Project 1	
Browser	

Now the Arrange options include two Set Custom Layout options. Using the Option key to choose this menu indicates you want to *set* a custom layout, not recall one.

3 Set Custom Layout 2 and make sure you release the mouse before releasing the Option key.

4   To return to the Standard editing layout, choose Window > Arrange > Standard, or press the shortcut Ctrl-U.

Let's make some changes to the standard interface and save it as Custom Layout 1 so that you can get to it easily using a shortcut.

5   Move the pointer over the intersection of the Browser and Viewer windows. When you see the resize pointer appear, drag left to make the Browser more narrow. Make the Viewer and Canvas windows larger by dragging down on the Timeline window boundary line.

6   Press Option and choose Window > Arrange > Set Custom Layout 1. Release the mouse and then release the Option key.

7   To work with your wide Browser layout (Custom Layout 2), choose Window > Arrange > Custom Layout 2, or press Option-U.

> **TIP** The Browser window is so wide that it may have come up behind the Viewer and Canvas windows. Click any portion of the Browser window you see to bring it to the front. Or press Cmd-4 to make the Browser the active window.

8   Choose Window > Arrange > Custom Layout 1, or press Shift-U, to return to the saved layout.

9   Press Cmd-S to save the project with its current Browser and layout settings.

> **NOTE** ▶ Changing the track height in the Timeline is not a saved layout feature.

Project Tasks

1   Take a minute to set up your Browser columns the way you would like
    to work with them.

2   Press Ctrl-U to restore the Standard window layout, or choose that
    option from the Window menu.

Using Button Bars

Although there are many keyboard shortcuts in Final Cut Express, it's
sometimes easier just to click a button to make something happen. In
the upper-right corner of each window in the interface is a button bar. A
button bar is an area where you can place representative buttons for Final
Cut Express functions. In the Timeline button bar, two buttons always
appear as a default: the Snapping button and Linked Selection. Let's add
some editing buttons to the Canvas window.

1   Choose Tools > Button List, or press Option-J.

A window opens with a list of functions and commands organized first by main menu topics and then alphabetically by function.

2   Below the main menu listings, find the Editing topic. Click once on Editing.

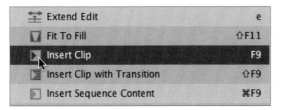

3   When the Editing functions are revealed, scroll down until you see Insert Clip.

4   Position the Button List so you can see the Canvas window. Drag the Insert Clip icon into the Canvas button bar and release it.

The button bar brackets open up and bookend the new button.

5   Now scroll down the Button List until you see the Overwrite Clip button. Drag it into the Canvas button bar and release it to the right of the Insert Clip button.

6   Hover the mouse pointer over it until you see the tooltip appear.

7   To change the color of the button, Ctrl-click the Overwrite Clip
    button and choose Color > Red. Ctrl-click the Insert Clip button
    and choose Color > Yellow.

8   To separate these buttons with spacers, Ctrl-click the Overwrite Clip
    button and choose Add Spacer. Repeat this to add additional spacers.

    Button bar layouts can be saved and recalled, just like window layouts.
    You can even use your own custom layouts and button bars on another
    computer by transferring that file to the other computer.

9   Save this button layout by Ctrl-clicking the Canvas button bar and
    choosing Save All Button Bars.

    A Save window appears. The default is for you to save this layout as
    Custom Button Bars in the Button Bars folder. This folder is automat-
    ically created during the save process and resides in the Final
    Cut Express User Data folder.

10 Enter a new name for your button bar, such as *Edit Buttons*, then
    click Save.

11 To remove a button from a button bar, drag it away from the button
    bar and release it, just as you would drag an icon from the OS X Dock.
    Close the Button List.

    NOTE ► Layouts are personal to Users on OS X and can be found at
    the User level on your hard drive. Go to Macintosh HD > Users >
    (User Name) > Library > Preferences > Final Cut Express User Data >
    Button Bars to locate the saved layout.

Working with Master Clips

A clip in a project represents media captured on your hard drive. The first appearance of the original clip in a project is referred to as the *master clip*. In this exercise, you will work with one master clip in different ways, and copy and paste it from one project to another so that you can apply some of these steps to your own projects.

1   Create a new project by choosing File > New Project, or pressing Shift-Cmd-N. In the new project, change the view to View as List.

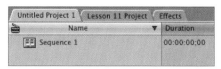

When a new project is created, it is given a default name, Untitled Project, and a sequential number, just like sequences and bins. The first project you create is Untitled Project 1, the second is Untitled Project 2, and so on. In the Browser, the default sequence, *Sequence 1*, appears in the new project. This empty sequence automatically opens in the Timeline.

2   To save the untitled project with a new name, choose File > Save Project As. In the Save window, name the project *Copied Clips*. Select a folder where you would like this project to be saved, perhaps with your other Final Cut Express project files or on your Desktop, and click Save.

3   In the Lesson 11 Project tab in the Browser, select the **nose riding** clip. Drag the horizontal Browser scroll bar to the right until you see the Master Clip column heading.

This clip, and the other clips in this project, are master clips. Currently, there are no other uses of these clips in the project.

4 Double-click the **nose riding** clip to open it in the Viewer. Mark an In point where Jimbo first stands up on the board and an Out point when he reaches the nose of the board.

5 Select the *Starting* sequence tab in the Timeline, and drag the marked clip into the *Starting* sequence as an Overwrite edit.

6 In the same master clip in the Viewer, mark a different In point just before Jimbo starts to walk to the back of the board and a new Out point after he starts to go down behind the wave. Drag the newly marked clip to the Timeline as an Overwrite edit following the first clip.

Although you have two separate clips in the Timeline, they both refer back to the same master clip in the Browser. These clips are referred to as *sequence* clips.

A sequence clip is an *affiliate* of a master clip. You always have the full length of the master clip available to you when you want to trim or slip the sequence clip, as you have already experienced in previous lessons.

7   In the Timeline, double-click the first sequence clip to open it into the Viewer.

In the scrubber bar, you see the In and Out points you marked to define the portion of the master clip you are using in the sequence.

8   In the Browser, copy the **nose riding** clip by selecting it and choosing Edit > Copy, or pressing Cmd-C.

The clip is copied, but you won't see anything until you paste it.

NOTE ▶ In Final Cut Express, you can copy and paste just about any item from one project, such as a clip, sequence, or bin, and paste it in another as long as both projects are open. The clips in the Copied Clips project link back to the same media files that the clips in the **Lesson 11 Project** do.

9   Click the Copied Clips project tab, and choose Edit > Paste, or press Cmd-V, to paste this clip into this project. Drag the Browser scroll bar to the right until you see the Master Clip column heading.

This clip is also considered a master clip because it is the first use of this clip in this new project.

TIP ▶ If you want to make changes to a master clip but not affect the affiliate clips created from it, you can duplicate the clip and choose Modify > Duplicate as Master Clip, and make changes to that clip.

Working with Subclips

In the next lesson, you will begin to capture source material you have shot with your digital camera. When you capture footage, the duration of each clip is up to you. You might capture everything from your camera in one very long clip. Or you might start and stop a few times to create several shorter clips.

When you start editing, working with one long clip may not be as convenient as working with shorter clips. Even though you can mark different clips from one master clip, as you did in the previous exercise, the marked clips in the sequence will all share the master clip's name, which could become confusing if you are using several marked portions from one master clip.

The solution to working with longer clips is to break up the master clip into *subclips* of specific shots you want to use. When you create a subclip of a master clip, you can determine just the length of the shot you want to work with and give it its own unique name. This subclip becomes a separate clip, with its own icon, that you can name and work with in the Browser. In fact, a subclip becomes its own master clip because it is the first use of *that* clip in the project.

Making a Subclip

Creating a subclip begins with marking In and Out points on a clip in the Viewer to identify the material you want to use. But this clip will stand alone, unlike sequence clips that always refer back to the full length of the master clip. Therefore, you might want to give yourself a little extra space, or handles, on either side of the portion you want to edit, to be able to make editing adjustments or add transitions in the future.

1   In the Browser, click the Lesson 11 Project tab and close all open bins except the Relaxing Weekend bin.

2   Double-click the **couple at beach** clip to open it in the Viewer. Play the clip.

This two-minute master clip has several shots you can use in a sequence. However, all the shots were so close together on tape that they were captured as one long clip. Let's subdivide each usable shot into its own separate subclip.

3   Mark an In point at the head of the clip and an Out point on the last
frame of the shot of the couple drinking a toast.

4   Choose Modify > Make Subclip, or press Cmd-U.

> **TIP** If this menu option is not available, make sure the Viewer window is active or selected. You can press Cmd-1 to select the Viewer.

The Browser window becomes active, and a new icon appears under the
master clip in the Relaxing Weekend bin. The subclip icon has jagged

edges, as if it had been torn or cut from the original clip. It also shares the master clip's name for the moment, but the filename is highlighted, awaiting a name change.

5   Rename the subclip *toasting*.

6   Double-click this new subclip to open it in the Viewer, and play it.

The clip is only as long as the distance between the In and Out points you marked to create it.

7   Open the **couple at beach** master clip, and mark In and Out points to identify the next shot, immediately after the toasting shot.

   TIP ▶ If the playhead is already parked at the last Out point, press the right arrow key to move the playhead forward one frame, and mark a new In point there.

8   Choose Modify > Make Subclip. In the Browser, enter *tilt down patio* as the new subclip name.

9   To see the thumbnail images of these subclips, Ctrl-click the Duration column and choose Show Thumbnail from the shortcut menu.

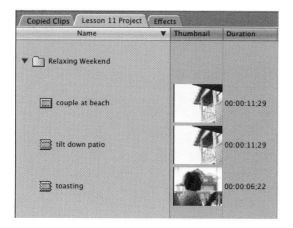

In the Thumbnail column, the different images of the new subclips help to identify them further.

NOTE ▶ The master clip's thumbnail changes to reflect the new In point.

Project Tasks

1   Follow the guidelines in steps 3–5 in the preceding exercise to create subclips from every potential shot in the **couple at beach** master clip. Use the following naming suggestions:

   ▶   **walk to beach wide**

   ▶   **walk medium shot**

   ▶   **pan to chairs**

   NOTE ▶ The Browser is automatically selected after a subclip is created so you can enter a new name. To mark the next subclip, you have to click in the Viewer window to make it active again. You can also use the keyboard shortcut Cmd-1 to select the Viewer from the Browser or another window. Look at the Window menu to see the shortcuts for the other interface windows.

2   Open the **nose riding** clip from the Browser. Make one subclip out of the section where Jimbo walks to the nose, and another subclip where he falls behind a wave toward the end of the clip.

3   Press Cmd-S to save the project.

   TIP ▶ If you use a subclip in a sequence and find you need more material to extend or adjust the clip, you can remove the subclip limits, taking it back to the master clip length. Select the clip in the Timeline and choose Modify > Remove Subclip Limits.

Working with Markers

Markers are location indicators that you can place on a clip or in the Time-line ruler area to help identify a specific frame while you edit. Markers can be helpful if you want to identify beats of music, moments in a narration or interview, or any specific action.

Creating and Naming Markers

A marker can be placed on a clip or in the Timeline ruler area. If a marker is attached to a clip, the marker will stay at that location on that clip even if the clip is moved elsewhere in the sequence. If a marker is not attached to a specific clip, it will be created in the ruler area of the Timeline and become a reference to that specific location in the sequence.

1   In the Timeline, click the *Marking* sequence tab and play the sequence.

    You will use markers to align specific action points in the video clips with specific music beats.

2   To focus on just the video, click the A1 and A2 Audible controls to turn off sound from those tracks.

3   Play the **back up again** clip in the Timeline, and park the playhead where Jimbo first jumps up on the surfboard.

4   To set a marker on this clip at this location, select the clip and press M.

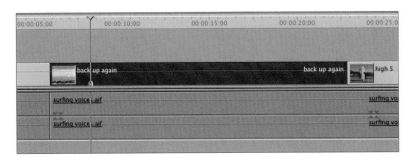

A marker appears on the clip at this location because the clip is selected.

5   Press M again to open the Edit Marker dialog. Type *up on board* in the
     Name field and click OK.

The Edit Marker dialog has additional options to explore, such as
adding a chapter marker or compression marker if you're going to
be creating a DVD. You can create scoring markers if you are working
with the Apple music composition application, Soundtrack. You can
also delete a marker in this dialog.

6   Continue playing the **back up again** clip, and stop where Jimbo is belly down on the board, at about 13;27 in the sequence.

7   With the clip still selected, press M to set a marker and M again to open the Edit Marker dialog. Name this marker *belly down*.

8   Play the clip and stop where Jimbo touches the wave with his hand at about 21;05. Create a marker and name it *touches wave*.

9   Ctrl-click the **back up again** clip, and from the bottom of the shortcut menu choose "belly down" to go to the "belly down" marker location.

10 Select the **high 5** clip, and set a marker where Jimbo and his dad touch hands. Name the marker *high 5*.

> **TIP** You can delete a marker in the Edit Marker dialog. Or you can go to a marker and choose Mark > Markers > Delete. Here you can also delete all the markers in the Timeline.

11 Deselect the **high 5** clip and toggle back on the Audible controls for the A1 and A2 tracks.

This time, you can play the music track and create markers on the fly by pressing M several times while the clip is playing. If you want to follow the beat of the music and place markers on the fly, just listen and mark every eight beats, which is about three seconds. Or you can simply move the playhead forward three seconds at a time, and place a mark at those locations.

12 Mark the first strong beat of music where the voices come in, at around 9;10. Then mark every eight counts, or three seconds, after that point until the end of the clip.

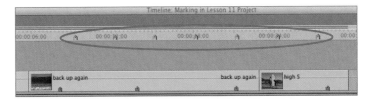

Since you did not select the clip, you should have about seven markers in the Timeline ruler area (and Canvas scrubber bar), representing the place where the strong beats occur in this music track. These markers are not attached to the music clip but to the sequence itself.

NOTE ▶ When the playhead is over a marker in the Canvas scrubber bar, the marker appears yellow and the name of the marker appears in the image area.

Editing with Markers

Now that you have markers set in clips and in the sequence, you can begin to align some of the action points of a clip with beats of music. Since the clips are already in the sequence, you will use the Slip tool to make the adjustments.

1   In the Timeline, drag the playhead over the sequence markers and see how it snaps to each marker in the ruler area.

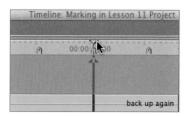

2   Select the Slip tool from the Tool palette, or press S.

3   Drag the **high 5** clip left and right.

The clip marker moves with the clip as it is adjusted.

4   Now click with the Slip tool directly above the marker in the **high 5** clip, and drag left over the last sequence marker in the ruler area.

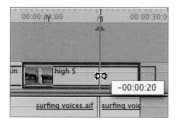

The clip marker snaps to the sequence marker.

5   Play the clip to see the alignment of the two marker points.

6   Ctrl-click one of the visible markers in the **back up again** clip. From the shortcut menu, choose "belly down."

The playhead goes to that marker.

7 With the Slip tool, click above the "belly down" marker and drag left. Snap it to the second sequence marker and play the clip.

8 Press A to change the pointer back to the default Selection tool and play the sequence.

Project Tasks

Markers can be placed in clips in the Viewer, in selected clips in the Timeline, or in the sequence in the Timeline. There are different ways you can move to a marker or delete it once it's been placed.

1 Move the playhead to the beginning of the sequence and press Shift-Cmd-A to deselect all clips. In the main menu, choose Mark > Next > Marker, or press Shift-M. The playhead moves to the next sequence marker. Repeat this to move through the rest of the markers.

> **NOTE ▸** You can also press Shift-up arrow or Shift-down arrow to move the playhead backward or forward to a marker.

2 Choose Mark > Previous > Marker, or press Option-M, to move backward through the sequence from marker to marker.

3 Move to the first sequence marker, press M to open the Edit Marker dialog, and name it *voices in*. Name the other sequence markers for practice.

Using Markers to Create Subclips

You have created subclips by marking In and Out points in the Viewer. But you can also create a subclip from a marker placed in a clip in the Viewer.

1 In the Browser, Ctrl-click the Thumbnail column head and choose Hide Column.

2 Open the **couple at beach** master clip into the Viewer.

This is the clip you used to make subclips earlier in this lesson.

3 In the Viewer, place a marker at the beginning of each scene change. Give each marker an appropriate name.

4 In the Browser, click the disclosure triangle next to the **couple at beach** master clip.

Name	Duration	In	Out
▼ ☐ Relaxing Weekend			
▼ ☐ couple at beach	00:01:10;09	Not Set	Not Set
🔖 toasting	00:00:00;00	00:00:00;00	Not Set
🔖 tilt down patio	00:00:00;00	00:00:06;22	Not Set
🔖 walk to beach wide	00:00:00;00	00:00:18;22	Not Set
🔖 walk medium shot	00:00:00;00	00:00:43;05	Not Set
🔖 pan to chairs	00:00:00;00	00:00:58;07	Not Set

5 Select one of the markers under the clip and choose Modify > Make Subclip.

A new subclip is created that begins where this marker is located in the master clip and continues to the next marker in that clip.

TIP ▶ To convert a group of markers into subclips at once, create a new bin and drag a group of markers into that bin. Final Cut Express will automatically convert the markers to subclips.

6 Quit Final Cut Express by pressing Cmd-Q, or close this project and continue with the next lesson.

Lesson Review

1. How do you hide or show a column in the Browser?
2. Which column allows you to scrub through a clip in the Browser?
3. How would you sort the contents of a bin by duration?
4. What criteria can you use to sort or find project elements in the Browser?
5. How do you save a custom window layout?
6. True or false: The Find function works only in the Browser.
7. What different things can you do to customize a button bar?
8. How do you add a marker in the Timeline and then name it?
9. How do you create a subclip?

Answers

1. To hide a column, Ctrl-click the column head you want to hide and choose Hide Column. To show a column, Ctrl-click the column head where you want the new column to appear and choose the column from the shortcut menu.
2. The Thumbnail column.
3. Click the Duration column heading.
4. Any criteria that appears in one of the Browser columns.
5. Hold down the Option key and choose Window > Arrange, then choose one of the Set Custom Layout options.
6. False. You can also use it to find a clip in the Timeline.
7. Add and delete buttons, colorize buttons, add spacers between buttons, arrange buttons in any order, and save button bars.
8. Press M where you want the new marker to appear. Press M again to open the Edit Marker dialog, and enter the desired name.
9. Open the clip in the Viewer, mark an In and Out, and choose Modify > Make Subclip. You can also select a clip marker in the Browser and choose Modify > Make Subclip.

Keyboard Shortcuts

Cmd-F	Opens a Browser or Timeline Find window, depending on which window is active
M	Adds a marker at the playhead location in the Viewer or Timeline
MM	Adds a marker and then opens the Edit Marker dialog
Shift-M	Moves the playhead forward to the next marker
Option-M	Moves the playhead backward to the previous marker
Shift-up arrow	Moves the playhead backward to the previous marker
Shift-down arrow	Moves the playhead forward to the next marker
Cmd-U	Makes a subclip from a marked clip or a clip with a marker

12

Lesson Files   None

Media   Your own

Time   This lesson takes approximately 60 minutes to complete.

Goals   Capture digital video

Set capture bins

Log clips and add notes

Set markers in clips while logging

Choose user preferences

Set system settings

Choose Easy Setup preset

Transfer from an AVCHD source

Autosave a project

Capturing Digital Video

Capturing digital video is where all the fun of editing begins. But capturing doesn't stand alone—its partner is *logging.* If you just want to get to it, you can capture with default settings and very little logging information. If you want to work more professionally, you can experiment with different capture settings and organize your clips with loads of logging information. As you learned in working with the Browser, this logging information can be helpful when sorting and finding clips in your projects or sequences.

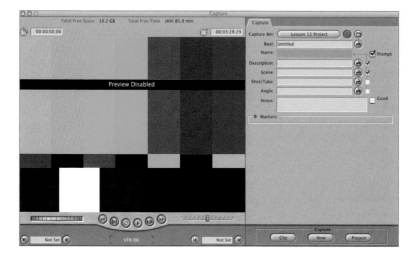

Preparing the Project

There is no project file for this lesson. Instead, you will capture and save clips into a new project file.

1   Launch Final Cut Express by clicking its icon in the Dock.

When Final Cut Express opens, any project that was active when you last quit the program will open along with the program.

2   Close any open projects, including any untitled projects.

Remember that when no sequences are open, the Canvas and Timeline windows close because they have nothing to display.

Before you create a new project, think about the standard you used to shoot the material you want to capture. Was it shot with NTSC or PAL equipment? Since the media in this book was captured with DV-NTSC equipment, the projects and sequences were created using the DV-NTSC preset. Final Cut Express allows you to play back a combination of formats in one sequence, including DV, HDV, and AVCHD. However, it's a good idea to choose an Easy Setup and to match the majority of your footage before you create a new project or sequence.

TIP In the Easy Setup dialog, each option controls presets for your sequence, capture, and device controls to capture and output media in the appropriate standard.

3   To choose a different option, choose Final Cut Express > Easy Setup, or press Ctrl-Q.

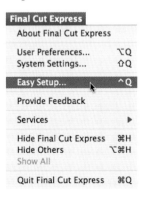

NOTE ► All the Final Cut Express settings windows use the shortcut letter Q.

4   Click the Use pop-up menu and choose a preset that is appropriate for the media you are capturing. In addition to DV and HDV, you can also choose a setup for working with a DV converter. If you change the preset, an External A/V dialog will open. Click Continue.

TIP ► To streamline your search for the correct preset, you can use the Format and Rate pop-ups to choose a specific type of media and frame rate. These filters reduce the number of options you see in the Use pop-up menu.

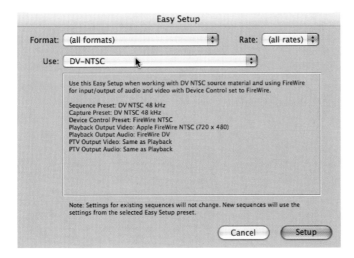

The details of the selected preset appear below the pop-up menu. Choosing a different preset affects only new sequences, not those you have already created.

5   Choose File > New Project, or press Shift-Cmd-N, to create a new project, and choose View as List in the Browser.

An Untitled Project tab appears in the Browser window along with a default sequence, *Sequence 1*.

6   To rename this project, choose File > Save Project As, and enter
Lesson 12 Project as the new name. Navigate to the Lessons folder
on your hard drive and click Save to save the project there.

> **NOTE** ▶ What you are saving here is just the project file, not the place
> where the media will be stored. You will set that destination
> later in this lesson.

Connecting Sources for Capture

The first step in capturing your source material is to properly connect your
digital camera or digital tape deck to the computer through a FireWire
cable. The FireWire cable has a different connector on each end. The smaller
FireWire connector on one end goes into the camera or deck. The larger
connector goes into your computer's FireWire-port.

1   Connect your DV or HDV camera or other DV or HDV source to
your computer's FireWire port.

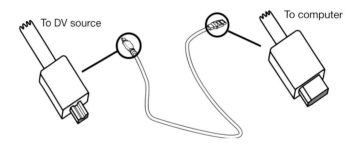

2   Put a source tape in your camera or deck.

You can also connect your camera or deck to a separate video monitor,
television set, or VCR, just as you would if you were simply screening your
tape. However, this is not necessary because there is a preview image area
within the Final Cut Express Capture function.

To capture material from an older, nondigital tape source, such as VHS, Betamax, or Hi8, you must connect that source to a separate digital converter box. The digital converter box converts the material into a digital source, which you can then capture into your computer through a FireWire cable.

> **NOTE ▶** If you are using an AVCHD source, follow the steps in the "Transferring AVCHD Footage" section in this lesson to transfer the clips into a Final Cut Express project.

Previewing and Marking Your Source

Once your video source is connected, you can screen your material and mark the areas you want to capture. Marking source material for capture is very similar to marking clips for editing.

Opening and Sizing the Capture Window

All capturing is done in the Capture window in Final Cut Express. The Capture window has two main areas: the Preview area, where you screen and mark your source tape, and the Logging area, where you log your clips.

1   Choose File > Capture, or press Cmd-8.

Preview area   Logging area

TIP If you see the following message, double-check that you have properly connected your source to your computer's FireWire port.

> ! Unable to initialize video deck. You may still log offline clips or use Capture Now.
>
> OK

The Preview area of the Capture window defaults in size to that of the Canvas window. If you change the size of that window, the Capture window changes to match. But you must first close the Capture window, readjust the Canvas, and then reopen the Capture window for it to resize.

2 Close the Capture window by clicking the Close button in the upper-left corner of the window, or by pressing Cmd-8.

3 To enlarge the Capture Preview area, first choose Window > Arrange > Custom Layout 1 to recall the saved layout with the larger Viewer and Canvas windows.

4 Choose File > Capture, or press Cmd-8, to reopen the Capture window.

   The Capture Preview area now matches the larger Canvas window size.

Playing Your Source Tape

Playing and marking In and Out points in your source material is done in the Preview area of the Capture window.

The Preview area has certain functions similar to the Viewer window. For example, it has Duration and Location fields above the image area, transport controls under the image area, a shuttle slider, and a jog wheel. The Mark In and Mark Out buttons are next to the In Point and Out Point fields, where you can see your Mark In and Mark Out location numbers. The Go to In Point and Go to Out Point buttons are on the other sides of those fields. In addition, the current total amount of free hard-drive space and time appear in the upper portion of the screen.

Duration field   Location field

Total Free Space 4.1 GB   Total Free Time (AV) 18.2 min

00:00:00:00   00:10:13:12

Preview Disabled

Go to   Mark In   Transport   Mark Out   Go to
In point   controls   Out point

1   In the Preview area, click the Play button to play the tape.

> **TIP** ▸ As you capture, you preview the audio through your camera
> or other playback device.

Rewind   Stop Play   Fast Forward

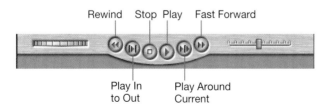

Play In   Play Around
to Out   Current

2   Click the Stop button to pause the tape.

3   Click the Stop button again to stop the tape.

When a tape in a camera or deck is stopped, the tape unwraps off the video heads. The image in the Preview area is the most recent frame played.

TIP It's more efficient to play and pause your tape rather than to stop it completely. But you don't want to leave your tape in a pause mode for very long, or the picture quality could be affected.

4   Press the spacebar to play the tape; the Play button is highlighted.

5   Press it again to pause the tape; the Stop button is highlighted.

6   Click the Rewind and Fast Forward buttons to stop the tape and move it quickly backward and forward.

TIP If you started shooting material at the head of the tape, it's always a good idea to rewind to the beginning before logging and capturing.

7   Rewind your source tape to the beginning of the tape or to where you want to begin capturing footage.

Marking a Source for Capture

Marking a source tape is similar to marking a clip in the Viewer. In fact, you can use the same Mark In and Mark Out buttons or shortcut keys, I and O.

The primary difference is that when you mark a clip in the Viewer, you make edit points around the action you want to use. But when you capture a clip, you mark a few seconds before the action you want to use and a few seconds after, creating additional padding, or handles, to use when adjusting your edits in the Timeline.

1   Play the tape to where your usable material begins.

2   Press the spacebar, click the Stop button, or click the Play button to pause the tape at this point.

3 Click the Mark In button, or press I, to set an In point.

NOTE ▸ You can also mark your In point on the fly as the tape source is moving.

When you mark an In point, that number is also entered into the Out Point field until you mark a specific Out point.

4 To adjust this edit point and create a two-second clip handle, click in the In Point field, type –2. (minus 2 period), and press Return.

Typing –2. sets a new In point two seconds earlier than where the desired action begins in your material.

5 Press the spacebar or click the Play button to move forward to where this portion of the action ends.

6   Click the Mark Out button at this point, or let the tape continue to play
     a few seconds past the usable material and then mark an Out point.

NOTE ▶ You can also mark an Out point and then type *+2.* (plus 2
period) in the Out Point field and press Return to push the Out point
two seconds later.

Viewing a Marked Source

Once you've marked your edit points, you can view the source material
between them to see if that's the material you want to capture. To do this,
you use the same play buttons as you did in the Viewer to preview the portion of the clip you want to use in an edit. You can use the Play In to Out
button to see the entire selection, or you can jump to edit points by using
the Go to In Point or Go to Out Point buttons.

1   Click the Play In to Out button in the Preview area.

2   Click the Go to In Point button next to the In Point field.

3   Click the Go to Out Point button next to the Out Point field.

4   Click the Play Around Current button.

As in the Viewer, the Play Around Current command will play material a little before and after the playhead's current location—in this case, the Out point.

TIP ▶ You can use the Play Around Current command to play around the In or Out point if you want to mark a new edit point.

Logging Your Clips

Now that you have marked your source, you are almost ready to capture. Here comes the little or lots question in regard to logging. The more information you log about the clip at this point, the more information you will have in the Browser columns to distinguish the really good clips from the OK clips. But as you learned in the previous lesson, you can add some logging information after you have already captured the clip. So the choice is yours.

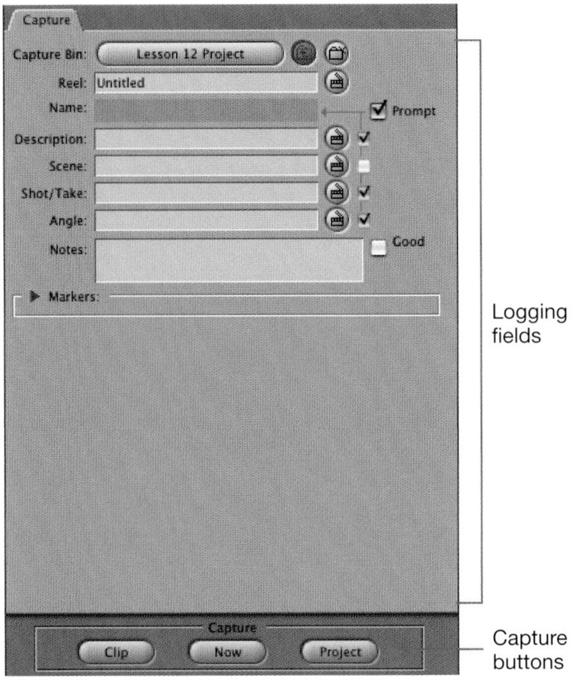

Logging fields

Capture buttons

Look at the fields in the Capture tab and see if you recognize any of the logging information topics you saw as Browser columns in the previous lesson.

Setting a Capture Bin

When you capture a clip, the actual media will be saved to your hard drive, but the clip icon linking you to that media will be saved to the current project in the Browser. Now you have a choice as to how you'll organize the new clips. You can send the clips to a new bin as you capture, or you can capture the clips into the project tab area and organize them into appropriate bins later.

In either case, Final Cut Express needs to know where to place the clip icons. This destination is called the *capture bin*. There can be only one capture bin active at any given time, no matter how many projects you have open. If you just want to get going with your capturing, you can capture all your clips into your project in the Browser and organize them later. If you feel adventuresome, you can experiment with creating and assigning new bins as capture bins.

1   Make sure you can see both the Capture and Browser windows at the same time while doing these steps.

   In the Capture tab of the Capture window, the project name, Lesson 12 Project, appears on the long, oval Capture Bin button.

   In the Browser window, in the far left of the Name column heading, a tiny *slate* appears, indicating that this project is the current capture bin.

   NOTE ▶ At this point, you can begin capturing all your clips into your project tab, which is set as the capture bin. However, if you want to explore another option for capturing directly to a new bin, continue with the following steps.

2   Click the New Bin button to the far right of the Capture Bin button.

A new bin is created in the current project with the default name Bin 1.

The Capture Bin icon now appears next to this bin in the Browser to identify it as the target location for your new clips.

3   In the Capture tab, click the large Capture Bin button with the new bin name on it.

The new bin opens as a separate window, allowing you to view just the new clips you're capturing without mixing them up with other clips already in your project.

4   Click the Close button in the upper-left corner to close this window.

5   In the Capture tab, next to the Capture Bin button, click the Up button (the button with an upward arrow on a bin).

This takes the Capture Bin destination up to a higher level—in this case, *back* to the project level.

6   To return the capture bin to the new Bin 1 you just created, Ctrl-click
Bin 1 in the Browser. Choose Set Capture Bin from the shortcut menu.

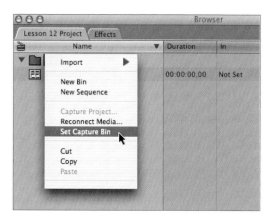

The tiny Capture Bin icon attaches to Bin 1 in the Browser.

TIP ▶ This is how you set any bin in your project as the capture bin.

7   In the Browser, rename Bin 1 *Test Capture*.

Logging Clip Information

Some information is required before you can capture a clip, and other information is not. For example, you must enter a reel number and a clip name,
or Final Cut Express won't capture the clip. You can use a simple numbering
system for reel numbers or enter a reel name. The clip name is drawn from
the Description, Scene, and/or Shot/Take information you enter.

1   Enter an appropriate reel number or name for your source tape.

2   Try to click in the Name field.

The Name field is not for entering information, just displaying it. The name is actually compiled from any combination of the three descriptive fields below it.

3   In the Description field, enter a description for the clip, such as *Dan teaches surfing.*

> **TIP** When naming a clip, think of a descriptive name that will help you distinguish it from the other clips while you're editing.

4   To the right of the Description field is a tiny *feeder* check box next to the tiny Slate button. Make sure there is a checkmark in that box. If there's not, click it.

5   Press Tab or Return.

The Description information now becomes part of the name. The arrow leading upward from the check box feeds into the Name field.

6   Enter Scene information, such as *malibu beach.*

> **TIP** Sometimes it's helpful to create a naming system. For example, for the lessons in this book, all clips are labeled with lowercase words and names, and sequences are upper- and lowercase. This can be a visual aid when working with different elements in the Browser.

7   Enter the number *1* as a Shot/Take number.

8   Click the feeder check boxes next to each line to see how the name changes in the Name area.

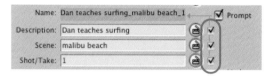

Any one, or all three, of the descriptive entries can feed into the full clip name. This name is what will appear on the clip in the Browser and in the Timeline.

TIP ▸ Although it is nice to have a lot of information attached to the clip, a really long clip name may be difficult to read when it is displayed on the clip in the Timeline.

9   Next to the Shot/Take entry, click the Slate button, also called a *clapboard*.

Every time you click any of the Slate buttons, the next consecutive number is added to the descriptive entry, even if no number was originally entered.

NOTE ▸ If you are working with more than one camera, you can enter the specific camera angle in the Angle field, such as 1, 2, or A, B. You can also enter a note about the clip, which will appear in the Log Note column in the Browser. Clicking the Good box will place a checkmark in the Good column.

10 Make sure the Prompt check box next to the Name area is selected.

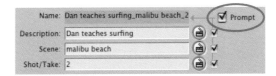

With the Prompt box selected, Final Cut Express will display the information you've entered before logging the clip so that you can change it or add to it before you complete the logging process.

As you learned in the previous lesson, if there are markers present in a clip, those markers can be used to create shorter subclips. Setting markers in a clip during the capturing process can be a convenient way to begin organizing because it is the first step to screening your material. As you think about how to use the material, you can set a marker and name it, and then later create a subclip if you want to work with that portion of the clip separately.

11 Click the Markers disclosure triangle to display the marker controls. Cue the tape to the place *within* the logged clip where you want to set a marker, and then click the Marker In button. Enter a name for the marker in the Marker field. To enter the marker information, click the Set Marker button.

NOTE ▶ A subclip is created from one marker to the next, or from a marker to the end of the clip. Depending on how many markers you set within a clip, you may or may not need to set Marker Out points.

Capturing Options

There are three Capture buttons in the lower portion of the Logging tab area, which represent three capture options: Clip, Now, and Project. Each of these options converts footage from your tape source into computer media files, such as the QuickTime files you worked with in Lesson 2. Although all the capture options create media files, they go about the process differently. For example, to capture DV footage, you use the Capture Clip option. To capture HDV, you capture the footage first, then enter any log information in the Browser columns.

Capturing a Clip

When working with DV, you play the footage, mark In and Out points to define the clip, and log the clip information before capturing it. If you have marked In and Out points on your DV source footage, you have identified a specific clip. The Capture Clip option will capture just the marked portion of your source material.

1   Mark a new clip from your source footage, or use the clip you marked in previous exercise steps.

2   Enter or amend the logging information for your clip.

For example, you may want to deselect the slate boxes for Scene and Take so that information is not included in the clip name. You may also want to select the Mark Good box if it's a really good clip.

3   In the Capture tab, click the Capture Clip button.

If the Prompt check box in the Name area was selected, the Log Clip window appears with the new clip's name, Log Note entry, and Mark Good check box.

```
┌──────────────────────────────────────────────────┐
│                     Log Clip                       │
├────────────────────────────────────────────────────┤
│   Name: Dan teaches surfing          🖮            │
│                                                     │
│ Log Note: teaches how to nose ride    ☑ Mark Good  │
│           ┌──────────────────────┐                  │
│           │                      │                  │
│           └──────────────────────┘                  │
│                         ( Cancel )  ( OK )          │
└──────────────────────────────────────────────────┘
```

4   If necessary, make changes to the Name or Log Note, and click OK.

When capturing begins, a window appears that displays the material you are capturing. Don't worry if it looks jagged at this point. The display during capturing doesn't always reflect the quality of the captured image. When the capture process is complete, the clip appears in the Browser Capture bin.

5   To stop the capture process manually at any time, press the Escape key on your keyboard.

Capturing Now

The second way to capture is to use the Capture Now option. This option is helpful when you want to capture unmarked portions of your source tape as one long clip, or when you don't have FireWire control over a source device, such as a VHS VCR or Hi8 camera, playing through a digital converter box.

1   Enter a clip name and reel number.

2   Cue the source tape about 10 seconds before the action begins in the footage you would like to capture.

3   Play the tape from that point.

4   In the Capture tab, click the Capture Now button to begin capturing.

> **TIP** ▶ This is a less-exact method than the Capture Clip option, so make sure you give yourself adequate pre-roll time before the action you want to capture.

5   To stop capturing, press the Escape key on your keyboard.

Capturing HDV Footage

To capture HDV footage, you begin as you would with DV. You connect your camera via FireWire to your computer, turn it on and switch it to VCR mode, then launch Final Cut Express. At this point, the capture process is more similar to Capture Now in that you do not mark In or Out points or enter detailed clip information before you capture.

1   Choose Final Cut Express > Easy Setup and choose the appropriate HDV preset.

2   Cue the HDV tape up to the area you want to capture, giving it a few extra seconds of handles before the desired material begins.

3   Choose File > Capture.

In the dialog that appears, you can name the clip you are going to capture.

4   Enter the clip name and click Capture.

Final Cut Express automatically plays the HDV camera and begins to capture from its current location. As the footage is being captured, the computer image may lag behind, so use your camera monitor as a reference.

5   To stop capturing, press the Escape key on your keyboard.

Each captured clip appears in the capture bin after capturing is complete.

NOTE ▶ HDV cameras use the MPEG-2 compression format to compress HD footage. This format records audio and video files separately. During the capture process, Final Cut Express joins the audio and video together and creates QuickTime movies out of these files so you can work with them as single clips, as you do DV footage. This is why the capture process is different for HDV.

Working with Long Captured Clips

If you capture a portion of your tape or the entire tape in one long clip, there are a few ways that material can be divided into smaller clips. First, you can always create subclips from that clip before you begin editing. Second, if there are places in your source tape where the camera stopped and started again, the timecode will have changed. Final Cut Express can detect when the timecode changes and will create a new clip as it captures the material. You will work with this setting in the section on User Preferences.

TIP ▶ There is also a feature called DV Start/Stop Detect in the Mark menu. After capturing a long clip, you can open that clip into the Viewer and select this feature. The clip (QuickTime movie) will be scanned for where the camera stopped and started, and markers will automatically appear in the Viewer scrubber bar at those locations. You can then use those markers to create subclips.

Mark	
Mark In	i
Mark Out	o
Mark Split	▶
Mark Clip	x
Mark to Markers	^A
Mark Selection	⇧A
Select In to Out	⌥A
Set Poster Frame	^P
DV Start/Stop Detect	▸
Clear In and Out	⌥X
Clear In	⌥I
Clear Out	⌥O
Clear Split	▶
Clear Poster Frame	
Markers	▶
Play	▶
Go to	▶
Previous	▶
Next	▶

The third capture option, Project, is used once you have completed editing a project. This option will be covered in Lesson 16.

Choosing Preferences and System Settings

Let's take a look at some of the Final Cut Express settings that will affect how you capture your video and affect your project. There are two places you can change settings: in User Preferences and System Settings. The User Preferences window is where most of your editing settings and some capture settings are stored. You have already worked with a few preferences and changed a few settings in previous lessons, and you will work with still others in later lessons.

Exploring User Preferences

The User Preferences window has four tabs. Each tab organizes settings related to specific functions of Final Cut Express.

1   Choose Final Cut Express > User Preferences, or press Option-Q.

The User Preferences window opens with the General tab in view. The General tab is where you choose assorted preference settings for capturing and saving your project.

2   Click the Editing tab.

This is where you choose settings for several editing functions, such as the length of your Pre-rolls, Freeze durations, Multi-Frame Trim Size, and so on.

3   Click the Timeline Options tab.

This is where you choose settings for all *new* Timelines. Any changes made here will not affect existing sequences in the Timeline.

> **TIP** To change Timeline settings for an active sequence, choose Sequence > Settings, or press Cmd-0 (zero), and make adjustments in that window.

4   Click the Render Control tab.

Final Cut Express has numerous effects that can be applied to an edited clip. These effects are discussed in more detail in Lesson 14. Some of these effects are real-time effects, referred to as RT. This means that the effect can be viewed immediately after applying it. Other more complex effects may need to go through an additional step of creating a new media file of the effect in order to be viewed in real time. This process is called *rendering*. You can set controls for the rendering process in this tab.

5   Select the General tab, where you will set preferences for capturing.

Setting General Preferences

Many of the General Preferences options are personal preferences, such as the number of undos you want to work with or the number of recent clips available in the Viewer's Recent Clips pop-up menu.

Auto
Render
area

User Preferences

General \ Editing \ Timeline Options \ Render Control

| Levels of Undo: | 10 | actions | ☐ Prompt for settings on New Project |
| List Recent Clips: | 10 | entries | ☐ Prompt for settings on New Sequence |

Real-time Audio Mixing: 8 tracks
Audio Playback Quality: Low (faster)
☐ Limit real-time video to: 20 MB/s

☑ Report dropped frames during playback
☑ Abort capture on dropped frames
☐ Do not show A/V Device Warning on launch

☑ Show Tooltips
☑ Bring all windows to the front on activation
☑ Open last project on application launch
☑ Autosave Vault

Browser Text Size: Small

☑ Auto Render

Autosave
Vault area

Save a copy every:	30	minutes	Start Render after:	45	minutes
Keep at most:	40	copies per project	Render:	Open Sequences	
Maximum of:	25	projects	☑ Render RT Segments		

Cancel   OK

TIP ▶ Final Cut Express opens with the above standard default preference settings. If you are ever unsure about how to set your preferences, make sure your settings match these and then make changes from there.

1   Review your personal preferences in the upper left of the General tab.

2   Look in the lower-left Autosave Vault area of the General tab.

Many computer programs have the capability to save your work automatically and create a backup copy of your document for you. Final Cut Express does this as well in its Autosave Vault. You can choose how frequently a project will be saved, how many versions of the project will be saved, and the maximum number of projects saved.

☑ Autosave Vault
Save a copy every: 30 minutes
Keep at most: 40 copies per project
Maximum of: 25 projects

If you have named a project, you have begun the saving process. Final Cut Express quietly saves the project at specified intervals. There can sometimes be a slight hesitation in your editing operations while the project is being saved.

NOTE ▶ If you are working in a new project and have not yet begun the saving process by naming it, the Final Cut Express icon in the Dock will start bouncing to get your attention. The program really wants to save your project for you, but it can't until you name it and decide where you will place it. If the following message appears on the screen, click Yes and name the project.

Final Cut Express cannot autosave your project unless you save it first. Would you like to save it now?

No | Yes

Setting Capture Preferences

On the right-hand side of the Preferences window is an option that relates to capturing: "Abort capture on dropped frames." This option does not have to be changed unless you run into difficulty capturing your source material. Let's look at what this capture setting does.

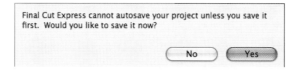

☑ Abort capture on dropped frames

If Final Cut Express notices any frames of video being dropped or left out while capturing your source material, it will stop the capture process and report the dropped frames in a message onscreen.

NOTE ▶ Use the default settings when you start to capture. If you find there is a problem with dropped frames, deselect this option and try again.

Exploring System Settings

Another set of options you can use to set up your project is the System Settings. These settings affect where you will be saving your media files during the capture process, as well as other settings used throughout your editing.

1 Close the User Preferences window, and choose Final Cut Express > System Settings, or press Shift-Q.

The first tab, Scratch Disks, is where you specify the location or drive where you want to save media files during the capture process, and where you want to save render files during the editing process.

2 Click the Search Folders tab.

If your clips should become disconnected from their media files, you can limit the search for them to specific folders or media drives. Reconnecting files is covered in Lesson 16.

3 Click the Memory & Cache tab.

This is where you make changes to memory usage while in Final Cut Express. Generally, you will use the default settings.

4   Click the Playback Control tab.

This is where you make choices about playing back effects in real time (RT) and the playback quality of the effects. This will be discussed in more detail in Lesson 14.

5   Click the External Editors tab.

In this tab, you can set other software applications as external editors and access them directly from within Final Cut Express.

Setting the Capture Destination

Some computers have large hard drives that give you plenty of room to capture footage for your editing project. Others, perhaps certain laptops, may not give you quite enough room to store all your source material, especially if you're working on a larger project or several projects at one time.

If you are going to work with an additional internal hard drive or an external FireWire hard drive to store your QuickTime media files, you will need to direct Final Cut Express to that drive as the destination for your captured clips. The destination drive is called the *scratch disk*. The program defaults to your main hard drive unless you redirect it to a different location.

1   If you're working with an external FireWire drive, make sure the drive is connected to your computer before setting the scratch disk.

2   Select the Scratch Disks tab in the System Settings window.

When you begin creating new render files of clips with effects, they can be stored in a different location. For now, let's capture everything to the same location.

TIP The Scratch Disks tab always tells you how much hard-drive space you have available for capturing.

3   In the first line, click the Set button.

The Choose a Folder window appears, where you can navigate to a different destination for your captured media.

NOTE ► The default scratch disk is your internal hard drive. More specifically, it is the Final Cut Express Documents folder, located in your home Documents folder.

4   In the Choose a Folder window, scroll to the left until you see all of the storage devices attached to your computer and all of your hard-drive options.

5   Select the hard drive you want to capture your media to and click Choose.

The Choose a Folder window closes and returns you to the Scratch Disks tab of the System Settings window. Leave this window open through the next exercise.

In the lower portion of the Scratch Disks tab, you can also set a different destination for other items such as Thumbnail Cache and Autosave Vault. The Autosave Vault is just a folder located on your hard drive. You can change the destination of this folder just as you chose a scratch disk in the previous steps.

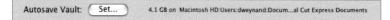

NOTE ► *Caches* are temporary files that Final Cut Express creates when it needs to generate information on the fly. For example, when you use the Show Thumbnail command in the Browser, Final Cut Express has to create tiny versions of your video clips to display in the Thumbnail column. It then stores those thumbnails in a cache on disk so that it doesn't have to generate them all over again every time you expand the bin that contains those clips.

Limiting Capture Now

Capture Now is one of the three capture options covered in the "Capturing Options" section earlier in this lesson. Part of the Scratch Disks tab information includes an option to limit the amount of video you can capture in one stretch while using the Capture Now option.

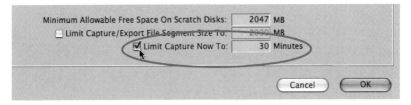

To limit the capture time, click the Limit Capture Now To checkbox, and enter the number of minutes you want to capture. The default is 30 minutes.

You may want to practice logging clips and capturing them different ways, or just dive in and practice as you go. Just make sure you keep an eye on your available hard-drive space so that you have room to capture the really good shots into your project.

Transferring AVCHD Footage

Since the AVCHD format records footage as digital files, you don't capture the footage as you would from a tape source. Instead, you transfer the files using the Final Cut Express Log and Transfer window. During the transfer, the AVCHD footage, which is recorded originally as MPEG-4, is converted to the Apple Intermediate Codec. (AVCHD is supported only on Intel-based Macs.)

1   Connect your AVCHD camera using a USB cable, and switch your camera to PC mode.

2   To open Log and Transfer, choose File > Log and Transfer, or press Shift-Cmd-8.

    The Log and Transfer window opens and automatically detects your clips, listing them in the left clip Browse area.

Browse area   Preview area

Transfer Queue area   Logging area

3 In the Browse area on the left side, click a clip to load into the Preview area on the right side.

You can play a clip to preview it. However, unlike tape, you cannot mark an In or Out to transfer a portion—you must transfer the entire clip. You can also use the Logging area beneath the Preview area to name your clip and enter additional clip information.

4 Enter a reel number or ID, and enter a name for the clip in the Name field. Then enter any additional clip information, such as Scene, Shot/ Take, Log Note, and so on.

5 To transfer the clip, click the Add Clip to Queue button (between the Preview and Logging areas).

The clip is added to the queue (list) in the lower-left Transfer Queue area, and the Status icon indicates that the clip is being transferred.

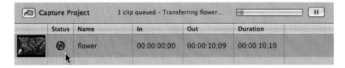

Final Cut Express transfers the clip to your scratch disk and automatically imports the clip into your project.

NOTE ▶ When you capture videotape, you cannot perform any additional functions as the clip is being captured. With AVCHD, you can preview and add additional clips to the queue while the transfer is in progress.

Saving and Quitting

When you save your project now, you will be saving the setup of the capture bin and whatever clips have been logged and captured. But you will not save whatever logging information may be in the Capture window.

1   If you made changes in the System Settings window that you want to keep, click OK. If not, click Cancel.

2   If the Capture window is still open, close it by clicking the Close button, or pressing Cmd-8.

3   Save the current project one last time by pressing Cmd-S.

4   Quit Final Cut Express by pressing Cmd-Q, or close this project and continue with the next lesson.

Lesson Review

1.   What must you do with your camera before you begin capturing footage?

2.   Where does the logged information appear after a clip has been captured?

3.   Can you set markers when you capture? If so, why would you want to do this?

4.   What happens when you select the Prompt box in the Capture tab?

5. What are the three capture options?

6. When you do not have control over a device, such as a VHS player, which capture option do you use?

7. What logging options do you have when you capture HDV footage?

8. Where do you choose a different scratch disk to store captured media?

9. If you've shot material using the AVCHD format, how do you bring it into Final Cut Express?

Answers

1. Turn on your camera, switch it into VCR mode, and make sure the FireWire cable is connected to your computer.

2. In the Browser columns.

3. Yes, you can. Remember you can use markers to create subclips from longer clips.

4. After you choose Capture Clip, a dialog will appear that prompts you to confirm or change the existing clip information.

5. Capture Clip, Now, and Project.

6. Capture Now.

7. You can enter a name only in the Capture dialog.

8. In the System Settings window.

9. You choose File > Log and Transfer, and transfer the clips you want to edit into the project.

Keyboard Shortcuts

Cmd-8	Opens and closes the Capture window
Shift-Cmd-8	Opens and closes the Log and Transfer window
Esc (Escape)	Stops the capture process when capturing HDV or using the Capture Now option
Option-Q	Opens the User Preferences window
Shift-Q	Opens the System Settings window

13

Lesson 13
Working with Audio

So far, a lot of attention has been paid to the video portion of a sequence. However, all the editing, marking, trimming, and adjusting covered so far also applies to audio clips. In this lesson, you will work with different ways to see and hear the audio portion of a clip, adjust audio levels, make audio-only edits, keep audio in sync, and work with stereo pairs. You will also learn how to record a narration track, or voice-over.

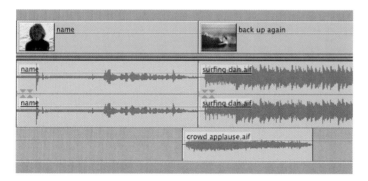

Preparing the Project

To get started, launch Final Cut Express and then open the project for this lesson.

1   From within Final Cut Express, choose File > Open, or press Cmd-O, and select the **Lesson 13 Project** file from the Lessons folder on your hard drive.

2   Close any open projects.

3   In the Timeline, play the *Audio Needs Work* sequence.

In this sequence, the audio levels are not very consistent and are not mixed together well. They need some adjusting, which you will do throughout this lesson. You are working with three audio tracks. In this lesson, tracks 1 and 2 are used for stereo music and DV clips; track 3 is used for single-channel sound effects.

Hearing, Seeing, and Selecting Audio

As you work with audio in Final Cut Express, sometimes you will want to hear the sound, and other times you will want to see a visual representation of the sound. And sometimes you will want to select just the audio portion of a clip.

Scrubbing and Shuttling Audio

You have been scrubbing through clips by clicking and dragging the playhead within the scrubber-bar area in the Viewer and Canvas windows, and even in the Timeline. Scrubbing helps you to find where a specific sound starts and stops while screening or editing a clip. But it isn't the best choice if you actually want to understand what's being said.

1   Drag the playhead through the *Audio Needs Work* sequence.

You hear the sound of the clips at whatever speed you drag the playhead. This digitized audio isn't always understandable, but it can be used as a reference to where audio starts and stops.

2   To turn this function off, choose View > Audio Scrubbing, or press Shift-S. Now drag the playhead through the sequence again.

There is no sound as you drag the playhead across the clips.

TIP ▶ If you are focusing on the visual aspect of your sequence, you may want to work with audio scrubbing off so that you don't hear the digital audio track as you drag the playhead through the sequence.

3   Choose View > Audio Scrubbing again, or press Shift-S, to turn scrubbing back on.

4   In the Canvas window, use the shuttle slider to run the audio from the clip back and forth. Shuttle slowly enough that you can hear syllables spoken.

NOTE ► Another way to use the shuttle is to click and hold the pointer on either side of the slider. The farther away you click, the faster you will shuttle.

TIP ► Use the shuttle slider when you need to understand what's being said, such as a specific word or phrase. Scrub the playhead when you want to get quickly to a specific point, such as where music or sound starts or stops.

Using the Audio Meters

Although audio is the part of the clip you usually hear rather than see, there are two visual aids that can help you *see* what the audio portion of your clip is doing. One of those visual aids is the Audio Meters window.

The Audio Meters measure the volume of a clip in decibels (dB). When editing your sequence, keep an eye on the Audio Meters window to ensure that the final sound is consistent and not distorted. You may have a good sound level on one clip, but when you combine it with music or sound effects, the level can go over the acceptable level. A good target for audio is about –12 dB. Some sounds will fall above or below that, and some audio can *peak* at around –3 dB. But if any sound reaches 0 dB, it will be distorted and will not sound good in the final output. Always try to be consistent.

> **NOTE** ▸ If the sound level of a source clip peaks at 0 dB, the sound may have been recorded too high or loud during the original shoot. Changing the level as outlined in this lesson might help but will not always correct the problem.

1   If the Audio Meters window is not showing in your Final Cut Express interface, choose Window > Audio Meters, or press Option-4.

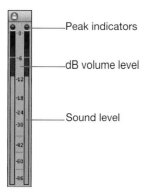

The Audio Meters window contains two vertical audio meters. The small numbers down the middle are used as a reference point for measuring dB levels.

> **TIP** ▸ Keep in mind as you work with volume levels that raising or lowering the volume on your computer speakers or external monitors has no effect whatsoever on the audio level of a clip. The audio on the clip is still at the same level at which it was recorded and captured.

2 Play from the head of the sequence and watch the Audio Meters.

Some of the audio clips are in the correct range; others have audio levels that are too high or too low.

When working with audio, be consistent throughout your project. For example, if you set the audio of Jimbo talking between −12 dB and −9 dB early in the sequence, make sure that the similar Jimbo talking clips later in the sequence are at that level as well.

Viewing an Audio Waveform

Another way Final Cut Express allows you to *see* your audio is to display a visual representation of the audio levels. This visual display is called a *waveform display* and can appear in two places: the Viewer and the audio tracks in the Timeline. You will work with audio in the Viewer later in this lesson. Here, we'll look at waveform displays in Timeline clips.

1 Click the Timeline to make sure it is the active window, and press Shift-Z to bring the sequence into full view.

2 Press Cmd-Option-W to turn on the audio waveform display in the Timeline audio tracks.

A waveform representing the clips' audio appears in all the audio tracks.

A waveform displays an audio level from a central reference point. A higher audio volume is displayed as a taller waveform. A lower volume is displayed as a shorter waveform. When there is no volume, as in the A2 track of the **no leash LOW** clip, the display is a flat line.

3   Observing the height of the waveform display in each clip, determine which clip in the sequence is the loudest. Which is the softest? Play the sequence to see if you're right.

4   Drag the playhead through the sequence across the audio where the volume changes.

5   To make just the audio tracks taller and allow room for a larger waveform display, press Option and drag the A1 track boundary line down.

NOTE ▶ Changing the track height makes the waveform display bigger but does not affect the sound level in any way.

6   Move the playhead to the beginning of the sequence. Drag the Canvas shuttle slider slowly to the right to hear Jimbo speak very slowly. Watch the clip's waveform as you drag.

7   Press Shift and drag any Timeline track boundary line to make all tracks uniform. You can also click one of the Track Height control columns.

TIP ▶ Another way to turn off and on audio waveforms is by clicking the Timeline Layout Popup control (arrow) in the Timeline and choosing Show Audio Waveforms from the pop-up menu.

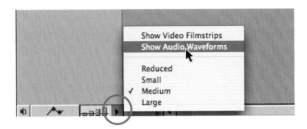

Selecting Linked Clips

When you capture a clip, you generally capture one track of video and two tracks of audio. These three tracks are linked together to form a single clip. Once this clip has been edited to the Timeline, you can select and adjust all three tracks of the clip at once. But you may at times want to select or adjust the tracks individually. To do this, you must turn off a function that automatically selects linked clips.

1   In the current sequence, click the **back up again** clip in the video track.

Only the video portion of this clip was used in the sequence, so it does not naturally link to the music beneath it.

2   Click the **surfing dan.aif** music track beneath it.

This audio came from a CD. Since it is not linked to the video, you can select it separately.

3   Click the video portion of the **name** clip.

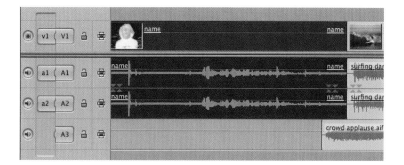

If both the audio and video are being used from the originally captured clip, all three tracks become highlighted when any one track
is selected.

TIP ▶ A line beneath the clip name indicates that the tracks are
linked together.

4   Deselect the **name** clip.

In order to select just one of the clip's tracks by itself, such as the video
portion of the clip, you must turn off the Linked Selection control in
the Timeline button bar.

5   Click the Linked Selection control to turn this default function off.
You can also press Shift-L to toggle this function off and on.

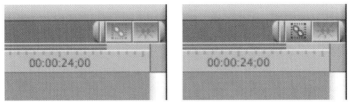

Linked Selection on   Linked Selection off

The Linked Selection control looks like two green chain links. When Linked Selection is on or enabled, you can click any track of a linked clip in the Timeline, and all of the clip's tracks become highlighted. When it's off or disabled, the control appears black and convex, and only the individual track you select becomes highlighted.

6   With Linked Selection off, click the **name** video track again to select it.

This time you can select the video or audio portions of the clip separately.

Just like video clips, audio clips can be cut, copied, and pasted. For example, now that you can select these tracks separately, you could delete the **name** video track, replace it with a video cutaway, or copy and paste it elsewhere in the sequence.

7   For now, click the Linked Selection control in the Timeline to turn it back on.

TIP ▶ It's a good idea to work with the Linked Selection function turned on in the Timeline. When you need to select or adjust a clip's audio or video, you can easily turn Linked Selection off to make your selection or adjustment and then turn it back on again.

Project Tasks

1   In the current sequence, make sure the audio waveform is still displayed. Make the audio tracks taller, and zoom in to the **name** clip so that you can see an expanded waveform for this clip.

2   Using the waveform of the audio as a guide, use the Ripple Edit tool to trim the In and Out points of the **name** clip so that you hear only Jimbo saying, "My name is … since I was 5 years old."

3   Press A for the default Selection tool and drag the **crowd applause.aif** clip to the left to reposition it so that the sound of this clip begins immediately after Jimbo finishes talking. Use the waveform in both clips as a guide.

The **crowd applause.aif** clip now overlaps the two clips above it.

4   Again with the waveform as a guide, use the Slip tool (keyboard shortcut, S) to slip the **surfing dan.aif** clip left until the music waveform begins exactly at the clip's In point.

5 Toggle off the A3 Audible button. Then trim a little off the end of the **no leash LOW** clip so that it ends when Jimbo stops talking.

> **TIP** Since this is the last clip in the sequence, you can just drag the clip's Out point left to trim this clip. Make sure the default Selection tool (keyboard shortcut, A) is selected.

Currently, Jimbo's audio is very low, but you will fix it in the next exercise.

6 After you've trimmed the **no leash LOW** clip, trim the **water lapping.aif** clip to end at the same location.

7 Enable the sound for all clips and play the sequence.

> **TIP** Working with the audio waveform display in the Timeline is like working with thumbnail images in that it uses additional computer RAM. When you do not need to see the waveform display, it's a good idea to turn that option off.

8 Press Cmd-Option-W to turn off the audio waveforms in the Timeline.

9 Press Cmd-S to save these changes to your project.

Adjusting Audio in the Timeline

You can adjust the audio level of a clip directly in the Timeline after editing it into the sequence, or in the Viewer before placing it in a sequence. Adjusting levels in the Timeline adjusts audio for each sequence clip but does not change the audio level for the master clips in the Browser. Let's adjust the audio levels of the current sequence clips in the Timeline.

Working with Clip Overlays

To adjust the audio level in the Timeline, you first need to see a visual representation of the overall audio level. To do this, you will work with the Clip Overlays function in the Timeline. As a viewing option, clip overlays can be turned off and on whenever you like during the editing process.

1   If you completed the previous "Project Tasks" steps, continue working in the *Audio Needs Work* sequence. If not, open the *Changing Audio Levels* sequence, which has the "Project Tasks" changes already made.

2   Find the Clip Overlays control in the Timeline next to the Track Height control.

3   Click the Clip Overlays control to turn on the clip overlay lines.

Volume level overlay lines

A thin pink line appears in each audio clip, representing the overall volume of that clip. This line is called the volume level overlay line. There is also a black overlay line for the video portion of the clip, but you will work with that in a later lesson.

4   Press Option-W to turn the overlay lines in the Timeline off and on. Leave clip overlays on.

NOTE ▶ In the Timeline, the control appears to be sunken or depressed when active and raised when not active or selected.

You can adjust the overall volume of a clip by dragging the volume level overlay line up and down. Let's correct the out-of-range audio clips in the current sequence.

5   Play the **name** clip in the sequence, and look at its current audio level in the Audio Meters.

This clip is at a good level. It does not need adjusting.

6   Play the **surfing dan.aif** clip and look at its level in the Audio Meters. To hear it by itself, turn off sound for the entire A3 track.

TIP ▶ The sound bites and music are the primary audio tracks in this short sequence. It is important to set their levels first. Then you can add or mix in the desired levels of the two sound effects.

This music clip is so loud that it's peaking at a constant 0 dB in the Audio Meters. The audio level must be brought down to an acceptable range.

7   Move your pointer over the clip's pink volume level overlay line in the A1 track of the **surfing dan.aif** clip.

The pointer turns into the up-down resize arrow.

8   Begin to drag the line down to lower the sound.

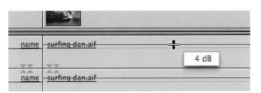

As you drag down, an information box appears, indicating the new dB level. This is a relative level of sound for just this clip.

NOTE ▶ As you move one volume level line, the line on A2 also moves. This will be explained in the following exercise.

9   Drag the volume level line down to 0 dB and let go. Play the clip again and watch the Audio Meters to see if the sound is in the proper range.

The audio level is still a little too high.

10   Drag the volume level line down until the clip's audio level plays back between −12 and −9 dB in the Audio Meters.

Working with Stereo Pairs

When you edit a stereo music track from a CD, a clip with two tracks will appear in the Timeline because it's a stereo track. When you capture from sources such as DV, HDV, or AVCHD, the audio is captured as a stereo pair. In the Timeline, whenever you select one of the tracks in a stereo pair, both tracks are selected. Also, adjustments made to one track of a stereo pair are automatically applied to the other track. There are times, however, when you need to work with only one track of the stereo pair.

1   Play the **no leash LOW** clip in the Timeline.

The audio level for this clip is too low and needs to be adjusted.

2   Select the A1 track of this clip.

If Linked Selection is active in the Timeline, all the tracks of the clip will be highlighted.

3   Click the Linked Selection control to turn it off, or press Shift-L.

4   Deselect the **no leash LOW** clip and then reselect the A1 track.

Both of the audio tracks are selected together.

Between the two audio tracks are stereo pair indicators. These triangles indicate that the two tracks are bound together as a stereo pair.

5   Raise and lower the audio level on the A1 track or the A2 track.

The volume level lines in both tracks move when you adjust either one of the stereo pair.

6   To take a closer look at the audio levels, turn on the waveform display by pressing Cmd-Option-W.

The flat line indicates that there is no audio on the A2 track. All usable audio is on the A1 track.

7   Turn off the waveform display, and bring the audio volume level line of the stereo pair back to 0 dB.

Separating a Stereo Pair

In the preceding steps, the **no leash LOW** clip was originally recorded with a single microphone feeding only one channel. But when it was captured, both channels of the tape source were captured together. The goal now is to separate out and delete the A2 track, which doesn't have any audio, and duplicate the A1 track to help pump up the volume on this clip. In order to do this, the stereo pair indicators must be turned off so that you can access each of these tracks separately.

1 With the **no leash LOW** audio tracks selected, choose Modify and look at the Stereo Pair menu option. If a checkmark is present, select the option to turn it off.

This option will turn *off* stereo pair status on two clips that are currently a stereo pair. Or it will turn *on* stereo pair status for two clips that are not currently a stereo pair. The check indicates that stereo pair is the current status of the selected clips. When you select this option, the checkmark is removed, and the stereo pair status is turned off for the selected items, allowing you to make changes to individual audio tracks.

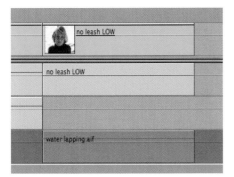

The stereo pair indicators have disappeared from between the two tracks. The two tracks can now be adjusted separately.

NOTE ▶ If you select a clip in the Timeline with just one audio track, such as one of the mono sound effects, the Stereo Pair menu option is dimmed.

2 Deselect the tracks, and click the A2 audio clip to select just that one track. Delete the A2 audio clip.

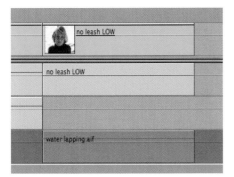

3   To duplicate the good audio, click the A1 audio clip and press Cmd-C to copy it. Move the playhead to where you will edit the copied clip, at the head of the **no leash LOW** clip.

The next step is to paste the audio clip you just copied to the A2 destination track. Since this is not a new source, you do not use the clip's source control to patch it to the A2 track. Instead, you use the Auto Select controls to indicate which track will be used. When copying and pasting clips *within* the Timeline, the clip is automatically placed on the highest track for which the Auto Select control is turned on. For this exercise, you will toggle off the Auto Select control for all audio tracks other than A2.

4   Toggle off the Auto Select controls for each audio track except A2.

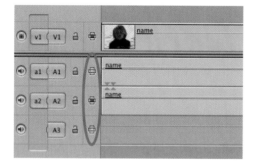

5   Press Cmd-V.

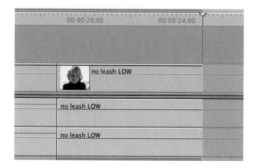

The copied clip from the A1 track is pasted onto the A2 track at the playhead location.

6   Play this clip and look at the Audio Meters.

Notice that both tracks are playing on the same side or channel of the Audio Meters. In the next step, you will change this.

7   To make these two audio tracks a stereo pair, Shift-click the A1 track so that both A1 and A2 are selected, and choose Modify > Stereo Pair, or press Option-L.

Now, if you click just one audio track, they are both selected again.

TIP ▶ All the linking keyboard shortcuts involve the letter L.

8   Press Cmd-S to save these changes to your project.

9   Now turn the Linked Selection function back on in the Timeline.

When you click the V1 portion of this clip, all three tracks are highlighted.

10   Toggle all Auto Select controls back on.

Boosting and Panning Audio

The **no leash LOW** clip sounds louder now that you doubled the A1 track. Whenever adjusting any volume levels, however, you must be careful not to peak the audio, or it will become distorted. Final Cut Express includes an automated feature that increases the volume of a clip without any worry of peaking.

1   From the Browser, open the *Normalize Levels* sequence.

This sequence is the same sequence you were just working on prior to copying and pasting the A1 clip into track A2.

2   In the Timeline, select the **no leash LOW** A1 audio clip.

3   Choose Modify > Audio > Apply Normalization Gain.

```
                      Apply Normalization Gain
        Normalize to:  ‹————|————————›        0 dBFS

                            ( Cancel )    (    OK    )
```

Notice the "Normalize to" scale is measured in dBFS (decibels of full scale). In this feature, you will be setting how loud you want the highest peak of the clip to be.

4   Drag the "Normalize to" slider to the left until it reads –6 dB, and then click OK.

5   Play back the **no leash LOW** clip in the Timeline and watch the Audio Meters.

Now the highest levels of the clip reach –6 dB on the Audio Meters. This function allowed you to successfully increase Jimbo's voice without any risk of peaking the audio.

Final Cut Express made this audio change by adding a Gain filter to the audio portion of the clip.

MORE INFO ► You can work with filters more in the "Working with Filters" appendix, which you can find on the DVD that came with this book.

6   To see the Gain filter, double-click the **no lease LOW** clip in the Timeline.

7   In the Viewer, click the Filters tab.

```
  Video    Stereo (a1a2)   Filters   Motion
Name                Parameters              Nav        2:0
▼  Video Filters
▼  Stereo 1 Filters
▼  ☑ Gain                                    ⊗  ☑▾
   Gain(dB)            ‹——|——›      4.29      ◁◉▷
```

Final Cut Express calculated the needed Gain amount to boost Jimbo's loudest audio up to –6 dB.

Keeping Linked Clips in Sync

When video and audio are captured together, the audio is in sync with the video, meaning that when someone speaks, the correct sound comes out of that person's mouth at the correct time. With Linked Selection on, the video and audio portions of a clip are always adjusted together. They will get out of sync only if you lock one track and make an adjustment to other tracks in the same clip. But if Linked Selection is off, adjusting just the video or audio portion of a clip can cause the tracks to go out of sync from each other.

1   Copy the **name** clip and paste it about five seconds past the end of the current sequence. Deselect the clip.

   NOTE ▶ It might be helpful as you are working through this exercise to turn off the clip overlay and waveform displays. They are not required and may make certain items harder to see.

2   Toggle off Linked Selection in the Timeline.

3   With the default Selection tool, drag the video of the **name** clip to the right about two seconds and play the clip. Deselect the clip.

A red out-of-sync indicator appears with a positive duration in the video track, indicating the amount of the forward move. In the audio tracks, a negative duration of the same amount appears, indicating how far behind or out of sync the audio tracks are from the video.

4   Press Cmd-Z to undo this move.

> **TIP** An easy fix for any mistake, such as when you throw your clips out of sync, is to undo what you just did by pressing Cmd-Z.

5   Choose Edit > Redo, or press Shift-Cmd-Z, to redo the move and return the clip to its previous out-of-sync configuration.

In the out-of-sync clip, if you really don't want to move the video from this location, you must decide what to do with the audio. You have three choices:

▶   Leave the audio where it is, and it will remain out of sync.

▶   Move the audio's position in the Timeline to be aligned with the video again and return to sync.

▶   Slip the audio so that the portion under the video clip is in its original sync.

6   Ctrl-click the red out-of-sync indicator in one of the audio tracks and choose Move into Sync from the shortcut menu.

Both audio tracks are literally moved in the Timeline to catch up with the video. The red out-of-sync indicators are removed from the clip.

7   Now drag the audio portion of the clip to the right two seconds and play the clip.

The audio is obviously out of sync from the video.

8   Ctrl-click one of the audio out-of-sync indicators, and this time choose Slip into Sync from the shortcut menu. Play the clip.

Slipping a track back into sync will not change its location in the Timeline. This adjusts the selection of audio material so that it slips back into sync with the video.

9   Turn Linked Selection back on and delete this extra **name** clip.

Adjusting Audio in the Viewer

You can also make audio adjustments in the Viewer when you first screen a clip. The Viewer contains additional options that appear on the audio tab of the window. Any audio adjustments made to a master clip in the Viewer will remain with that clip for future uses until it is changed.

Working in the Audio Tab

When you open a clip in the Viewer, the video portion of the clip is displayed in the Video tab. The audio attached to that clip is displayed in the Stereo or Mono audio tab, depending on whether the source audio is stereo or mono. If the audio portion of the clip is a single track of audio, a single waveform is displayed. If it is a stereo pair, two waveforms are displayed, one for each track of audio.

1   From the Clips bin in the Browser, open the **name** clip into the Viewer.

2   Select the Stereo (a1a2) tab. Click back and forth between the Video and Stereo tabs to see what parts of the Viewer are similar and what parts are different.

The two tabs share the same controls from the scrubber bar and below, as well as the Duration and Location fields in the upper part of the Viewer.

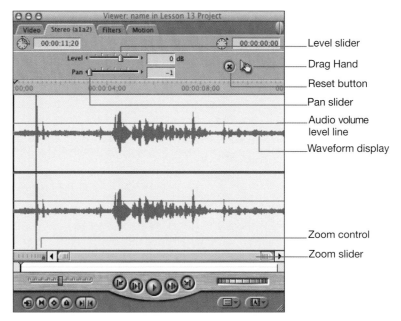

3   From the Music and Sound Effects bin, open the **crowd applause.aif** clip.

This clip has only one audio track so there is only one waveform display. Also, a Mono tab appears because the source audio is mono. In the Timeline, only an a1 source track control appears.

4   Beneath the waveform, drag the Zoom control left to zoom in or expand the waveform display. Leave the display in an expanded view.

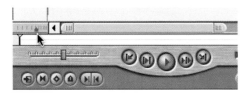

5   Drag the Zoom slider to view a different portion of the waveform display.

The Zoom control and slider operate in the Audio tab just as they do in the Timeline.

6   Drag the Zoom control to the left as far as possible to zoom in to the waveform. Then click in the scrubber-bar area to see the playhead.

When the clip's waveform is expanded, the stem of the playhead expands to indicate how much of the waveform equals a full video frame. In a fully expanded view, there is a wide black bar attached to the playhead stem to indicate the width of a single frame.

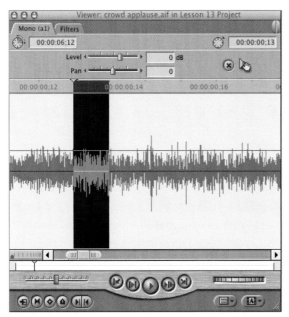

7   Press Shift-Z to bring the entire audio track of the clip into view.

8   Drag the shuttle slider left and right. Drag the jog wheel left and right.

All the Viewer play keys and mark buttons are used in the same ways as in the Video tab.

Adjusting Audio Levels in the Viewer

You can adjust audio levels in the Viewer by dragging the pink volume level line up or down, using the Level slider, or entering a dB value in the numerical entry box. You can also pan the channels of audio in a clip using the Pan or Spread slider beneath the Level slider.

1   Open the **name** clip from the Recent Clips pop-up menu in the Viewer and select the Stereo tab.

2   Move the pointer over one of the pink volume level lines in the waveform display area.

Just as it did in the Timeline, the pointer changes to the up-down resize arrow to raise or lower the level.

3   Drag the volume level line up and down.

As you drag, the Level slider moves, and the numbers in the numerical entry box next to the Level control change to reflect the new adjustment. Also, the level lines in both tracks move in tandem because they are a stereo pair.

4   Now click in the numerical entry box, type –6, and press Return.

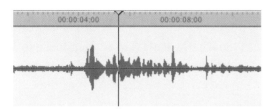

    After you press Return, the volume level line adjusts to the new level.

5   Drag the Level slider until the dB level is 0 (zero).

    When you stop dragging the slider, the volume level lines in the wave-
    form display adjust to reflect the change.

6   Play the clip and watch the Audio Meters to see if the levels are within
    the correct range.

    If you want to change the left and right channels of a stereo pair, you
    can adjust the Pan slider.

7   Open the **crowd applause.aif** clip in the Viewer. Play the clip and listen
    for the sound.

    The Pan slider should be set in the middle at 0. At this setting, you
    hear the sound equally distributed over both speakers.

8   Drag the Pan slider to the far left and play the clip again. Then drag it
    to the far right and play it.

    Adjusting the Pan slider places the sound of a mono track anywhere
    between the far left and far right, or –1 and 1. This can be used to
    control which speaker the sound plays through.

Making an Audio-Only Edit

When you worked with clips that had video, you dragged the image in the Viewer to the Canvas Edit Overlay or directly to the Timeline to make an edit. But you can't drag an audio clip the same way. To drag an audio clip to the Timeline, you have to drag from a special icon.

1   From the Browser, open the *Editing Audio* sequence.

    There is currently just one short clip in this sequence.

2   From the Music and Sound Effects bin, open the **water lapping.aif** clip into the Viewer and lower its sound level to –10 dB.

    In the Timeline, the a1 source track is automatically patched to the A1 destination track.

3   Make sure the playhead is at the head of the sequence, and that the a1 source track is patched to the A1 destination track.

4   Mark a two-second duration from the head of the **water lapping.aif** clip.

    You mark an audio clip in exactly the same way that you mark a video clip. The same buttons and shortcuts apply.

5   In the Viewer, locate the Drag Hand icon just under the Location field.

6   Drag the Drag Hand icon into the Canvas and drop it on the Overwrite section of the Edit Overlay.

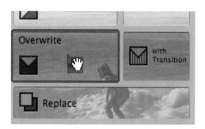

After you edit an audio clip into a sequence, you can double-click to open it and then make changes to it in the Viewer, just as you did with video clips. But remember, you can also change audio levels directly in the Timeline.

TIP ▶ If you want to use just the audio portion of an audio/video clip, unpatch the video source control. Then mark the audio in the Viewer and drag the Drag Hand icon from the Audio tab as you did in these steps.

Project Tasks

Let's edit just the audio portion of the **name** clip into the current sequence.

1   Open the **name** clip and mark the portion of the clip where Jimbo introduces himself. Use the waveform display as a reference.

2   In the Timeline, make sure that only the audio tracks are patched.

3   Edit just the marked portion of this clip into the Timeline after the **water lapping.aif** clip.

4   Extend the **back up again** clip to cover the length of the new audio.

5   Press Cmd-S to save your project.

Finding a Video Match

You might edit with just the video or audio portion of a clip but later decide to add back the missing track. For example, in the preceding project, you used just the audio of the **name** clip and not the video. But let's say you change your mind and decide to use Jimbo's video to match the audio. You begin by finding the video frame that matches the audio. This is called a *match frame* and can refer to any matching frame, audio or video, that shares the same location on the original master clip.

1   In the Timeline, move the playhead to the first frame of the **name** audio clip.

2   To find a match for the **name** audio clip frame and not the **back up again** video, click the V1 Auto Select control in the Timeline track area.

Clicking this control toggles off the selection of this track and directs Final Cut Express to look at the audio tracks as a reference.

3   Click the Show Match Frame button in the Canvas window, or press F.

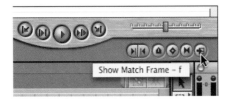

In the Viewer, the original **name** clip is opened and the playhead is parked on the matching frame of the audio clip in the Timeline.

NOTE ▶ In the Viewer scrubber bar, the lack of dots indicates that this is a source clip and not a sequence clip.

4   Click the V1 Auto Select control to toggle the status of this track back to normal.

5   To edit just the video of this clip, patch just the v1 source track and disconnect the a1 and a2 tracks.

6   Drag the clip image from the Viewer to the Canvas and drop it in the Overwrite section of the Edit Overlay. If you still have the Overwrite button in the Canvas button bar, you can click that instead.

7   Play the clip in the Timeline.

> **TIP** ▶ You can use the Match Frame button in the Viewer to find a matching frame in the sequence. You can also find a matching audio frame for a video clip.

Linking Clips

The audio and video from the previous exercise are now in sync, but they are not linked together, because they were edited separately. It isn't necessary to link the video and audio back together to use them in the sequence, but if you want to adjust them as one clip, it's a good idea to relink them.

1   Select the video of the clip.

Only the video portion of this clip becomes highlighted because you edited the video and audio separately, which broke the link between these tracks.

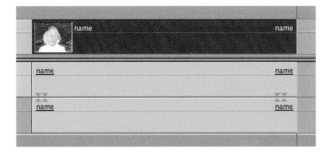

NOTE ▶ There is no linking line under the name of the video clip because it is currently not linked to the audio clip beneath it.

2   To relink the video of this clip back to the audio, Shift-click one of the audio tracks so that all tracks of this clip are highlighted.

3   Choose Modify > Link, or press Cmd-L.

The linking line now appears, and when you select just the video, all three tracks of the clip are selected.

Using the Voice Over Tool

As you edit, you may find you need to add a narration to your sequence. This is also called a *voice-over*, because you have a voice over your picture, or video clips. To record a voice-over, you can use your camera, an iSight camera, or other audio recording device, such as a USB microphone or internal mic on a laptop computer. Recording an audio track this way creates a new clip directly in the Timeline. This process uses the Voice Over tool.

1   If you are using an external mic, such as a camera, USB mic, or iSight camera, connect the device to your computer.

2   Open the *Voice Over* sequence from the Sequences bin in the Browser and play it.

The only clip in this sequence is the **back up again** clip of Jimbo surfing. It's about 27 seconds long. You will begin recording a voice-over and describe his ride when Jimbo first stands up, as though you were reporting a news story.

3   Move the playhead to where Jimbo first stands up on the surfboard and mark an In point. Then mark an Out point after he falls and gets back up again.

The voice-over clip will begin recording at the In point and continue until the Out point.

NOTE ▸ If no In or Out points are marked, the voice-over will begin recording at the playhead location and continue to the end of the sequence.

4   Choose Tools > Voice Over, or press Option-0, to open the Voice Over tool window.

If a warning appears saying, "No sound recording devices are available," make sure your microphone source is compatible, connected, and turned on.

If Final Cut Express detects a microphone source, a Voice Over tab appears in the Tool Bench window. The Voice Over information is divided into four areas: Status, Audio File, Input, and Headphones.

5   In the Audio File area, type *narrating surfer* as the name for this voice-over track.

NOTE ▶ Look at the Target information above the Name area to make sure it reflects Track A2 in the *Voice Over* sequence. The Voice Over function records only one channel of mono audio. It does not record in stereo. It also does not require that you patch or disconnect any other source tracks. It automatically targets the next available track or creates a new audio track if necessary.

6   In the Input area, select the correct source from the Source pop-up menu.

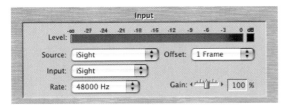

Final Cut Express will display a default Input configuration based on the audio recording device it detects or whatever device you selected. A recording offset amount and sampling rate are included as part of the default settings.

7   If you are using headphones, play the sequence and start talking to set the headphone and gain levels in the Input area.

You may want to turn off the sound for the A1 rack by clicking the A1 Audible control.

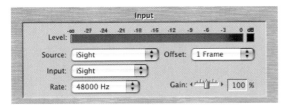

8   If you're using headphones, click the Sound Cues box. If you're not using headphones, make sure it's not selected.

Selecting the Sound Cues box will include beeps to count you in and out of the recording. They beep the first three seconds of the five-second pre-roll and countdown before recording. There is another beep at 15 seconds before the recording ends. The beeps come in again on the last five seconds of the recording to count you down and out.

TIP ▶ If you're not using headphones and you have Sound Cues selected, the beeps will be picked up and recorded as part of your clip. Deselect the Sound Cues option and instead watch the Starting countdown in the Status area to see when recording begins and ends.

9   Look for Ready to Record in the Status area, and when you're ready to begin, click the red Record button.

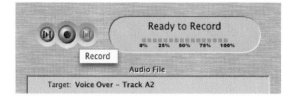

NOTE ▶ If Ready to Record does not appear, make sure your recording device is properly connected.

In the Status area, you will see a message counting you down, beginning with Starting…5, 4, and on until 1. When this message changes to Recording, you can begin your voice-over narration. The red Record button becomes a square black Stop button when you are in record mode.

10   The recording will end automatically if you let it continue to your Out point (or the end of the sequence). To stop before that point, click the square black Stop button, which toggles with the red Record button.

11   Play the clip back in the Timeline.

You can stop recording and start again by clicking the Stop button and then clicking the Record button. Each time you record a new version, a new clip is placed in another track in the Timeline and is labeled with the next-highest Voice Over number or take.

TIP ▶ You can also click the Discard button to discard an unwanted track. This step cannot be undone.

Project Tasks

1   Turn the audio of the back up again clip back on and adjust the sound level so that the sound is heard but doesn't overpower the new voice-over track.

2   Save the current project one last time by pressing Cmd-S.

3   Quit Final Cut Express by pressing Cmd-Q, or close this project and continue with the next lesson.

Lesson Review

1.   How do you turn off the digital sound of a clip as you drag through it?

2.   True or false: The Audio Meters are used to view just the audio from the Timeline.

3.   How do you toggle on the volume level lines in the Timeline?

4.   How can you view audio waveforms in Timeline clips?

5.   What must you do to select a single track of an audio/video clip?

6.   How do you drag an audio clip into the Canvas Edit Overlay?

7.   When a clip's audio and video become out of sync, how can you return them to sync?

8.   When audio tracks are captured as a stereo pair, can they ever be separated?

9.   What tool allows you to record a voice-over into your sequence?

Answers

1.   Choose View > Audio Scrubbing, or press Shift-S.

2.   False. You also view the audio levels from a clip in the Viewer.

3.   Click the Clip Overlays control in the Timeline, or press Option-W.

4.   Press Cmd-Option-W, or click the Timeline Layout Popup control and choose Show Audio Waveforms.

5. Toggle off Linked Selection in the Timeline button bar, then select the desired clip's track.

6. Drag from the Drag Hand icon in the Viewer.

7. Ctrl-click one of the sync indicators and choose Move into Sync, or Slip into Sync. You can also press Cmd-Z to return to the previous state.

8. Yes. You can select the two tracks and choose Modify > Stereo Pair to toggle that state to a mono status.

9. The Voice Over tool.

Keyboard Shortcuts

Shift-S	Toggles audio scrubbing off and on
F	Finds a match frame to a source or sequence clip
Option-4	Toggles on and off the Audio Meters
Cmd-Option-W	Displays audio waveforms in the Timeline
Option-W	Turns clip overlay lines on and off in the Timeline
Shift-L	Toggles Linked Selection on and off in the Timeline
Option-L	Toggles stereo pairs on and off
Cmd-L	Links selected tracks together
Option-0	Opens the Voice Over tool into the Tool Bench window

14

Lesson Files
Media
Time
Goals

Lesson 14 Project file

Scenic Beauty folder

This lesson takes approximately 90 minutes to complete.

Understand transitions

Apply audio and video transitions

Change transition durations

Change transition alignment

Copy and paste transitions

Use the Transition Editor

Work with different types of transitions

Preview and render transitions

Adjust edit points under a transition

Save favorite transitions

Applying Audio and Video Transitions

Now that you've explored the core principles of nonlinear editing, it's time to learn how to apply effects to your sequence. In Final Cut Express, there are two sets of effects: *transitions* and *filters*. This lesson covers transitions. To put it simply, transitions change how two clips meet in the middle. Does one clip cut to the next? Or does it dissolve over time to the next clip? Do you peel an image away to reveal the following image? Or wipe from one image to the next? Transitions are extremely versatile and can be used for many different purposes— for example, to smooth a jarring edit point, to indicate the passage of time, or to create a style in your sequence.

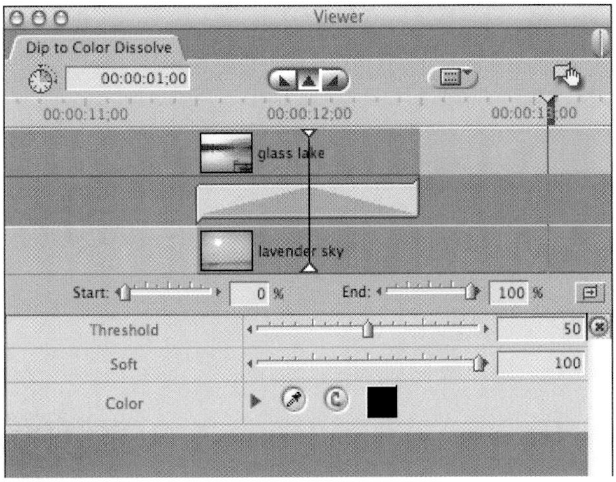

Preparing the Project

To get started in Lesson 14, you will launch Final Cut Express and then open the project for this lesson.

1   In Final Cut Express, choose File > Open, or press Cmd-O, and open the **Lesson 14 Project** file from the Lessons folder on your hard drive.

2   Close any other open projects.

Understanding Transitions

A transition is an effect that is applied to the edit point between two clips. When no transition effect is applied to the edit point, one clip will simply *cut* to the next clip. In all of the previous lessons, you have been cutting from one clip to the next in every sequence. And when you look at a film or television show, you see that cuts represent the majority of editing transitions. But you can apply a transition effect to an edit point to show time passing, cover a jump cut, change scenes, introduce a new topic, or create video art.

One type of transition used frequently in video editing is a *video dissolve*. A video dissolve gradually mixes the end of one clip with the beginning of the next clip. As the *outgoing* clip fades out, the *incoming* clip fades in. In audio, this same process is called a *cross fade*. The end of the outgoing audio clip fades out while the beginning of the incoming one fades in. This is where capturing additional clip *handles* becomes important. In order for the fade or dissolve to occur, there has to be enough material *past* the outgoing clip's Out point to continue and gradually fade out. Likewise, there has to be enough material *before* the incoming clip's In point to fade in gradually.

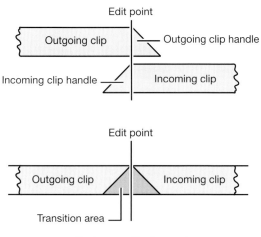

Center on edit alignment

1 Play the *Cuts* sequence in the Timeline.

   This sequence is a series of scenic beauty shots accompanied by sooth-
   ing music. Each clip cuts from one to the next, meaning that no time
   is spent transitioning between clips.

2 Play the *Dissolves* sequence in the Timeline.

   This is the same sequence as the *Cuts* sequence, but now each clip dissolves from one to the other over time. The way each clip transitions
   or dissolves to the next in this sequence creates a different look and
   feeling from the *Cuts* sequence.

Applying Audio Transitions

You have just looked at a series of video dissolve transitions. When you
create a dissolve between two audio clips, you lower the volume gradually,
or *fade down* on, the outgoing audio as you raise the volume, or *fade up,*
the incoming audio. These two fades overlap and create a cross fade. An
audio cross fade is the equivalent of a video dissolve. Both are considered
transitions and have their own folders of options. But there are fewer
options to setting up an audio cross fade, so let's start there.

Viewing the Effects Tab and Menu

The Effects tab in the Browser is where all the transitions are stored for both video and audio. But these same transitions can also be chosen from the Effects menu. Audio transitions, or cross fades, can be found in either of these locations.

1   From the Lesson 14 Project tab, open the *Audio Cross Fades* sequence and play it.

Different portions of the three-minute **vacation.aif** music track have been edited together so that each video clip has a different clip of music beneath it. Nice concept, but the music is abrupt as it cuts from clip to clip.

NOTE ▶ If you want to preserve the original *Audio Cross Fades* sequence to work with at another time, duplicate it and rename the copy *My Audio Cross Fades*.

2   Select the Effects tab in the Browser. If View as List is not selected for this tab, Ctrl-click in the Effects tab's empty gray area under the Name column and choose View as List from the shortcut menu.

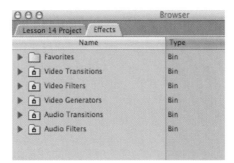

The Effects tab has six bins. All of the Final Cut Express effects are organized into these bins. There are three bins for video effects, two for audio effects, and one for favorite effects.

3   Click the disclosure triangle next to the Audio Transitions folder to view the contents.

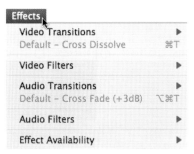

There are two audio cross fades in this bin: 0 dB and +3 dB. Notice in the Length column that each of the dissolves has a default length, or duration, of 00:00:01;00, or 1 second. The Cross Fade (+3 dB) transition is underlined because it is the default audio transition.

The two types of audio cross fades have a difference that may or may not be noticeable, depending on the material you are editing. A 0 dB cross fade has a slight dip in the audio level at the midpoint of the transition. The +3 dB cross fade is designed to produce a fade *without* having a dip in the middle of the transition.

TIP ▶ When working with audio, experiment with your options to get the best possible sound. At the end of this exercise, you can experiment with the 0 dB and +3 dB cross fades to determine which is the better choice for your sequence.

4   Choose the Effects menu.

Four of the Effects bin titles also appear here: Audio and Video Transitions and Filters.

5   From the Effects menu, choose the Audio Transitions submenu.

The two audio cross-fade options that appear here also appeared in the Effects tab in the Browser.

6   Slide the pointer off the menu and click back in the interface.

Applying a Cross Fade

Applying an audio cross fade is a good way to smooth out any rough sound you may have in your sequence. For example, you might have strong background noise in a clip (called *ambient sound*). Cutting to that clip might seem jarring. Or you could be working with different sources of music in a sequence but don't want to cut from one to the other. In both cases, creating a cross fade between two audio sources can be an effective solution.

Audio cross fades are applied to the edit point between two adjacent audio clips. If an audio clip has two tracks that are a stereo pair, applying a cross fade to one track will automatically apply it to the other track.

1   In the Timeline, park the playhead before the edit point between the first two clips, **bird fly by** and **boat dusk**. Press Option-+ to zoom in to that area of the sequence.

2   On the A1 track, click the edit point between these first two clips.

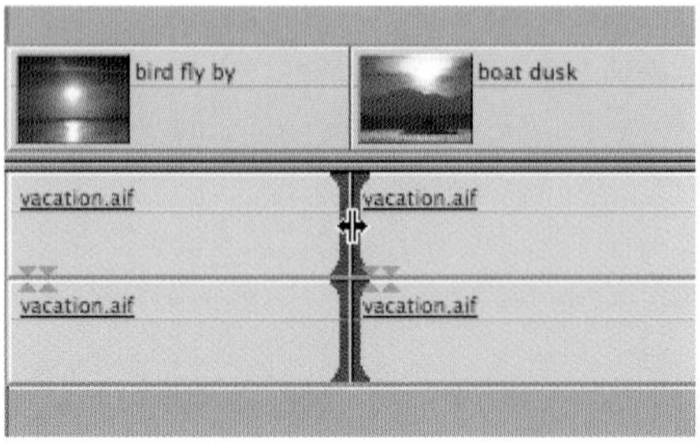

These two tracks are a stereo pair, so the edit points in both tracks become highlighted.

3   From the Effects menu, choose Audio Transitions > Cross Fade (0 dB).

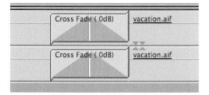

A transition icon appears over the edit point of both clips in the stereo pair. You may need to zoom into this area to see all the text on the Cross Fade icon.

4   Play this portion of the sequence to hear the cross fade.

The abrupt cut has been smoothed out considerably by the audio cross fade.

> **TIP** ▶ Sometimes it's easier to concentrate on just the sound if you're not seeing the video cutting abruptly in the V1 track. Try disabling the V1 track for these exercises by clicking the Visible control in the Timeline track area.

When you apply a cross fade from the Effects tab in the Browser, you don't have to select the edit point first. You can simply drag and drop it onto the edit point in the Timeline.

5   From the Effects tab in the Browser, drag the Cross Fade (+3 dB) icon onto the audio edit point between the second and third **vacation.aif** clips, under the **boat dusk** and **distant sunset** video clips, and release it. Play this transition.

6 Apply the same transition from the Effects tab to the audio edit point between **distant sunset** and **blue surf**.

> **TIP** If you are zoomed in to the Timeline, a convenient way of moving the sequence is to press H for the Hand tool and drag the sequence left until you see the next edit point. Don't forget to press A to return to the default Selection tool.

Project Tasks

1 Add the +3 dB audio cross fade to the remaining audio edit points.

2 Press Shift-Z to display the entire sequence in the Timeline, and play the sequence.

3 Press Cmd-S to save these changes to your project.

Changing Transition Durations

Once you have reviewed a transition, you might decide the transition rate or duration needs to be longer or shorter. The cross-fade transition you applied in the previous exercise had a default transition rate of one second. But you can give a cross fade whatever duration you want, as long as there is enough clip material or handles to cover it.

1 In the current sequence, double-click the right side of the second cross fade.

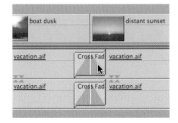

TIP ▶ Always click one side or the other of a cross fade. If you click in the middle, the edit point itself will be selected.

Duration
Duration: 00:00:01;00
Cancel   OK

A small transition Duration dialog appears with the default of 1 second. This duration is already highlighted, so you can begin typing a new duration without first clicking in the box.

2   Enter *2.* (2 period), and press Tab or Return to enter that amount. Then click OK to accept the duration change.

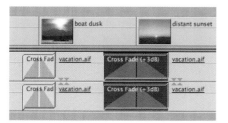

The second transition icon is twice as wide as the original one, indicating the longer transition duration. By comparison, the first cross fade in the sequence has a one-second transition.

3   Play the transition.

Another way to change the cross-fade transition duration is using a shortcut menu.

4   Ctrl-click one side of the first audio Cross Fade icon.

A shortcut menu containing several transition options appears.

5   Choose Duration.

The same Duration dialog appears for you to enter a new duration.

6   Enter *75* (frames) and press Return, and then click OK. Play the transition.

You can enter a duration by typing the amount in seconds using a period or zeros, or you can enter the total number of frames. For example, if your video is 30 frames per second, typing 75 would give you a 2.5-second transition.

There is a third way to change transition durations. This approach drags the edge of the transition, just as you drag the edge of a clip to lengthen or shorten it.

7   In the third cross fade, move the pointer over one of the cross-fade edges.

The pointer changes to a left-right resize arrow.

8   Drag the left or right edge out to extend the length of the duration
    to 1:20.

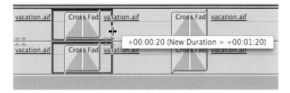

    The pop-up information box appears with the amount of the change
    and the new total transition duration.

9   Play the transition.

Copying and Pasting Transitions

If you have applied a transition to an edit point and like it enough to use it
elsewhere, you can copy and paste it to any other edit point in the sequence.
Or you can move it from one edit point to another.

1   Delete each cross fade in this sequence *except the second*. You can
    do this one at a time by selecting a cross fade and pressing Delete.
    Or you can Cmd-click each one until they are all selected and then
    press Delete.

2   Drag the edge of the remaining transition icon so that the cross fade
    has a 20-frame duration.

    TIP ▶ When dragging a transition to reduce its duration, you may
    want to turn snapping off temporarily (keyboard shortcut, N) to give
    you greater control. You can do this as you drag.

3   Select this transition, and press Cmd-C to copy it.

    You can also choose Edit > Copy, or Ctrl-click the transition and
    choose Copy from the shortcut menu.

4   Ctrl-click the next transition and choose Paste from the shortcut menu.

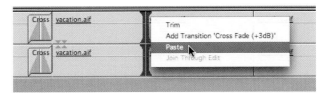

5   This time, select the next edit point and press Cmd-V to paste the transition. You can also choose Edit > Paste.

NOTE ▶ You can continue to paste the originally copied transition because it is held in the computer Clipboard until you copy something else.

6   Paste this transition to the remaining edit points in this sequence, and play the sequence.

Project Tasks

1   Change the first audio transition to one second.

2   Delete the other audio transitions in the sequence.

3   Copy the first transition and paste it to all the other edit points.

4   Close the current *Audio Cross Fades* sequence.

5   Press Cmd-S to save your project.

Applying Video Transitions

Video transitions are applied and adjusted in the same way as audio transitions. The only difference is that you are blending visual information between the outgoing clip and the incoming clip. Also, there are just two audio transitions, but there are numerous video transitions, organized into 10 different bins.

Some Final Cut Express transitions are real-time (RT) effects, meaning they can be played at normal play speed after you apply them. But some transitions must first be rendered to view in real time. As you work with video transitions in this lesson, you will learn how to render your transitions so that they can be screened in real time.

1   In the Browser, click the Lesson 14 Project tab and display the contents of the Sequences bin. Duplicate the *Cuts* sequence and name the duplicate *My Video Dissolves*. Open the new sequence and play it.

Duplicating the *Cuts* sequence will allow you to add transitions to the duplicate sequence and still have a version without transitions to use again later in the lesson.

2   In the Browser, click the Effects tab and close any open bins so that you see only the six primary Effects bins.

3   Display the contents of the Video Transitions bin.

▼ 🔒 Video Transitions	Bin
▶ 🔒 3D Simulation	Bin
▶ 🔒 Dissolve	Bin
▶ 🔒 Iris	Bin
▶ 🔒 Map	Bin
▶ 🔒 Page Peel	Bin
▶ 🔒 QuickTime	Bin
▶ 🔒 Slide	Bin
▶ 🔒 Stretch	Bin
▶ 🔒 Wipe	Bin

There are nine different types of video transitions organized into bins.

4   Display the contents of the Dissolve bin.

▼ 🔒 Dissolve	Bin	
🔲 Additive Dissolve	Video Transition	00:00:01;00
🔲 Cross Dissolve	Video Transition	00:00:01;00
🔲 Dip to Color Dissolve	Video Transition	00:00:01;00
🔲 Dither Dissolve	Video Transition	00:00:01;00
🔲 Fade In Fade Out Dissolve	Video Transition	00:00:01;00
🔲 Non–Additive Dissolve	Video Transition	00:00:01;00
🔲 Ripple Dissolve	Video Transition	00:00:01;00

There are seven different video dissolve transitions. The one that most resembles the audio cross fade is the Cross Dissolve. The Cross Dissolve is underlined, meaning it is the default video transition. It is also in boldface. When a transition appears in boldface, it can be played in real time with the current configuration.

Applying Video Dissolves

The most popular type of video transition is the *cross dissolve.* A cross dissolve is like a cross fade in that it blends out or dissolves away from the first clip as it blends or dissolves into the second clip. The cross dissolve is the default video transition in Final Cut Express. As with audio transitions, you choose the type of video transition in either the Effects tab or Effects menu. But there are additional ways you can add a transition.

1 Select the edit point between the **bird fly by** and **boat dusk** clips.

2 Choose Effects > Video Transitions > Dissolve > Cross Dissolve, and play the dissolve.

   You may see a colored *render bar* appear in the ruler area above the transition in the Timeline. See the "Rendering Transitions" section later in this chapter for a more in-depth discussion.

   NOTE ▶ Remember, boldface effects can play in real time and do not need rendering. If these effects do not appear in boldface and a colored render bar appears in the Timeline after the effect has been applied, click the Real Time pop-up menu in the Timeline and choose Unlimited RT.

Another way to add a transition is from the shortcut menu that
appears when you Ctrl-click an edit point.

3   Ctrl-click the second edit point, between the **boat dusk** and **distant
    sunset** clips, and choose Add Transition 'Cross Dissolve.' Play through
    the dissolve.

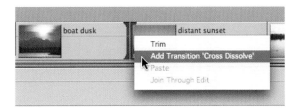

You can also use a keyboard shortcut, which adds the default transition to the edit point.

4   Select the third edit point, or move the playhead directly over it, and
    press Cmd-T to add the default transition.

   TIP ▶ To add the default cross fade to an audio edit point, select
   the edit point, or move the playhead directly over it, and press
   Option-Cmd-T.

    You can also drag and drop a video transition as you did the audio
    cross fades.

5 From the Dissolve bin in the Effects tab, drag the Cross Dissolve icon to the fourth edit point, between **glass lake** and **lavender sky**, and release the mouse.

As you move the transition over an edit point, make sure the transition is lined up over the edit point's center. It can be lined up on the left to end on the transition point or on the right to begin there. This is called *transition alignment* and is used when a clip doesn't have enough handle material to cover the full length of a centered transition.

TIP To change the transition alignment, Ctrl-click the transition and choose Transition Alignment from the shortcut menu.

6 To make the first clip in the sequence fade in from black, drag the Cross Dissolve icon from the Effects tab to the head of the clip and then release the mouse.

When there is only one clip involved in the edit point, the cross dissolve creates a fade-in from black to that clip.

TIP ▸ If you want to apply this type of fade-in on a clip somewhere within the sequence, hold down the Command key as you drag the Cross Dissolve icon to the edit point.

You can also edit a new clip to the Timeline and add a transition at the same time. This is done by dragging a clip to one of the Edit Overlay sections in the Canvas.

7   Place the playhead at the end of the sequence to edit a new clip.

8   Open the **waterfall pond** clip in the Viewer. Drag it to the Canvas and drop it on the Overwrite with Transition section of the Edit Overlay.

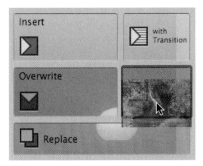

In the Timeline, an edit is made with a dissolve leading into it, all in one step. You can also insert an edit and add a transition at the same time.

NOTE ▸ When working with your own video, if a dissolve does not attach to an edit point, make sure there is enough handle material on both sides of the clips.

Adjusting and Copying Video Transitions

You can copy video dissolves and then paste them to other edit points, just as you did audio cross fades.

1   Ctrl-click the Cross Dissolve icon between the **boat dusk** and **distant sunset** clips.

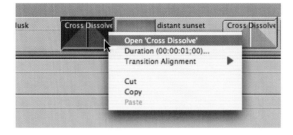

The menu contains many of the same options that are in the audio transitions shortcut menu.

2   Choose Duration.

A Duration dialog appears, just as it did for audio transitions.

3   Enter a new duration of 2 seconds and click OK.

NOTE ▶ If there is not enough clip handle to cover the length of the transition, the longest duration that the clip *can* accommodate will be entered.

Once a transition has been placed on an edit point, it can be replaced with a different transition from either the Effects menu or Effects tab.

4   Select the next Cross Dissolve in the sequence between **distant sunset** and **glass lake**. To replace this transition, choose Effects > Video Transitions > Dissolve > Dither Dissolve.

5   In the Effects tab in the Browser, make sure you can see all the Dissolve transitions. Drag the Dip to Color transition to the edit point between **glass lake** and **lavender sky**, release it over the current transition, then play the new transition.

The new transition replaces the old one without having to delete it first. You will learn how to make changes to this transition in the following exercise.

TIP ▶ Dip to Color is a good transition to use when you want to create the effect of a camera flashing between two clips.

Project Tasks

If you need to make changes to the actual edit point between two clips, you can use some of the editing tools even while a transition is present.

1   Move the pointer to the center of a Cross Dissolve transition.

The pointer temporarily changes to the Roll Edit tool so that you can adjust the edit point.

2   Drag left and right to roll the edit point between the two clips.

As you drag, the transition moves along with the edit point.

3   Use the Ripple tool (RR) to change the length of the glass lake clip.

4   Slip the boat dusk clip so that the boat begins out of frame on the right.

5   Slide the blue surf clip left one second.

6   Select A to return your pointer to the default Selection tool.

7   Press Cmd-S to save your project.

Using the Transition Editor

The transitions you've worked with so far have been relatively simple and have only required adjusting durations or possibly changing the transition alignment. But there are several video transitions that are much more complex and have several attributes that can be adjusted. To make these adjustments, you will work with the Transition Editor in the Viewer window. You can open the Transition Editor from the transition's shortcut menu or by double-clicking the transition in the Timeline.

1   Ctrl-click on one side of the transition between the **distant sunset** and **glass lake** clips. Choose Open 'Dither Dissolve' from the shortcut menu.

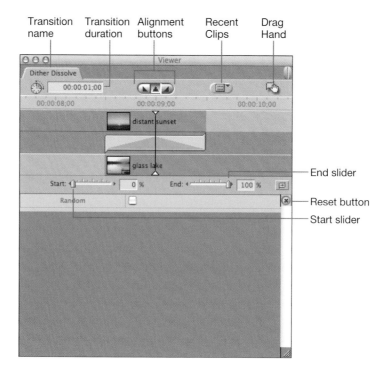

The Transition Editor opens as a tab in the Viewer with a graphic display of the current transition. There are some familiar properties you will recognize from the Video or Audio tab, such as the Duration field for the transition length, a Recent Clips pop-up menu, and a Drag Hand icon for dragging transitions to other edit points. There is also a set of alignment buttons above the graphic display. Beneath the graphic are Start and End sliders. These determine whether the transition begins at 0% and ends at 100%, which is the default, or whether you want to have the transition begin or end as a mixture of the two sources.

2   To see the graphical layout of the transition change, click each of the alignment buttons.

In the Viewer, the graphic changes to reflect the selected alignment. In the Timeline, the transition reflects whatever changes you make in the Viewer.

TIP ▶ Use the Start on Edit alignment when the incoming clip doesn't have enough handle material prior to the In point to dissolve into the clip. This will start the dissolve on the In point of the incoming clip. Likewise, use End on Edit when the outgoing clip doesn't have enough handle material to transition past the Out point.

3   Make sure the Center on Edit alignment is selected, and enter 15 frames as the new transition duration. Press Tab or Return to enter this change.

The width of the transition icon changes in the Timeline.

Another way to open the Transition Editor is to simply double-click a transition in the Timeline.

4   Double-click the Dip to Color transition between the **glass lake** and **lavender sky** clips in the sequence. Remember to double-click the side of the transition. Double-clicking the edit point itself would open the Trim Edit window. (To work with the Trim Edit window, refer to the "Advanced Trimming" PDF on the DVD that comes with this book.)

NOTE ► Double-clicking an audio transition opens a Duration dialog. Double-clicking a video transition opens the Transition Editor.

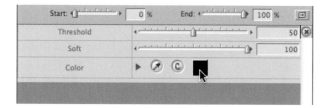

Notice that additional color information appears below the Start and End sliders.

5   To change the color the images dip to, click the Color box.

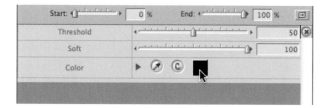

A Colors window opens with five different color palette layouts for choosing a color. Each layout appears as an icon at the top of the window. Click each icon to familiarize yourself with the various color palette layouts.

6   Click the Crayons icon and then click the whitish crayon in the lower-right corner. The word *Snow* will appear above the crayons. Click OK and play the transition.

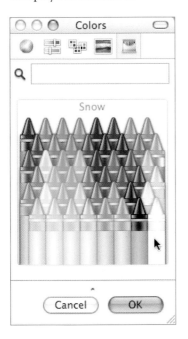

7   Now change the duration of this transition to 5 frames.

You can also make editing changes in the Transition Editor.

8   In the Transition Editor, move your pointer over the transition icon in the graphic. When the pointer changes to a Roll tool, drag left or right.

In the Canvas, a two-up display shows the outgoing clip's new Out point and the incoming clip's new In point.

9   Drag the Drag Hand icon (which looks like a hand on a transition icon) from the upper-right corner of the Transition Editor to the edit point between **lavender sky** and **blue surf**.

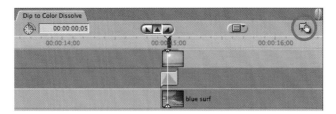

The Dip to Color transition with the properties you just set is applied to the new edit point.

Working with Wipe Transitions

Sometimes a transition is a blending process, as in dissolves and cross fades, and sometimes it's a replacement process, in which part of the outgoing clip is replaced by the incoming clip through the form of a geometric shape, such as a circle, box, or line. These are called *wipe transitions* and may be familiar to you because they have been used for many years in video and film editing.

Applying Wipe Transitions

You apply a wipe transition the same way you apply a dissolve or a cross fade. There are many fun and useful wipe transitions. The following steps will help you to become familiar with a few.

1   In the Browser, duplicate the *Cuts* sequence and rename it *My Sunset Wipes.* Open the sequence and play it.

2   In the Effects tab in the Browser, collapse the Dissolve bin and display the contents of the Wipe bin. Scroll down to see the complete contents of this bin.

▼ 🔒 Wipe	Bin	
🔲 Band Wipe	Video Transition	00:00:01:00
🔲 Center Wipe	Video Transition	00:00:01:00
🔲 Checker Wipe	Video Transition	00:00:01:00
🔲 Checkerboard Wipe	Video Transition	00:00:01:00
🔲 Clock Wipe	Video Transition	00:00:01:00
🔲 Edge Wipe	Video Transition	00:00:01:00
🔲 Gradient Wipe	Video Transition	00:00:01:00
🔲 Inset Wipe	Video Transition	00:00:01:00
🔲 Jaws Wipe	Video Transition	00:00:01:00
🔲 Random Edge Wipe	Video Transition	00:00:01:00
🔲 V Wipe	Video Transition	00:00:01:00
🔲 Venetian Blind Wipe	Video Transition	00:00:01:00
🔲 Wrap Wipe	Video Transition	00:00:01:00
🔲 Zig-Zag Wipe	Video Transition	00:00:01:00

Remember, all the wipes you see in boldface in your own Wipe bin can play in real time on your computer.

3   Look in the Length column in the Browser.

Each wipe transition has a default duration of one second. This is true for all cross fades and cross dissolves as well.

4   Drag the Checker Wipe icon from the Wipe bin to the edit point between the first two clips, **bird fly by** and **boat dusk**, and play the transition.

NOTE ▶ Depending on the processing speed of your computer, and the current settings in the RT pop-up menu, you may see a colored render bar appear above this transition. You will learn to preview and render effects in the "Rendering Transitions" section of this lesson.

5   Drag the Band Wipe to the edit point between the **boat dusk** and **distant sunset** clips in the Timeline, and play it.

As with video dissolves, the name of the specific wipe appears on the transition icon in the Timeline.

6   Drag the Jaws Wipe to the next transition point, between the **distant sunset** and **glass lake** clips.

Adjusting Wipes in the Transition Editor

Like dissolves, wipe transitions can also be adjusted in the Transition Editor. In fact, several additional options are available because there are simply more properties that can be changed in a wipe than in a dissolve.

1   Double-click the Jaws Wipe transition icon in the Timeline.

> **NOTE** ▶ Wipe settings are specific to a particular wipe. But if you look at this and other wipe transitions in the Viewer, you will find that most of the settings are self-explanatory.

2   In the Timeline, park the playhead in the middle of the wipe.

> **TIP** ▶ Always park your playhead on the clip or transition you are adjusting so that you can see a visual display of the adjustment in the Canvas.

3   Drag the Angle pointer to about 8 o'clock, or enter *–130* in the number box and press Return.

4   Drag the Tooth slider to the far right to create 10 teeth.

5   Enter a Sharpness number of *25* and press Return.

> **NOTE** ▶ It doesn't matter whether you enter a number or move the slider. One always affects the other.

6 Drag the Border slider to 11 or enter *11* in the number field, and press Return.

> **TIP** Click the tiny triangles at the end of each slider to change the numerical value of an effect by single increments.

7 Click the black Color box to open the Color window. Choose the Crayons icon at the top of the window, click the brightest yellow color (named Lemon) for the wipe border, and click OK or press Return.

You can also pick a color for the border from an image. Choosing a color from an image involved in the transition can be very effective.

8 Click the Select Color tool (eyedropper) in the Color parameter. In the Canvas, click the dark peach color in the **glass lake** clip.

> **TIP** To search or preview different border colors, select the eyedropper and click and drag around the Canvas image area without releasing the mouse. The border will reflect whatever color the eyedropper picks up. When you see the color you want, release the mouse.

9 Reverse the direction of this wipe by clicking the tiny Reverse Transition button to the right of the End slider.

10 To reset the Jaws Wipe parameters to their original default settings, click the Reset button (which has a red X) beneath the Reverse Transition button.

Rendering Transitions

Rendering a transition is the process of taking just the transition area between two clips and making a completely separate clip out of it. That clip is stored in your Render Files folder on your scratch disk and played back in your sequence as a separate but invisible clip—meaning that it does not appear in the Browser along with your master clips, but it does exist as a separate media file.

1 Press Shift-Q to open the System Settings dialog.

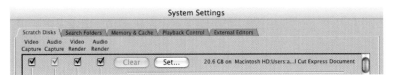

In the Scratch Disks tab, the default setup is for all your render files to be saved to the same location as your audio and video clips, although you can change the destination to a different scratch disk if you prefer.

2 Click Cancel to close the System Settings dialog without changes.

If you are working on a computer that supports real-time effects, you will see a thin green line in the ruler area of the Timeline when you add a cross dissolve to an edit point. If your computer doesn't support real-time effects, you will see a thin red line in the same position. Remember, all transitions that can play in real time on your computer appear in bold type either in the Effects tab or Effects menu.

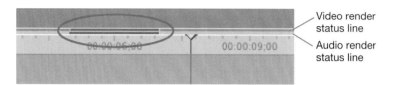

If you look closely at the render line above the clip, you will see that it is one of two thin lines. The upper line represents video, and the lower line, audio. If the render bar appears on the upper line, it is a message about the render status of the transition or effect applied to the video of that clip. If it appears on the lower line, it pertains to the audio. There are different colored lines that might appear in this render status area:

▶   Dark gray   No rendering is required.

▶   Green   Transition is a real-time effect and does not need rendering.

▶   Yellow   Transition can play in real time but may approximate certain attributes.

▶   Orange   Transition will play in real time if Unlimited RT effects is selected in the Timeline RT pop-up menu, but may drop frames.

▶   Red   Transition needs to be rendered to play in real time.

▶   Blue   Transition or effect has been rendered.

These colored render status lines also appear in the Sequence > Render Selection submenu. Selecting one of the render status options in this submenu will turn on rendering for that render level.

> **TIP** You can hover your mouse pointer over the render status lines for more information about a clip's playback performance.

Previewing Transitions

Rendering a transition makes a separate clip out of just the transition portion of your sequence. But before you begin taking up hard-drive space with lots of render files, let's explore some ways to preview your transitions. Taking a moment to preview your clips before rendering them can help you manage your hard-drive space as you edit.

If you have real-time capability on your computer, you will not see a red render line from any of the Cross Dissolve transitions you have applied to the current sequence. In fact, in the Unlimited RT mode, most transitions can play in real time, even if they have to drop a few frames to do it. For this exercise, you'll change the RT status to Safe RT so you can experiment with previewing and rendering effects.

1   In the Timeline, click the RT pop-up menu and choose Safe RT.

2   Add the Jaws Wipe to the edit point between the **glass lake** and **lavender sky** clips, and play the transition.

NOTE ▸ Adding a transition where one already occurs simply replaces the original transition.

The name of the transition appears on the transition icon in the Timeline. In the Safe RT mode, this is not a real-time transition effect, therefore you should see a red render bar in the ruler area of the Timeline above the transition.

In the Canvas, you no longer see the image. Instead, *Unrendered* appears in the image area.

3   Place the playhead a few seconds before the Jaws Wipe in the sequence.

4   To preview this transition, press Option-P. You can also select this option by choosing Mark > Play > Every Frame, or by pressing Option-\ (backslash).

The clip plays at normal play speed until the playhead reaches the transition. At that point, the play speed slows down to process every frame of the transition, then picks up again when it has passed the transition area.

TIP ▶ Option-P is a great way to check the placement of a video transition. However, it may not be as helpful if you are testing for timing. Also, it does not play back audio.

5 Double-click the transition to open it in the Transition Editor. Change the parameters however you'd like and preview the transtion again by pressing Option-P.

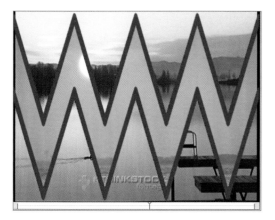

6 Drag the playhead manually through the transition area. This is some-what like scrubbing an effect.

> **TIP** ▶ Dragging through a transition is a good way to identify how specific frames of the two clips are blending together, or even how they will look at the midpoint of the transition.

7 Park the playhead just before the transition. Press the right arrow key to step through the transition frame by frame.

This allows you to see every frame of the transition.

Rendering Options

Once you have made the desired changes to a transition and it looks good in preview, you can render the transition to make a permanent file of the transition so that it will play in real time. You have several render options. The two basic options utilize the shortcuts Cmd-R to render a selected item or items, and Option-R to render everything in the sequence.

1   To render the Jaws Wipe transition, select it and choose Sequence > Render Selection. Make sure the render level of your transition is selected in the Render Selection submenu. Then choose Sequence > Render Selection > Both, or press Cmd-R.

> **NOTE ▶** If a transition has already been rendered, changing its duration or any other aspect will require it to be rendered again.

As the effect is being rendered, a dialog containing a progress bar appears.

In the Timeline, a dark blue render bar indicates the effect has been rendered.

2   To render all unrendered transitions in the sequence, choose Sequence > Render All > Both, or press Option-R.

NOTE ▶ The more complex the transition, the longer it takes to pre-view and render.

Applying Other Video Transitions

Dissolves and wipes are just two of the different types of transitions you can apply to clips in your sequence. But there are eight other Video Transition bins to explore. Some of the transitions, such as Iris, act like a wipe and replace one clip's material with another's through a specific pattern. Others, such as 3D Simulation transitions, Page Peel, Slide, and Stretch, make changes to a clip's size and shape. Let's experiment with a few.

1   Duplicate the *Cuts* sequence and name the duplicate *My Sunset Fun.* Open the sequence and play it. In the Timeline, click the RT pop-up menu and choose Unlimited RT to view more real-time effects.

2   In the Browser Effects tab, collapse the Wipe bin and display the con-tents of the Page Peel bin.

TIP ▶ Collapse the current transition bin before opening the next so you can access other transition bins more easily.

3 Drag the Page Peel transition icon to the second edit point, between the **boat dusk** and **distant sunset** clips. Play this effect.

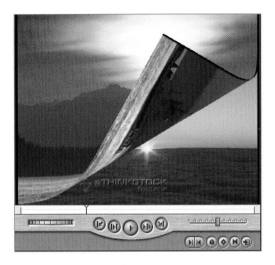

4 Click the next edit point, between the **distant sunset** and **glass lake** clips, and this time choose Effects > Video Transitions > 3D Simulation > Cube Spin. Play this effect, or preview it by pressing Option-P.

Like cross dissolves, all other transitions can be applied by dragging an icon from the Effects tab directly to an edit point, or by selecting the edit point and choosing a transition option from the Effects menu.

5   From the Video Transitions > QuickTime bin in the Effects tab, drag the Explode transition to the next edit point, between the **glass lake** and **lavender sky** clips, and play or preview it.

6   From the Slide bin, drag the Multi Spin Slide icon to the next edit point, between the **lavender sky** and **blue surf** clips, and preview it.

Saving a Favorite Transition

The Effects tab in the Browser contains a bin called Favorites. This is where you save your favorite transitions. But what constitutes a favorite transition? If your favorite transition is a one-second cross dissolve, there's no point in making it a favorite because that's its default configuration. Use the Favorites bin for transitions you have tweaked to your liking and think you would like to use again at a later time. Once saved, these transitions can be applied to any sequence in any open project.

1   In the Browser Effects tab, display the contents of the Favorites bin.

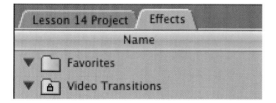

At this point, there are probably no favorite effects stored here, so nothing will be revealed.

2   Double-click the second transition in the current sequence, the Cube Spin, to open it in the Transition Editor. Park the playhead over this transition in the Timeline.

3   In the Duration field, enter *90* frames, or 3 seconds (*3.*), and press Return.

In the Timeline, the Cube Spin icon has stretched to cover a three-second duration.

4   In the Transition Editor, click the Spin Direction pop-up menu and choose Down. Leave the View on Outside.

5   Change the Border setting to 10, and give the border the golden color of the setting sun in the **distant sunset** (lower) clip.

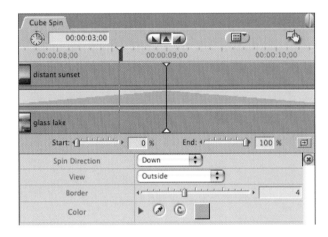

6   To save this transition with its new parameters, drag the Drag Hand icon in the upper-right corner of the Transition Editor window to the Favorites bin. When the bin becomes selected, release the mouse.

The new Cube Spin transition is added to the Favorites bin. The Length column displays the three-second length you entered. You can apply it as you would any other transition.

7   Drag the Browser scroll bar right until you see the Comment 1 col-
    umn. If necessary, move this column to follow the Length column.
    Click in the Comment 1 line of the new Cube Spin favorite transition
    to activate the text field, and enter *sunset yellow*. Press Return.

> **TIP** ▶ You can also drag a transition directly from the sequence
> into the Favorites bin. That transition, along with all its properties,
> is saved.

Project Tasks

The more familiar you are with the different transitions and their parameters, the better choices you can make during the editing process. Take a
minute to test the different transitions to see what each can do.

1   Duplicate the *Cuts* sequence and rename it *Transitions Project*.

2   Apply one transition from each transition bin not covered in this
    lesson to acquaint you with that type of transition.

3   Open each transition in the Transition Editor and edit at least one of
    its parameters.

4   Save three of your favorite transitions as practice. If you don't like
    one, delete it by selecting it and pressing Delete.

5   Press Cmd-S to save your project.

6   Quit Final Cut Express by pressing Cmd-Q, or close this project and
    continue with the next lesson.

Advanced Editing Techniques

Many editing projects can be completed with basic editing techniques and some transition effects, like those you have learned so far. However, you can also apply a second type of effect called filters. Whereas a transition is applied to an edit point between two clips, a filter is applied to the entire body of a clip. Filters can be used to change the look of an image or give it style, such as adding a border around the image, mirroring it, or replicating it (as in the following image). Filters can also be used to correct the color of an image or to create a "composite" of multiple images through the use of a color screen or matte.

You can also adjust the speed of a clip and create a "freeze frame" in Final Cut Express. And you can change a clip's motion parameters, which allow you to change the size or position of an image in the screen. As you change the size of an image, you can combine several images together to create a multilayered look (as in the following image), which you may have seen in some television shows and commercials.

And finally, some sequences may require additional audio tracks to add
music or sound effects underneath the primary audio track in your
sequence. Once you edit the audio tracks into your sequence, you can mix
those tracks together.

> **MORE INFO** ▸ The DVD that comes with this book includes additional lessons where you can learn how to apply filters, change motion parameters, and work with multiple video and audio tracks. The lesson project files and media are already in the FCE 4 Book Files folder on your hard drive.

Lesson Review

1. What are the two ways you can apply a transition?
2. Is there a difference between how you apply an audio transition versus a video transition?
3. What set of keyboard shortcuts are used to copy and paste a transition?
4. How do you access the Transition Editor?
5. In what ways can you change the duration of a video transition?
6. Are wipe transitions applied differently than dissolves?
7. In the Timeline Real Time pop-up menu, which setting allows you to work with the most real-time effects: Unlimited RT or Safe RT?
8. When a transition can't play back in real time, how can you preview it?
9. How do you render a single effect?
10. How do you save a transition as a favorite?

Answers

1. From the Browser Effects tab, drag a transition directly to an edit point, or select an edit point and choose a transition from the Effects menu.
2. No. You apply audio and video transitions the same way.
3. Cmd-C copies a selected transition, and Cmd-V pastes the transition to the selected edit point.
4. Double-click one side or the other of the transition icon.

5. You can drag the edge of a transition icon, right-click the transition and choose Duration from the shortcut menu, or change the duration in the Transition Editor.

6. No. Wipes are applied the same way as dissolves. They do however have more parameters that can be adjusted.

7. Unlimited RT.

8. To preview the effect, press Option-P, choose Mark > Play > Every Frame, or press Option-\ (backslash).

9. Select the transition and choose Sequence > Render Selection, or press Cmd-R.

10. Drag the transition from the Transition Editor, or from the Timeline, into the Favorites bin in the Effects tab.

Keyboard Shortcuts

Cmd-T	Applies the default transition
Option-P	Previews a transition (Play Every Frame command)
Cmd-R	Renders a transition
Option-R	Renders all transitions
Cmd-C	Copies a selected transition
Cmd-V	Pastes a copied transition

15

Lesson Files	Lesson 15 Project file
Media	Surfing folder
Time	This lesson takes approximately 60 minutes to complete.
Goals	Understand and work with video generators
	Add Bars and Tone to a sequence
	Add titles to a sequence
	Create lower thirds
	Work with the Controls tab
	Superimpose a title
	Add a scrolling text credit roll

Adding Titles and Other Items

No matter how simple or complex a sequence is, adding a title can give it that personal touch. But creating titles in Final Cut Express isn't just about putting the show's name at the beginning of the sequence. It's about giving your visuals voice, identifying who is talking, creating an impressive roll of credits as in a feature film, and even adding to your sequence other items, such as color backgrounds and shapes, that are generated from within the program.

Preparing the Project

As a change of pace, in this lesson you will launch Final Cut Express by opening the project file for this lesson.

1 Navigate to the Lessons folder and double-click the **Lesson 15 Project** file.

2 Play the *15-Finished* sequence to see what you will create in this lesson.

> **NOTE ▶** If you see red render bars in this sequence, click the RT pop-up menu in the Timeline and choose Unlimited RT. To improve the performance further, open the User Preferences and deselect "Report dropped frames during playback."

This is the completed sequence from the lessons "Working with Multiple Tracks" and "Creating Motion Effects" on the book's DVD. Motion parameters were changed on the **dad about jimbo** clips to resize and reposition them. By placing those clips on the V2 track, you can see the Jimbo surfing clips beneath them on the V1 track. Then the motion was animated to bring the clip on and off the screen. To recreate this sequence, follow the steps in those lessons.

In this lesson, you will learn how to add titles and other items to a sequence.

3 Play the *15-Starting* sequence to see where you will be starting out in this lesson.

The surfing clips in this sequence do not appear in the Browser, but they link back to the Media > Surfing clips used throughout the book.

4 If you want to preserve the starting sequence for use at another time, duplicate the *15-Starting* sequence in the Browser and name it *My Titles*.

5 To make sure you have plenty of Timeline room, choose Window > Arrange > Standard, or press Ctrl-U.

Working with Video Generators

So far, you have been working with footage that was shot with a camera and captured as clips to edit. But now you will work with different types of clips that are generated from within Final Cut Express. Clips that are made within the program are referred to as *generator* clips. There are different types of video generators, each generating a different type of clip, such as text or a color background or matte. Some generator clips might stand alone; others might be used in conjunction with the video clips you captured. None of the generator clips have audio, except for Bars and Tone and Slug, which have special purposes explained later in the lesson.

Selecting Video Generators

Like filters and transitions, video generators can be selected from two different places: one is the Effects tab in the Browser; the other is a pop-up menu in the Viewer.

1   Find the Generator pop-up menu button in the lower-right corner of the Viewer. It is to the right of the Recent Clips pop-up menu button.

2   Click the Generator pop-up menu button to see the list of options.

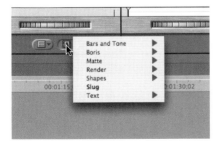

The video generators appear as a list with submenu arrows next to those generators that have additional options.

3 Slide down to Text and look at its submenu options, but don't choose any just yet. Move the mouse away from the pop-up menu.

4 Now click the Effects tab in the Browser.

5 Display the contents of the Video Generators bin.

These are the same options as in the Generator pop-up menu in the Viewer. But here, submenu items are organized by bin, and individual items are represented by clip icons. There are two new clip icons used for generated items.

Using a Color Reference

When you walk into an electronics store and look at television monitors, it is sometimes difficult to find two monitors that have the same color qualities. In fact, the color in each seems to be set a little differently. In the video world and in television broadcasting, a color reference is used to ensure that the edited piece or sequence will look exactly as intended regardless of what monitor is used. This color reference also has a tone attached as a sound reference.

If you are going to be the only person looking at your video, you can easily adjust your own television set to make your edited piece look the way you want. You can add more color or brightness, or adjust the color hue. But if your final tape will be viewed on someone else's monitor, or even by a professional, you will want to add the color and sound reference at the beginning of your sequence. This will allow outside viewers to set up their own television monitors appropriately before viewing your sequence.

This color/sound reference is called *Bars and Tone*, sometimes *colored bars and tone*, or just *color bars*, and is created as a generated item within Final Cut Express. If you are going to use color bars, they are usually the first thing seen on a tape before your sequence plays. Therefore, they would be the first edit in your sequence.

1   In the Browser Effects tab, click the disclosure triangle for Bars and Tone and select the **Bars and Tone (NTSC)** clip.

TIP ▶ As you edit Bars and Tone to your own sequences, choose whichever standard or format matches your source material and project settings. Since the media for this exercise was captured in NTSC, that is the correct option for this step.

2   Press Return to open the selected clip into the Viewer, or double-click its clip icon, just as you would with a normal video clip.

The image in the Viewer is made up of a group of individually colored bars that set a reference for video color, including saturation (amount of color), hue, luminance (brightness), and black.

3   Play the **Bars and Tone** clip in the Viewer.

The color bars do not change. Neither does the constant −12 dB tone. You use this constant tone as a reference to set proper monitor or recording levels.

4   Click the Viewer Stereo (a1a2) tab to see the volume level.

5   Although the clip opened with a marked duration of 10 seconds, enter 30 seconds (type *3000* or *30.*) in the Duration field, and press Tab or Return.

6   In the Timeline, park the playhead at the head of the sequence and make sure the source tracks are patched to the V1, A1, and A2 destination tracks.

7   Drag the clip into the Canvas and drop it in the Insert section of the Edit Overlay to place it before the sequence begins.

The **Bars and Tone** clip is edited at the beginning of the sequence, and all other sequence clips are moved down 30 seconds, the length of the clip.

Adding Slugs

Final Cut Express plays through any gap in a sequence as though it were black video. But you may not want to leave a gap or hole between clips. You may prefer putting something in the gap as a filler clip. This can be done using the slug generator. A *slug* is one track of black video and one set, or two tracks, of stereo audio. However, there is no recorded audio on the tracks.

You can use a slug clip when you want to hold a place for another clip in the sequence. Maybe someone is working on a great graphic for you, but it isn't ready to edit just yet. You can place a slug clip where you want the graphic to go, to hold its place. In this sequence, you want two seconds of black after the color bars clip has finished playing. You can either move all the clips in the sequence down two seconds and leave a two-second gap, or insert a two-second slug after the color bars.

1   In the Viewer, click the Generator pop-up menu button and choose Slug.

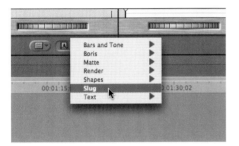

2   Play the **Slug** clip in the Viewer.

This is a two-minute clip of black video and stereo audio tracks.

3   Click the Stereo tab to view the volume level for the **Slug** clip.

The volume level is at 0 dB. Pan is at its default setting.

4   Click the Video tab and enter a two-second duration for the **Slug** clip in the Duration field.

Slugs have a 10-second marked duration just like Bars and Tone.

5   In the Timeline, make sure the playhead is parked at the end of the **Bars and Tone** clip.

6   Drag the **Slug** clip from the Viewer into the Canvas Edit Overlay as an Insert edit. Play the clip.

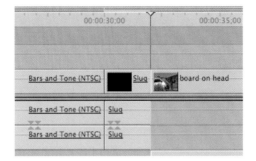

The audio/video **Slug** clip is edited into the sequence and plays back as black video with no sound.

Creating Text Edits

Text is another video generator that generates clips from within Final Cut Express. Text in video can appear in different ways at different times throughout a story or sequence. For example, it can appear before the story begins to identify the name and date of the sequence, at the first frame of the sequence as a title, during the sequence to identify the person speaking, or at the end to credit the "stars" and of course you, the editor. Final Cut Express gives you lots of options to create or control text edits. Many of the font and style options will be familiar to you from other word-processing or graphics programs.

Adding a Slate

A simple way to approach your first text edit is to create a slate for your sequence. A slate is another piece of information you can add in the *leader* portion of your sequence, or prior to where the story clips begin. In film and television productions, slates are placed in front of the camera to identify the scene and take number before the actors begin delivering their lines. The Final Cut Express icon is modeled after such a slate.

In editing, the slate that appears before the sequence begins is simply a list of information that describes certain aspects of the sequence, such as the sequence name, length, date recorded, and any other information you think might be helpful or required. Slates are generally simple in style and stand alone without other visuals. But you can spice them up to your liking. Let's begin creating a slate by setting up a basic text edit.

1   In the Viewer, click the Generator pop-up menu button.

The most recent item selected, in this case Slug, appears at the top of the list for easy access.

2   Choose Text, and choose Text from the submenu.

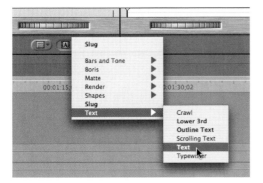

In the Viewer, the words *SAMPLE TEXT* appear over the image area. This is a default text line. There are In and Out points in the scrubber bar that create a 10-second duration.

3   Press Option-X to remove the marks, and look at the duration in the Duration field.

All generator items have two minutes of material in their total length, and all open with a 10-second marked duration. You can change the default duration in the User Preferences window (Option-Q).

4   Press Cmd-Z to add back the marked duration.

An important trick to working with text clips is to edit the clip into the sequence first. Once the clip is in the Timeline, you can open the clip into the Viewer and edit the text there. This allows you to view the clip in the Canvas as you make changes. Let's edit the text into the sequence.

5   To insert the **Text** clip between the **Bars and Tone** and **Slug** clips, park the playhead at the beginning of the **Slug** clip in the sequence.

6   Drag the **Text** clip into the Canvas and drop it in the Insert section of the Edit Overlay.

All text clips are video-only and are lavender in color, as opposed to the light blue video clips you have been seeing.

7   Move the playhead to the center of the **Text** clip in the Timeline.

You see the same *SAMPLE TEXT* block in the Canvas that you see in the Viewer.

8   In the Timeline, double-click the **Text** clip to open it in the Viewer.

Now the *SAMPLE TEXT* clip from the Timeline appears in the Viewer.

Controlling Text Options

When you open the text video generator in the Viewer, a new tab, called Controls, appears in the Stereo tab position. This is where you make changes, or *control* the generator. When you work with text, many of the options are about text style and font selection. When you work with other generators, there will be different choices.

1 In the Viewer, click the Controls tab.

Look at some of the familiar text parameters, such as Font, Size, Style, and Alignment. Use the Viewer scroll bar to reveal other Text generator parameters.

2 Click the *SAMPLE TEXT* block to select it, and type all the following information, using the Return key to move to the next line:

"New Kid in Malibu"
Length: 1:08 min/sec
Editor: Your Name
Date: Today's Date

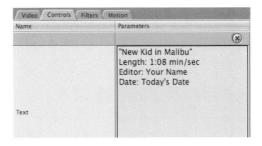

This text option allows you to enter multiple lines of text.

3   Press Tab to apply this information.

With the playhead over the text clip in the Timeline, you see in the Canvas what you have just typed.

4   Using the controls beneath the text box, format the text as follows:

▶   Font: *Arial Black*

▶   Size: *40*

▶   Alignment: *Center*

▶   Origin: *–70* (in the second field for vertical placement)

5   In Font Color, click the color tile box.

The system color picker opens as a Colors window. You can select from several color models at the top of the Colors window.

TIP ▶ When you make the text dark or black, you may need to change the color of the Canvas background from black to a lighter color to see the text more clearly. If necessary, choose View > Background and select a lighter color or one of the checkerboard options.

6   Click the third option, Color Palettes, and choose Apple from the List pop-up menu. Choose Yellow and click OK.

NOTE ▶ If you want to reset your text parameters to their default status, click the red X in the upper-right corner of the Controls tab as you did in the Filters and Motion tabs. Also, Cmd-Z will undo the most recent text change.

7   Adjust the Tracking, Leading, and Aspect sliders to see how they affect the text in the Canvas. If you want to return to your previous settings, press Cmd-Z.

8   To double-check that the text is within the title safe area, click the Canvas View pop-up and choose Show Title Safe. Turn Title Safe off when you finish viewing the text.

The three clips you've created make up the *leader* portion of your sequence, before the story begins.

Adding a Title over a Background

The slate you just created stands alone as its own clip. It is not combined with any other clips. You may want the title of your show to have a similar look. But you can also place the sequence title *over* another clip, using that clip as the text background. When a text clip is placed over another clip in the Timeline, the text remains, but the area around the text drops away and reveals the clip beneath it.

The reason this occurs is that the text clip has an *alpha channel.* All video clips have three channels of color information: red, blue, and green. Images are formed by the combination of these three colors. But some clips, such as text clips in Final Cut Express, have a fourth channel called an alpha channel. The alpha channel cuts a hole around the text information so that just the text can appear over a different background.

Since there are surfing clips on V1 and all the **dad about jimbo** clips on V2, a good way to organize the titles within the body of this sequence is to place them all on the V3 track. When you place a title on the V3 track, that title will appear over any other clip on any track below it at that location.

1   In the Timeline, Ctrl-click in the video track area, above the V1 and V2 tracks, and choose Add Track from the shortcut menu to add a V3 track.

2   Move the playhead to the first frame of the **board on head** clip. Press I to mark an In point.

NOTE ▶ You will be directed to place all the text clips within the body of this sequence on the V3 track. You could place them in the V2 gaps, but placing them together on V3 is a better organizational approach.

3   Press the down arrow key to go to the next edit point and then press the left arrow key to move back one frame, so that you are on the last frame before the **dad about jimbo** clip begins. Press O to mark an Out point at this location.

You will place the title of the sequence over this portion of the **board on head** clip.

4   In the Viewer, click the Video tab and then the Generator pop-up menu, and choose Text > Text.

5   To patch v1 to the V3 track, drag the v1 source control up to the V3 destination level and release it.

6   To edit this clip into the Timeline, drag the *SAMPLE TEXT* clip from the Viewer into the Canvas and drop it into the Overwrite section of the Edit Overlay. To see the text, press the left arrow to move the playhead back one frame.

The **Text** clip appears on V3 above the **board on head** clip between the edit points. With the playhead parked on the **Text** clip, you see the default *SAMPLE TEXT* appear on top of the **board on head** clip in the Canvas.

7   In the Timeline, double-click the new text clip to open it in the Viewer.

8   In the Viewer, click the Controls tab.

9   Type a title for this sequence, *New Kid in Malibu*, and press Tab.

In the Canvas, text is automatically centered in the middle of the screen. If you add lines, they are added below, which is why in the previous exercise you had to raise the center point to include all the information.

10   Change the font to Arial Black and the size to 48, and press Tab.

11 To use the color of the surfboard as the font color, click the Select Color tool (eyedropper) in the Font Color parameter line, and then click the surfboard in the Canvas.

> **TIP** ▶ Remember, to see a sampling of different image colors, click the eyedropper and then drag in the image without letting go. As you drag over different colors, the text font color automatically changes.

In the "Advanced Titling" appendix on the book's DVD, you will learn to add motion effects to this text. For now, let's continue exploring other types of text clips.

Adding a Lower Third

If your sequence contains a clip of someone speaking, and you would like the audience to know who this person is and perhaps his or her title, you can add some identifying information over that clip. This is called a *lower third* because in order not to cover up the person's face, you must place the information on the lower portion of the screen. Final Cut Express has a Lower 3rd text option that automatically creates two lines of text in the lower left of the image area for this purpose.

You will use a different approach to editing this text clip into the sequence: You will use an existing clip as a reference for placement and length and superimpose the text clip over it. This is referred to as super-imposing a clip. Before you superimpose a clip, you patch the v1 source to the destination track *over which you want the superimposed clip to appear.* In the current sequence, there are clips on V1 and V2. You will patch v1 to V2 so that the text clips you superimpose will appear on V3.

1   In the Timeline, patch the v1 source control to the V2 destination track and move the playhead into the gap directly above the **waxing board right** clip.

NOTE ► The playhead only needs to be somewhere in the clip you are using as a reference. You do not need edit points to make a Superimpose edit.

2   Click the Video tab and then the Generator pop-up menu, and choose Text > Lower 3rd.

> ### Sample Text 1
> ### Sample Text 2

In the Viewer, two lines of sample text appear in the bottom third of the screen.

3   To superimpose this text over the gap above the **waxing board right** clip, drag the clip into the Canvas and drop it in the Superimpose section of the Edit Overlay.

The **Lower 3rd** clip is placed on the V3 track above the gap and is given the same length as the gap on V2.

4   In the Timeline, double-click the **Lower 3rd** clip to open it in the Viewer.

5   Click the Controls tab.

Video	Controls	Filters	Motion	
Name		Parameters		
				ⓧ
Text 1		Sample Text 1		
Font		Lucida Grande		
Style		Plain		
Size				36
Tracking				1
Font Color		▶		
Text 2		Sample Text 2		
Font		Lucida Grande		
Style		Plain		
Size				36
Tracking				1
Font Color		▶		
Background		None		
Opacity				100

The two lines of text are treated as separate blocks: Text 1 and Text 2. Each has its own set of formatting controls.

6   Enter *Jimbo Borland* in the Text 1 field and make it Arial Black, 40 point.

7   Enter *Professional Surfer* in the Text 2 field and make it Arial, 30 point.

8   If necessary, scroll down to see the Background parameter. Click the Background pop-up menu and choose Solid.

9   To match the **Lower 3rd** clip background color to an existing color scheme, move the playhead to one of the **dad about jimbo** clips. Find the Color parameter *beneath* the Background parameter and use that eyedropper to select the border around the **dad about jimbo** clip.

TIP ▶ Remember, you can click and drag with the eyedropper and continuously update the color you are sampling. Simply release the mouse when you see the color you want.

10 Move the playhead back over the **Lower 3rd** clip. Change the background Opacity setting to 20 and play this clip.

Project Tasks

Add a fade-in and fade-out to this text edit.

1 In the Browser, click the Effects tab and display the contents of the Video Transitions. Then open the Dissolve bin.

2 Drag the Cross Dissolve icon onto the beginning of the **Lower 3rd** clip.

3 Drag the Cross Dissolve to the end of the **Lower 3rd** clip to add a fade-out.

Outlining Text

The Outline Text generator adds a more robust look to your title. With it you can create a bold outline around the letters of your text and even fill the text or outline with a frame from another clip or graphic. There are numerous ways to adjust an Outline Text clip. This exercise will guide you through some of them.

1 Park the playhead over the **back up again** clip, in the second gap between the **dad about jimbo** clips.

2 In the Viewer, click the Video tab, and from the Generator pop-up menu choose Text > Outline Text. To see the outline around the text more clearly, choose View > Background > Checkerboard 1.

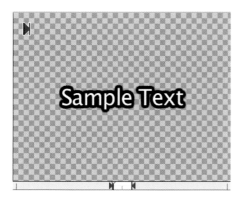

The default outline text is white text with a heavy black border around the letters.

3   Drag the image from the Viewer to the Canvas and drop it into the Superimpose section of the Canvas Edit Overlay.

4   In the Timeline, double-click the **Outline Text** clip to open it in the Viewer. Click the Controls tab.

5   Type the word *SURF* in the text field, and select Arial Black for the font and 148 for the font size. Press Tab to see the results.

6   Enter *.45* in the Aspect field to make the letters taller, and press Tab.

7   Scroll down to the Text Graphic parameter.

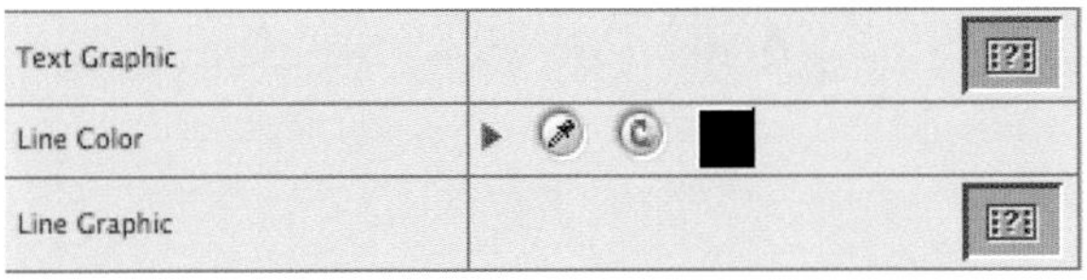

Text Graphic		📠
Line Color	▶ 🖊 Ⓒ ■	
Line Graphic		📠

In outline text, you can fill the letters *or* outline with a graphic or any frame from a video clip. Dragging the video clip from the Browser into the Text Graphic box will place the first frame of the clip in the outlined text. If you want a different frame, you can either set a marker and drag the marker into the Text Graphic box, or create a freeze frame and drag that.

8   In the Browser, click the disclosure triangle next to the **distant sun-set** clip to reveal the marker. Drag the Marker 1 icon into the Text Graphic clip box (with a question mark) and release it.

Without   Adding   With
image   image   image

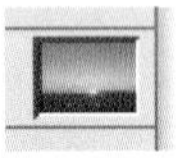

When you release the marker, the Text Graphic box displays the frame that will fill the text. In the Canvas, you see the outline text, filled with the **distant sunset** image, over the **back up again** clip.

NOTE ▶ You can also add a graphic or image frame to the outline area around the text. And you can create a separate background around the outlined text and add a frame to that background.

9   In the Timeline, click the Clip Overlays control, or press Option-W, to turn on the clip overlay lines.

Whereas the pink lines represent audio volume levels, the black lines represent opacity in the video clips. Dragging this line up or down will raise or lower the opacity of a clip. To work more with clip opacity, you can perform the exercises in the "Working with Multiple Tracks" appendix on the DVD.

10 Drag the opacity line for the new Surf **Outline Text** clip down to about 40%. Press Option-W to turn off the overlay lines and play the clip.

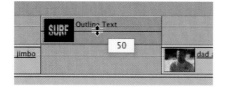

With the opacity lowered on this clip, you can see Jimbo surfing through the text.

TIP To replace an image in one of the Graphic boxes, just drag a new image and release it in the appropriate box. To remove an image, Ctrl-click the box and choose Clear from the shortcut menu.

An outline text edit can be superimposed over another clip, as in this exercise, or stand alone as the main title within a sequence.

Creating a Credit Roll

Let's face it—you've worked very hard to create a masterpiece sequence. You may as well put your name on it and get some credit for it. You can create credits as single edits with one name at a time on the screen. Or you can use the Final Cut Express animated Scrolling text option to roll the credits over the screen as they do in the movies.

1 Position the playhead at the end of the sequence and patch the v1 source control to the V3 track. In the Viewer, click the Video tab.

NOTE ► Even though this is the end of the sequence, placing the credit roll on the V3 track will keep the text in this sequence organized and allow you to place a background underneath the text on the V1 or V2 track.

2   Click the Generator pop-up menu and choose Text > Scrolling Text.

3   Make sure the duration is set for 10 seconds.

4   Drag the **Scrolling Text** clip into the Canvas, and drop it into the sequence as an Overwrite edit.

5   In the Timeline, double-click the **Scrolling Text** clip to open it in the Viewer, and click the Controls tab.

6   Scroll down to see the other formatting options.

TIP ► To better view the controls for this generator, you can also drag the lower-right corner of the Viewer window down to resize it. Afterwards, you can press Ctrl-U to restore the Standard window layout, or press Shift-U or Option-U to restore a saved custom layout.

7 Drag the playhead through the **Scrolling Text** clip in the Timeline to see the sample text scroll up. Then position the playhead in the middle of the clip.

NOTE ▶ The scroll is animated to move up from the bottom of the screen and then to roll off the top of the screen. If the playhead is parked at the end or beginning of the clip, the text will be out of view.

8   Enter the following information, including the asterisks, and press Tab:

> *Producer*Your Name*
> *Director*Your Name*
> *Editor*Your Name*
> (Press Return to add a line of space here.)
> *Cast*
> (Press Return to add a line of space here, too.)
> *Vicki*Susan Fielder*
> *George*Sam Rowdy*
> *Dorothy*Lynne Buckner*
> *Smokey*Himself*

When you press Tab, Final Cut Express will create two symmetrical columns separated by a gap where the asterisks were entered in the text. When no asterisk is entered, all the text is centered together.

9   Change the Font to Arial, the Size to 30, and the Style to Bold/Italic.

10   Scroll down to the lower Controls parameters and increase the Gap Width to 8%.

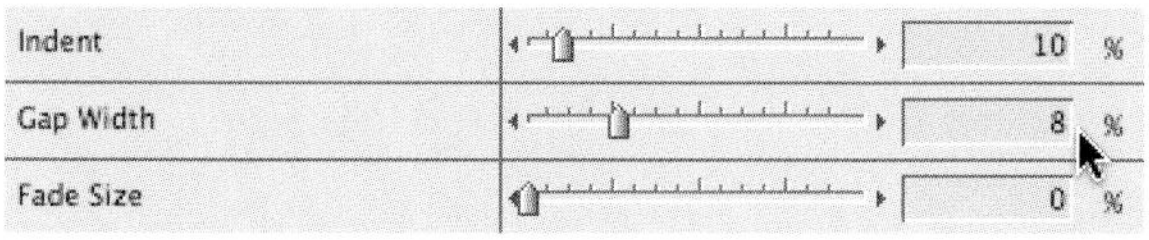

11   To see whether the text falls within the title safe area, click the Canvas View pop-up menu and choose Show Title Safe. Make any necessary changes to the gap width or font size, and then turn title safe off.

12   To see how the credits will scroll off or on screen, play the clip, or press Option-P to preview it.

Project Tasks

There are two other animated text edits you can try to spice up your sequences. These are the Crawl and Typewriter text options. Crawl reveals text horizontally across the screen from the left or right. You may have seen a weather warning broadcast this way. Typewriter reveals one letter at a time until the full text is revealed, as though a typewriter were typing the text. Let's apply a Typewriter text clip over a sequence.

> NOTE ▶ In the sequence you'll use for this exercise, we've applied some filters. If you'd like to learn how to do that, go to the appendix titled "Working with Filters" on the book's DVD.

1   From the Browser, open the *Blurry Workout* sequence and play it.

The video may stutter a bit because the clips have two filters applied.

2   Press Option-P to preview all three clips.

3   In the Viewer, click the Video tab, and then click the Generator pop-up menu and choose Text > Typewriter. In the Timeline, add a new video track, and edit the Typewriter text to the V2 track. Drag the Out point to the right until it covers the full length of the three V1 clips.

4   Park the playhead toward the end of the clip to see the full text. Double-click to open the Typewriter text clip into the Viewer and click the Controls tab. Make the text settings match the following image and play the new text edit:

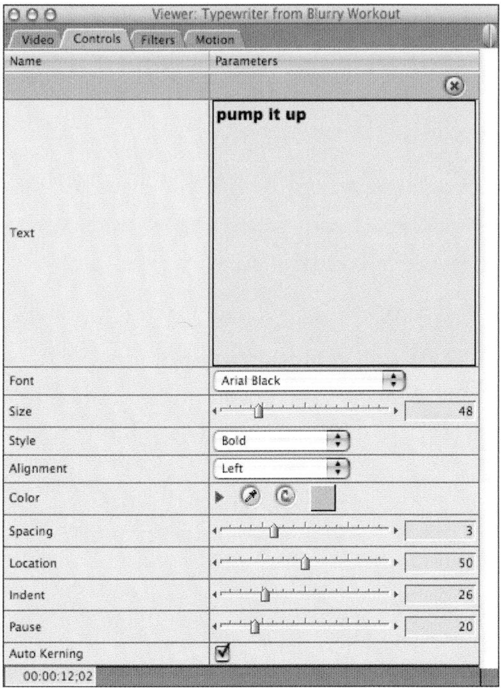

Project Tasks

1   Add a dissolve to any text edit that you would like to fade in or out.

2   Duplicate this sequence and name it *Advanced Titling*. You can use this sequence when you are ready to work on the exercises in the "Advanced Titling" appendix on this book's DVD.

3   Press Cmd-S to save the project.

Lesson Review

1.   Where do you access the Generators pop-up menu?

2.   Where are the parameters of a generator adjusted and controlled?

3.   Why are Bars and Tone edited into a sequence?

4.   When you play through a slug edit, what do you see and hear?

5.   Which text generator would you use to create a slate with several lines of text information?

6.   What type of text generator creates two lines of text automatically?

7.   If you want to superimpose a clip over the V2 track, what track must you target with the source control?

8.   What text does Final Cut Express animate automatically?

Answers

1.   In the Video tab of the Viewer window or in the Effects tab in the Browser.

2.   In the Controls tab in the Viewer.

3.   Bars and Tone give viewers a reference to set up their monitors properly before viewing your sequence.

4.   You see black video and hear nothing.

5.   The basic Text generator.

6. The Lower 3rd text generator.

7. Target the V2 track, and the superimposed edit will appear on V3.

8. Scrolling, Crawl, and Typewriter text.

Keyboard Shortcut

Option-P	Previews a clip that needs rendering

16

Lesson **16**

Finishing Your Project

The finishing stage can be a simple process of outputting your sequence to videotape so that you can screen it on your own TV. But it might also involve a number of other possibilities. For example, you may require other material to complete your sequence, such as additional clips or graphic files. You may need to fine-tune the audio or video in your sequence. Or you may need to export a sequence and burn it on a CD or DVD, or use it to author a DVD. You might also want to export a sequence to post it to the Web, view it on your iPod, or to create animated titles in the Apple LiveType application. All this is accomplished in the finishing stages of your project.

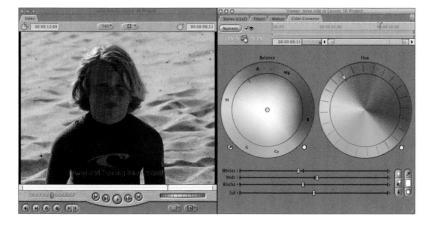

Preparing the Project

To get started, you will launch Final Cut Express and open the **Lesson 16 Project** file from the Lessons folder.

> **NOTE** ▶ Some of the exercises in this lesson use functions covered in the "Working with Multiple Tracks" and "Working with Filters" PDFs on the book's DVD.

1 In Final Cut Express, press Cmd-O and open the **Lesson 16 Project** file from the Lessons folder on your hard drive.

   This project has only one empty sequence and no clips. You will begin by importing clips into this project file from the Media folder on your hard drive.

2 Ctrl-click any open project tabs and choose Close Tab from the short-cut menu to close the projects.

Importing and Connecting Footage

Throughout these lessons you have worked with media files that you copied from the DVD over to your hard drive when you first started this tutorial. The clips and sequences that appear in the lesson project files are all connected, or *linked,* to those media files. If you want to access a media file but don't have a clip linking back to your media in your project, you must *import* a file. You can import a single file or an entire folder of files. In addition, when you move media or project files in your computer, the link between the clip and its media file can sometimes become broken, but there is a way to reconnect them.

Importing Clips

Importing a single clip file into a project creates a new link to existing media. Let's import different clips you can use to edit a sequence about vacations.

1   Choose File > Import > Files, or press Cmd-I.

2   In the Choose a File window, navigate to the following path: FCE 4 Book Files > Media > Scenic Beauty > **boat dusk**. Select this file and click Choose.

In the Browser, a new clip representing this media file appears. You can also Cmd-click files to import more than one at a time within the same folder.

3   Press Cmd-I to open the Choose a File window. Navigate to the Scenic Beauty folder again. Select the **bird fly by** file. Cmd-click the **glass lake** and **waterfall pond** files, and then click Choose to import these three files.

You can also import an entire folder of clips. This time, let's import using the shortcut menu in the Browser.

4   In the Browser, Ctrl-click in the blank gray area under the Name column and choose Import > Folder from the shortcut menu.

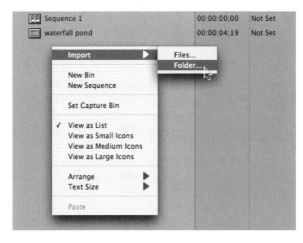

NOTE ▶ You can also use the shortcut menu to import a single file or files.

5   In the Choose a Folder window, navigate to the Media folder, and select the Vacation Fun folder. Click Choose.

With this import option, only the folders, not the individual clips, can be selected.

TIP ▶ Since the Import Folder command does not have a keyboard shortcut, you could make this command a button in the Browser button bar, if you think it's something you will use often.

6   Press Cmd-S to save this project with the new files.

Importing Audio from CDs

It's easy to use material from a CD in your sequence, whether it's music, narration, or sound effects. You can simply import an audio track from a CD directly into your project and then edit it into your sequence. But don't forget that as soon as you eject a CD, you no longer have access to the audio file. It's a good idea to take an extra step and copy the track or tracks you want to use to a folder along with your other media files, or import the files using the Apple music program, iTunes, before importing the track into your Final Cut Express project.

1   Press Cmd-H to temporarily hide the Final Cut Express interface.

2   Insert a CD into your computer that has an audio source you could use to enhance the vacation clips in your project. Double-click the CD icon to view its contents.

    NOTE ▶ If iTunes opens, click the window and press Cmd-H to hide it for the moment.

3   Press Cmd-N to create another Finder window. In this window, single-click the FCE 4 Book Files folder and navigate to the Media > Import-Export folder. Position this window so that you can also see the CD tracks in the other Finder window.

4   Drag the CD track you want to use in your sequence onto the Import-Export folder, and release it. After the track has finished copying, you can eject the CD.

5   In the Dock, click the Final Cut Express icon to make its interface visible.

6   Ctrl-click in the Browser blank area and choose Import Files from the shortcut menu.

7   Navigate to the Import-Export folder and select the CD audio track you just copied there. Click Choose to import it.

8   Select the music icon in the Browser and choose Edit > Item
     Properties, or press Cmd-9.

Item Properties: 5 Audio Track.aiff			
Format			
	Clip	A1	A2
Name	5 Audio Track.aiff	5 Audio Track.aiff	5 Audio Track.aiff
Type	Clip		
Creator	iTunes	iTunes	iTunes
Source	Macintosh HD:Documents:FCE HD Book F	Macintosh HD:Documen	Macintosh HD:Documen
Offline			
Size	20.7 MB	20.7 MB	20.7 MB
Last Modified	Today, 8:12 PM	Today, 8:12 PM	Today, 8:12 PM
Tracks	2A		
Vid Rate			
Frame Size			
Compressor			
Data Rate	172.2 K/sec	172.2 K/sec	172.2 K/sec
Pixel Aspect			
Anamorphic			
Field Dominance			
Alpha			
Reverse Alpha			
Composite			
Audio	1 Stereo	Left	Right
Aud Rate	44.1 KHz	44.1 KHz	44.1 KHz
Aud Format	16-bit Integer	16-bit Integer	16-bit Integer

Cancel   OK

The Item Properties window opens, listing information about the
selected item, including its file size and location. In this window, you
can see that this file has an Audio Rate of 44.1 kHz. Although this is
not as high as the DV audio rate of 48 kHz, the file can still be used in
the sequence without having to render it. It is ideal, however, to change
your audio rate to 48 kHz if you can, since Final Cut Express tends to
run smoother when the clip settings match the sequence settings.

TIP   In iTunes preferences, there is an importing option that will
convert CD tracks to 48 kHz as they are imported. See the iTunes
Help guide for directions.

9   Click Cancel to close the Item Properties window.

Importing Graphics

Final Cut Express can import many types of graphic files, such as TIFF, JPEG, and so on. You can import a single-layer graphic file or a multilayered graphic file created in Adobe Photoshop. When importing a multilayered file, it appears in Final Cut Express as a sequence icon, which allows you to edit each layer separately within Final Cut Express. You import and work with graphics just as you would work with other clips, but there are a few key things to keep in mind to make your graphics look their best.

Before you edit a graphic file into your sequence, be aware that the aspect ratio of a video pixel is different from a graphic file's pixel. This is because computers and graphics programs display square pixels, whereas digital video uses nonsquare pixels. If you create a graphic of a circle and import it into Final Cut Express, that circle will not look perfectly round in Final Cut Express. To be absolutely accurate, and to please those clients who use circles in their logos, you need to prepare your graphic files to accommodate this pixel difference.

A full discussion of importing graphics is beyond the scope of this book, but the following steps outline a common image preparation workflow that applies to both single-layer and multilayer graphics.

> **NOTE ▸** When you're working with graphics in video, the dpi (dots per inch) settings are irrelevant. A 300 dpi image will look the same as a 72dpi image. The pixel dimensions of an image—such as 1440×1080 or 720×480—determine the resolution of the video image.

1   In your graphics application, begin with a file image size that is 720×534 pixels for DV-NTSC or 768×576 for DV-PAL. These represent the square-pixel dimensions you should use in any still-image graphic program.

> **TIP ▸** Adobe Photoshop provides a project setting that automatically compensates for pixel aspect differences. If you use that setting, don't proceed with these steps.

2 When you have completed the graphic, save a copy of it and change the image size to 720 × 480 for NTSC or 720 × 576 for PAL.

3 Without making changes to the 720 × 480 (720 × 576 for PAL) file, import it into Final Cut Express.

The image will look as it did in the original version of your graphic file.

NOTE ▶ You can import and experiment with single layer and multi-layer graphic files from the Media > Import-Export folder.

Reconnecting Media

Clips in your project link back to specific media files on your hard drive. If you delete the media file or move it, you can break the link with the clip in the Browser because that clip no longer knows where to find its media file. The clip in the Browser becomes *offline,* and a red diagonal stripe appears over the clip icon. In order to use the media files, you must reconnect the clip icon in the Browser, or in the Timeline if it's already been edited into a sequence.

1 Press Cmd-H to hide the Final Cut Express interface.

2 Double-click the hard-drive icon to open the Finder window.

3 On your hard drive, navigate to FCE 4 Book Files > Media > Scenic Beauty.

4 Drag the **boat dusk** clip from the Scenic Beauty folder into the Media-folder so that the clip appears at the same level as the media folders.

Lessons	▶	Bad Audio	▶
Media	▶	boat dusk	
		Cooking	▶
		HDV Footage	▶
		Import-Export	▶

The **boat dusk** file is now in a different location than when you imported it into your project earlier in this lesson.

5   In the Dock, click the Final Cut Express icon to make the interface
visible again.

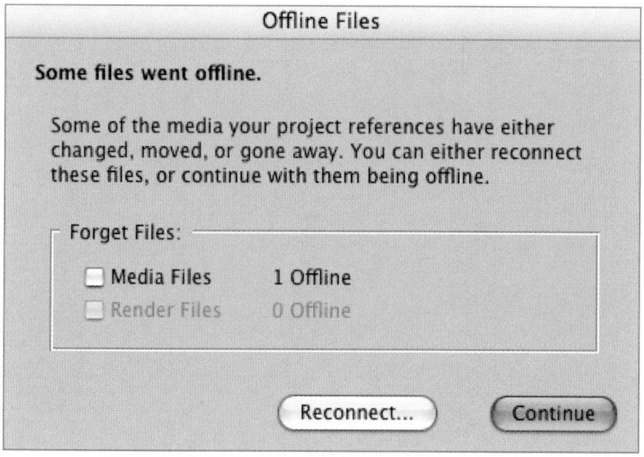

The Offline Files dialog appears, indicating "Some files went offline."
You can forget the movie (or render) file so that Final Cut Express
doesn't look for it again. Or you can reconnect to where the file is
currently located. Clicking Continue will postpone the decision. The
file will remain disconnected, and Final Cut Express will display the
Offline Files dialog the next time you open the project.

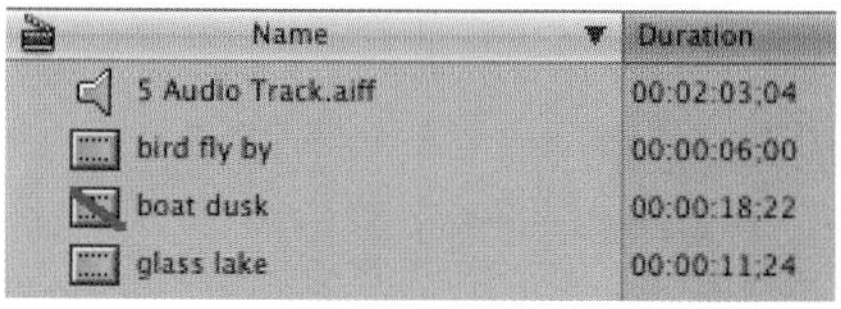

In the Browser, the **boat dusk** clip has a red diagonal line across it
indicating that it is offline or disconnected from its media file.

6   In the Offline Files dialog, click the Reconnect button to reestablish a
link between the clip icon in the Browser and the original media in its
new location in the Media folder.

The Reconnect Files dialog appears with the filename highlighted. The
previous path for this file appears above the name.

7   Click Search to have Final Cut Express look for the new location of the file.

The Reconnect browser window appears with the clip highlighted. You can also click the Locate button to locate the clip manually.

8   With the clip selected, click Choose. In the Reconnect Files window, the clip is moved from the upper Files to Connect area to the lower Files Located area. Click Connect to reconnect to the file at this location.

In the Browser, the red offline mark on the clip icon is removed, and you have access to that media once again.

TIP ▶ You can also initiate the reconnect process by Ctrl-clicking the clip in the Browser and choosing Reconnect Media from the shortcut menu or by selecting a clip in the Timeline and choosing File > Reconnect Media.

Project Tasks

You now have several clips in your project that you can use to build a sequence about vacations. Take a moment to organize your project elements.

1   Hide Final Cut Express and then put the **boat dusk** clip back in its original folder, FCE 4 Book Files > Media > Scenic Beauty.

2   Reconnect the Browser **boat dusk** clip to the media file in its original location.

3   In the Browser, create a new bin and name it *Vacation*.

4   Name the *Sequence 1* sequence *Vacation Images*.

5   Drag all the elements, clips, graphics, bins, and sequences into the Vacation bin. Collapse the bin so that you no longer see the contents.

6   Press Cmd-S to save your project.

Adding Finishing Touches

Before the actual outputting begins, there are usually a few finishing touches that can be applied to your sequence. Many times these adjustments are made during the editing process. But sometimes they are not made until you are ready to step back and think about the sequence as a whole, or rather as two halves—audio and video.

Making Audio Adjustments

When preparing the audio of your sequence for export or output, it's important to keep your eyes and ears open. You must look closely at the output level on the Audio Meters, making sure the combined audio tracks never peak at 0 dB. And you must listen closely to the mix level between tracks, making sure the primary audio is clearly heard over any background audio. (If you want to learn how to mix audio tracks together, read the appendix "Working with Multiple Tracks" on the DVD, where you will learn to raise or lower all the audio tracks in a sequence by the same amount.)

You will begin by opening a previous project, copying a sequence from that project, and pasting it into the current **Lesson 16 Project**.

1   Open the **Lesson 15 Project** file. In the Browser, copy the *15-Finished* sequence (Cmd-C), click the Lesson 16 Project tab, and press Cmd-V to paste it into this project.

2   Close the **Lesson 15 Project** file. In the Lesson 16 Project tab, double-click the *15-Finished* sequence to open it in the Timeline.

3   In the Timeline, press Option-W to reveal the clip overlays, and play the sequence.

     The music in this sequence is a little too loud in comparison with the dialogue clips. You will want to bring down the audio level for the music but keep the keyframes intact.

4   In the Timeline, select the **surfing voices.aif** music track.

5   Choose Modify > Levels, or press Cmd-Option-L. In the Gain Adjust dialog, enter *–2* in the "Adjust gain by" field. Leave the Make Changes pop-up on Relative. Watch the music tracks in the Timeline as you click OK.

The volume level lines of the music tracks move lower, but the change is made relative to the keyframes and levels that already exist in this clip.

6   Select both of the **big waves** clips. Choose Modify > Levels, and lower the relative volume on these clips by –4 dB.

> **NOTE ▸** The other Make Changes option, Absolute, will remove any keyframes in the clip and adjust the audio level an absolute or specific decibel amount from the original zero level.

7   Play the sequence and watch the Audio Meters. Make any additional changes in the audio levels to prepare this sequence for output.

Depending on your sequence, you may choose to adjust the Pan control in the Viewer to redirect the sound of a clip. A mono track can be *panned* or redirected to the left or right. With a stereo pair, one channel is panned to the left and one to the right. Wear headphones when making these adjustments to hear how the sound is being directed.

Making Video Adjustments

The finishing stage is a good time to do something about any clips that appear too dark or light on your monitor. As with audio monitoring, the way an image looks on your computer isn't always how it will look on your television monitor. The best way to check your sequence is to screen it on a separate video monitor before outputting it to tape. If this isn't possible, you can output a sequence to tape, view the tape, and then go back to the sequence and add a corrective filter to any clips that do not look good.

1   Ctrl-click in the Browser and choose Import Folder from the shortcut menu.

2   Navigate to Media > Surfing > Jimbo's Clips. Select the Jimbo's Clips folder and click Choose to import the entire folder of clips.

3   Display the folder's contents in the Browser. Double-click the **nose ride** clip to open it in the Viewer. Play the clip.

In this clip, there is a high *contrast* between the bright (white) and dark (black) pixels in the image. The pixels of the boy's face are too dark, and the pixels of the sand are too bright. The balance in this image can be improved by adding the Color Corrector filter.

NOTE ▸ In Lesson 14, you added transition effects to edit points. The other type of effect is a filter. Filters are applied just as transitions are but affect the entire body of the clip, not just the edit point. You look at and adjust filter parameters in the Filters tab in the Viewer. To learn more about filters, go through the exercises in the appendix "Working with Filters" on the DVD.

4   To apply a filter that will correct the color of this image, choose Effects > Video Filters > Color Correction > Color Corrector.

5   To see the clip's image as you make adjustments, drag the Video tab away from the Viewer and move it left over the Browser window. In the Viewer window, click the Color Corrector tab.

6   In the Video tab, move the playhead to the middle of the clip.

Changing the level of brightness for pixels in the middle range, or *mids*, in this image will raise the brightness level of the boy's face. Bringing down the white levels will decrease the brightness of the sand. This will improve the overall balance of lights and darks.

7   Drag the Mids slider to the right a bit until you see the boy's face look a little brighter. Then drag the Whites slider to the left to reduce the amount of brightness in the whites. Experiment with dragging the Blacks slider to the left a tad.

The adjustments you make in this filter apply to every frame in this clip.

8   To compare the effects of the color correction, click off and on the Enable box next to the Numeric button in the Color Corrector tab.

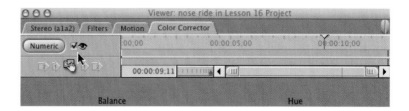

TIP ▶ If a clip needs color correcting, it may be easier to correct the original master clip before you start to use it in editing. Or you can copy and paste whatever color correction attributes you applied to one clip to other clips like it already in the Timeline.

Project Tasks

1   Improve some of the other clips in the Jimbo's Clips bin by applying a Color Corrector filter and following the steps in the previous exercise.

2   When you are through working with the clips in the Browser, click the Close button in the separate Video window to return it to the Viewer.

3   Play through the *15-Finished* sequence and see if any clips need adjusting before output.

4   Listen to the sequence and watch the Audio Meters to make sure the overall audio output will be balanced and within the desired range.

Exporting Sequences and Clips

The sequence is finished, and the tweaking has come to an end. Now it's time to decide just what you want to do with it. There are two things you can do to get your sequence out of your computer: export it as a file or output it to tape. Exporting a sequence as a computer file allows you to play the sequence on another computer, save it as a backup, add it to your project archives, or even import it into another application for further work.

There are three export options in Final Cut Express 4. Two of these options output the selected clip or sequence using the QuickTime format. The other option allows you to export a sequence for LiveType to use as a reference as you add titling effects.

Exporting a QuickTime Movie

When you want to export a clip or sequence exactly as it is, using its current settings, you export it as a QuickTime movie. There are two types of QuickTime movies; one is self-contained, and the other is not. A self-contained movie file contains a copy of the media itself. This creates a much larger file size but makes the file independent so that you can play it on other computers. When you export a QuickTime movie that is not self-contained, the movie file does not contain a copy of the media. This creates a much smaller file size, but you are limited to playing the sequence on the computer that also contains the media files.

1   Make sure the *15-Finished* sequence is active in the Timeline.

When you export from the Timeline, you can either mark In and Out points to identify the section you want to export, or remove any marks to export everything in the sequence.

2   Mark an In point at the beginning of the third clip (the slate) and an Out point at the end of the sequence after the final edit.

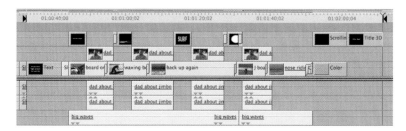

3   Choose File > Export > QuickTime Movie and enter *Self-Contained* as the name and the Import-Export folder as the destination. Choose Audio and Video from the Include pop-up menu, and None from the Markers menu. Make sure the Make Movie Self-Contained box is selected.

In this option, you can choose to export Audio and Video, or just one or the other. You can also choose to include specific sets of markers you may have created for the purposes of creating a DVD or to use in the Soundtrack application.

NOTE ▶ The following steps to save a QuickTime movie file may take about 500 MB of hard drive space. Before you click Save in the following steps, make sure you have enough hard drive space. You can also re-mark a shorter length of sequence, or simply read through the steps and apply them to your own files later.

4   To create a QuickTime movie of this sequence, click Save.

The Writing Audio and Video progress bar appears.

5   When the exporting is complete, press Cmd-I and select the **Self-Contained** movie to import this file into the project.

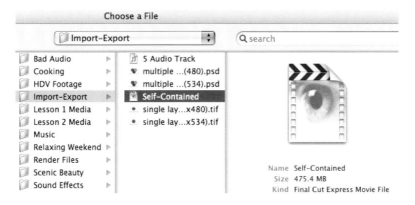

When you select the clip, you see a Final Cut Express movie icon. Look at the file size. In the Browser, the **Self-Contained** movie icon looks like any other clip icon.

NOTE ▶ Unlike other QuickTime media files, double-clicking this type of movie file from the Desktop will automatically launch Final Cut Express.

6 In the Browser, double-click the clip to open it in the Viewer. Play the **Self-Contained** movie.

> **TIP** ▶ Watching the movie play is a good double-check that everything is the way you want it to be before using or duplicating the file.

7 Click in the Timeline to make it active. Repeat steps 3 and 4, but this time enter *Not Self-Contained* as the name, and deselect Make Movie Self-Contained. To save this file, click Save.

When a movie is not self-contained, the saving is faster because only the sequence information is being saved, not the media itself.

8 Press Cmd-I and navigate to the **Not Self-Contained** file.

Compare the smaller size of this file to the **Self-Contained** movie file.

9 Open the **Not Self-Contained** movie and play it in the Viewer.

Both movies look exactly alike in the Viewer or Timeline. But the **Self-Contained** movie has the flexibility of being put on a CD or DVD and played independently on another computer. The **Not Self-Contained** movie can be played only on the computer that has the media to which it is linked.

> **NOTE** ▶ If you want to use a sequence or part of a sequence to author an iDVD project, you must export your material as QuickTime movies. You can even choose not to make the movie self-contained as long you will be working on the same computer that has the media files.

Exporting Using QuickTime Conversion

Exporting using the QuickTime Movie option maintains the sequence settings, such as frame rate and frame size. But you may need to export a clip or sequence with different settings, and for this you will use the Using QuickTime Conversion export option. Several situations may require changing settings. You may want to burn your sequence onto a

CD or DVD, perhaps requiring the frame size to be smaller; play it over the Web, requiring it to be smaller still; export it for use in authoring a DVD; export a single clip frame to use in a graphics program; or export the sound track alone as an audio file. Let's export the currently marked sequence so it can play easily on the Web.

> **NOTE** ▶ Exporting your sequence requires that it be compressed. When it plays back, it is decompressed. The method in which this process takes place is referred to as a *codec*, short for *c*ompression/ *dec*ompression. The QuickTime format supports a wide variety of compression methods, or codecs.

1   With the Timeline window active, choose Sequence > Settings, and click the Render Control tab.

Before you begin to output this sequence, make sure each of the checkboxes are selected, and that the Render pop-ups are each set at 100% for the best render quality. Then click OK.

2   In the Timeline, press Shift-I to move the playhead to the In point in the *15-Finished* sequence to see the first frame of your output section. Choose File > Export > Using QuickTime Conversion.

NOTE ▶ You can also export a clip or sequence from the Browser by selecting it and then choosing File > Export > and the appropriate export option.

3   In the Save dialog, click the Format pop-up menu and look at the different formats in which you can export your sequence.

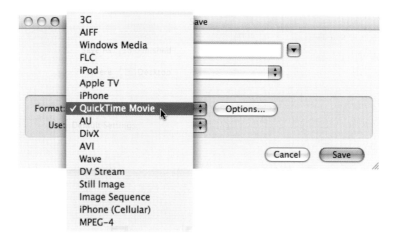

QuickTime Movie is the default format, but you can also export using 3G, iPod, Apple TV, Still Image, AVI, AIFF, and other format options. The options that appear in the Format pop-up may vary if you installed additional QuickTime plug-ins.

The Format option you choose determines what appears in the Use pop-up menu.

4   Select the AIFF audio format and then click the Use pop-up menu to
    see the default audio choices that appear. Click other formats and then
    the Use pop-up menu to see the default options for those formats.

    NOTE ▶ You may notice that one of the Format options is for iPod
    (320 × 240). Viewing a clip that was exported using this option opens
    the clip in iTunes.

    You can also change the options to conform to your specific needs.
    Let's export this sequence as a QuickTime movie file that can be easily
    posted to the Web.

5   Choose the QuickTime Movie format and click the Options button
    to open the Movie Settings dialog. Under Video, click the
    Settings button.

6   Click the pop-up menu at the top of the window and look at the dif-
    ferent codecs you can use to export this sequence.

    When you're selecting a codec, the three important considerations are
    file size, image quality, and file compatibility. Some codecs use very
    little compression, which produces an excellent picture quality but a
    very large file size. Other codecs use greater compression so the file
    size will be smaller and can be used more easily for other situations,
    such as the Web or CD.

7   In the Compression Settings dialog, choose MPEG-4 Video from
    the pop-up menu. Click the Frame Rate pop-up and choose 15 fps
    (frames per second), and enter 5 in the Key Frames field. In the Data
    Rate field, enter *700* as the kbits per second. Then drag the Quality
    slider to Best, and click OK.

    NOTE ▶ The MPEG-4 format is capable of high levels of compression
    while maintaining good image quality. This makes it a good choice for
    distributing media on the Web.

When you click OK, this dialog closes and returns you to the previous Movie Settings dialog.

8 In the Movie Settings dialog, in the Video section, click the Size button. When the Export Size Settings dialog appears, choose Custom from the Dimensions pop-up menu. Enter *320* for Width and *240* for Height, and click OK.

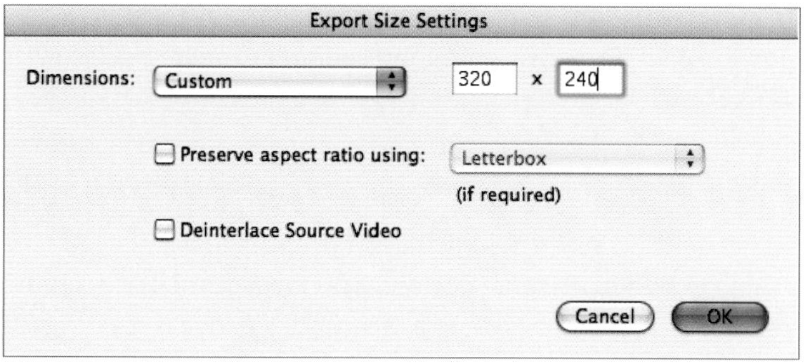

NOTE ▶ This is half the size of a typical television image, which when calculated in square pixels is 640 × 480. Changing the frame size will greatly reduce the size of the file. Depending on whether you burn the file to a CD (approximately 700 MB) or DVD (approximately 4.5 GB), you may not have to reduce the image size.

9 In the Movie Settings dialog, click the Settings button under Sound. In the Sound Settings dialog, choose or enter the following settings in this order, then click OK:

▶ Format: *AAC*

▶ Channels: *Mono*

▶ Target Bit Rate: *32*

10 Back in the Movie Settings dialog, deselect Prepare for Internet Streaming, and click OK.

11 In the Movie Settings dialog, click OK. In the Save dialog, change the name to *Surfing Web* and click Save if you want to create this file.

The saved file can now be posted to the Web.

> **TIP** ▶ Not all sequences have the same export requirements, so you may need to experiment with different options to find the best combination for your project.

Exporting for Other Apple Applications

LiveType is Apple's 32-bit animated application that creates animated titles. This application comes bundled with Final Cut Express, and you can find an introduction to it in the "Introduction to LiveType" appendix on this book's DVD.

Project Tasks

1   In the Timeline, park your playhead at 1:14;05.

2   To export this as a single frame, choose File > Export > Using QuickTime Conversion.

3   In the Format pop-up menu, choose Still Image. Click Options and select Photoshop or another type of file your graphics program can read. Export this image.

Outputting to Tape

It's movie time. You've exported files of the sequence and burned them to a CD or DVD to show others. You've gotten their final approval or given it your own green light, as it were. Time to move forward and output to tape. Before you begin outputting, hook up your DV source, whether it's a DV camcorder or a DV tape deck, through your FireWire connector in the back of your computer. Make sure it is on the VCR setting and not Camera. You can also output the tape manually to a non-DV device such as a VHS tape machine.

Recording Manually

An easy way to output to tape is simply to play the sequence and record it. This is referred to as a *manual recording* process. To record manually, you must have all the elements you want to see on tape, such as Bars and Tone, slate, and so on, edited into your sequence in the Timeline. If you have used effects in your sequence, you will want them to be rendered and appear at the highest possible quality. If you opened the program with no FireWire device attached, you may have to quit and relaunch for Final Cut Express to recognize the device.

> **TIP** ▶ When you were previewing effects, the Unlimited RT and Dynamic settings in the RT pop-up menu allowed you to see as many effects as possible. When you prepare your sequence for output, set the RT options to Safe RT and Playback Video Quality High by selecting those options in the Playback Control tab of the System Settings window. If any files in your sequence need rendering at these settings, press Option-R to render the sequence before moving on to the step of outputting.

1   In the Timeline, press End to move the playhead to the last frame of the *15-Finished* sequence. Press Option-X to remove the existing In and Out points.

   This sequence has the edits of Bars and Tone and slate you created. If you play this sequence, the playhead will stop on the last frame of the *The End* text clip. To start or stop on a frame of black, you must edit black to the head and tail of the sequence.

2   In the Viewer, click the Generator pop-up menu and choose Slug. Enter a 10-second duration. Patch the v1, a1, and a2 source tracks to the V1, A1, and A2 destination tracks, and edit this clip as an Overwrite edit at the end of the sequence.

3   Change the slug duration to five seconds, and edit this as an Insert edit at the beginning of the sequence before the Bars and Tone.

When you play back the sequence during the recording process, it will play exactly as it does on your computer monitor. For example, if there is an unrendered clip in the Timeline, that clip will be recorded unrendered.

4   Move the playhead back to the head of the sequence.

The output of the Timeline begins with a freeze frame of wherever the playhead is parked.

5   Put a tape in your recording device, cue it to the desired location, and begin recording.

6   Allow a few seconds for your recording device to get up to speed, and then play the sequence.

NOTE ▸ If you want the sequence to repeat, turn the Loop Playback option on in the View menu and place an appropriate amount of black at the end of the sequence.

7   Once the playhead has stopped at the end of the sequence and you've recorded the amount of black you want, you can stop the recording device and view your recording.

NOTE ▸ Manual recording works well if you are recording on a device, such as a VHS VCR, that can't be controlled through a FireWire connection.

Printing to Video

When you finish writing a document, you print it out. When you finish editing your sequence, you can *print* to video. Print to Video is another way you can output your sequence to tape. Just as you have certain choices about how you want to print your document, this option allows you to choose certain elements, such as Bars and Tone, slate, black, and so on, from a checklist, as opposed to having to edit them into the sequence in your Timeline before outputting.

1   In the Browser, duplicate the *15-Finished* sequence and rename the copy *15-Finished No Extras*. Double-click this sequence to open it into the Timeline.

2   Choose File > Print to Video, or press Ctrl-M.

The Print to Video dialog opens with items to select in four different areas: Leader (before the sequence begins), Media (the sequence or marked portion of the Timeline), Trailer (following the sequence), and Duration Calculator. You can also click the Automatically Start Recording box to initiate recording of your camcorder.

3   For now, click Cancel.

When you output using the Print to Video mode, you don't have to make the extra edits, such as Bars and Tone, to the sequence in the Timeline. They will be added automatically when you select the appropriate checkboxes and enter a duration for each element. Let's remove those generated clips you added manually in the previous lesson, such as Bars and Tone, slate, and black, so that you can add them automatically using the Print to Video options.

4   In the *15-Finished No Extras* sequence, use Shift-Delete to remove the unnecessary edits or gaps that are not part of the actual story. Make sure the first frame of the **board on head** clip is at the head of the sequence.

5   To ensure that your output will be at the highest possible quality, click the RT pop-up menu and choose Safe RT and Playback Video Quality High.

Now you're ready to output using the Print to Video option.

6   Choose File > Print to Video, or press Ctrl-M, and make the following changes in the Leader section: Color Bars = *20*, Black = *5*, Slate = *10*, Black = *5*, and Countdown = Built-in. Make sure each of these options is selected.

NOTE ▶ Do some tests to determine the best time combination for each element for your own sequences.

7   In the Slate pop-up menu, make sure that Text is selected and type the following slate information in the text box to the right:

16-Finished No Extras
Today's date
Your name and title

8 Click the Preview button to test the level of audio going into your recording device. If necessary, adjust the level using the slider.

9 In the Media area, choose Entire Media from the Print pop-up menu and make sure that Loop is set to 1 time only, or that it is not selected.

10 In the Trailer area, change the Black duration to *10* seconds.

11 If a tape is in your camcorder and cued, and you want Final Cut Express to automatically begin the recording process, make sure the Automatically Start Recording box is selected. Then click OK.

A progress bar appears as the output is configured and prepared. Final Cut Express will initiate recording if you selected the Automatically Start Recording box. If you did not, a message will appear telling you to begin recording.

> **TIP** ▶ If you are starting the recording process yourself, allow about five seconds for your recording device to pick up speed, and then click OK to start the playback and output of your sequence and elements.

Recapturing a Project

You've finished editing a project, output a finished copy to tape, and exported a QuickTime movie of the sequence. The next step is the most important thing you can do to back up your hard work: save a copy of your project file somewhere safe. Once you've saved your project file, you can delete the media files to free up hard-drive space and allow room for another project.

As soon as you delete the media files associated with a project, or even move them as you saw earlier in this lesson, the clips in the project will become offline. They will appear with a red diagonal line across them in the Browser and will be white clips in the Timeline. But the project file still retains all the information that was used when you originally captured the clips, all the Ins and Outs of the clips in the Timeline, all the filters used or effects created, and so on, even though the media is no longer available.

If you ever need to re-edit the original project, you won't have to re-enter any logging information. You can simply open the project file and *recapture* the media files, using the existing clip information in the project. When you have a need to recapture a project's media files, you can use the following steps as a guide,

> **NOTE** ▶ This process will work correctly only if there are no timecode breaks on your tapes.

1   Open the project file for the project whose media you want to recapture.

2   Choose File > Capture Project, or press Ctrl-C.

NOTE ► You can also choose Capture Project from within the Capture window (Cmd-8), which you worked with in Lesson 12.

```
┌─────────────────────────────────────────────┐
│                Batch Capture                 │
├─────────────────────────────────────────────┤
│                                              │
│     Capture:  [ All Items in Logging Bin ▼]  │
│                                              │
│     Options:  ☑ Use Logged Clip Settings     │
│                                              │
│               ☐ Add Handles:  [00:00:01;00]  │
│                                              │
│  Capture Preset:  [ DV NTSC 48 kHz       ▼]  │
│                                              │
│               Using DV Video for video input │
│               DCR-TRV900 using NTSC          │
│               29.97 frames per second        │
│               DV – NTSC at Best quality.     │
│               24 bits per pixel              │
│               720 by 480                     │
│               Using DV Audio for audio input │
│               Input: First 2 channels        │
│               Rate: 48.000 kHz               │
│               Speaker: off                   │
│               Volume: 100, Gain: 0           │
│               Capturing using logged clip    │
│               settings for picture, gain,    │
│               and media to be captured.      │
│                                              │
│                                              │
│                                              │
│  Total Media Time:  00:03:06:04              │
│                                              │
│  Total Disk Space:  589.0 MB needed / 2.3 GB │
│                     available                │
│                                              │
│            ( Cancel )    (  OK  )            │
└─────────────────────────────────────────────┘
```

The Batch Capture window opens, where you can choose to capture all or selected items in the project, add handles to the existing clip lengths, and choose a capture preset.

3   Click OK.

The Insert Reel dialog appears, indicating which tape reel to place in your playback source to begin capturing.

4   Insert the requested reel and click Continue.

When Final Cut Express has finished capturing all the necessary clips from the first tape, it will display the Insert Reel dialog again if a second reel was used. Insert the next tape in the list. Continue to insert tapes until Final Cut Express has finished capturing your entire project. When all the media has been captured, the clips will once again be linked to the media, and you will be able to continue working in your project.

5   Press Cmd-S to save the current configuration of the project.

Importing an iMovie Project

If you started a project in iMovie, and want to continue editing or finish the project in Final Cut Express, you can now import the iMovie project Timeline. The Timeline is exported and imported using Final Cut XML. An XML file is a text-based markup language format (think HTML for websites).

1 In iMovie, open your project and choose Share > Export Final Cut XML. Select a location for the XML file. This file does not contain clips, so you can safely save it to your Desktop.

2 In Final Cut Express, choose File > Import > Final Cut XML from iMovie.

3   Select the file you shared from iMovie.

After importing the XML file, you may delete the XML file if you will no longer use it in iMovie.

NOTE ▶ When importing an iMovie project into Final Cut Express, there are a few things to remember: All transitions in iMovie will be converted to cross dissolves, and many effects (such as titles, voice-overs, sound effects, music tracks, volume adjustments, cropping, Ken Burns effects, and color adjustments) are not exported.

Lesson Review

1.   What three ways can you import a file?

2.   When importing music tracks from a CD, what should you do first before you import the track into your project?

3.   After you've imported a multilayered graphic file, what type of icon will you see?

4.   What does it mean when you see a red diagonal line through a clip in the Browser?

5.   How do you open the Gain Adjust dialog, where you raise or lower the levels of all the audio clips in a sequence?

6.   What filter can you apply to a clip to correct its color?

7.   What format is frequently used to export a clip for the Web?

8.   When you output to tape, what are the two options?

Answers

1.   Choose File > Import > Files; Ctrl-click in the Browser and choose Import > Files from the shortcut menu; or press the keyboard short-cut, Cmd-I.

2.   You should copy the music track onto your hard drive, and then import it into your project.

3. A multilayered graphic file appears as a sequence icon, and each layer appears as a sequence layer.

4. That clip is not linking to its media file and will not play back.

5. Choose Modify > Levels.

6. The Color Corrector filter.

7. MPEG-4.

8. Play back the sequence manually or use the Print to Video option.

Keyboard Shortcuts

Cmd-I	Imports a file or files
Cmd-Option-L	Opens the Gain Adjust dialog
Ctrl-M	Opens the Print to Video dialog
Ctrl-C	Opens the Batch Capture dialog

Index

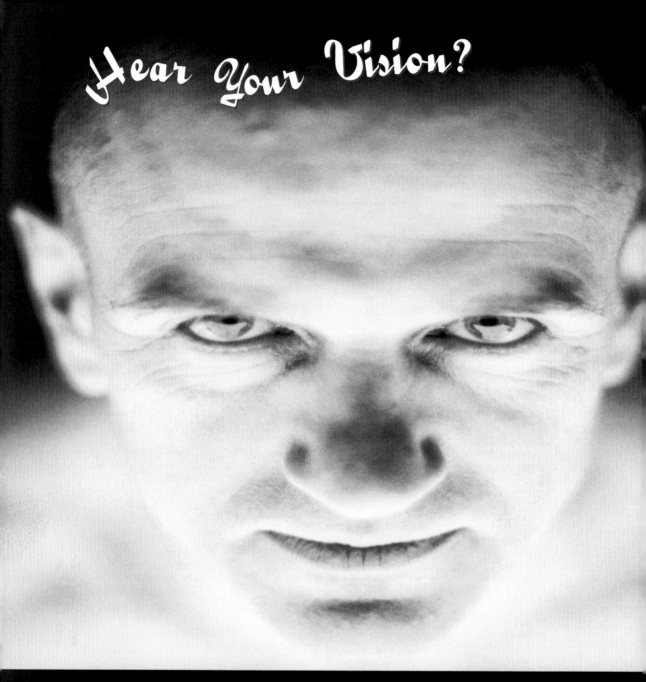

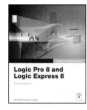

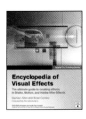